'This book takes us into uncharted terrain – exploring embodiment, what it means to 'optimise human potential', and 'the body-brain-environment person'. It challenges readers to learn, in a cautious, reflexive way, about how a scholarly marriage of the social and biological sciences can reshape what we know about education. An impressive *tour de force* by Deborah Youdell and Martin Lindley that displays their extraordinary encyclopaedic knowledge and imaginative rendering of biosocial education as a new field of research. The book brings readers to the forefront of contemporary thinking about what it is to be human and to learn.'

Madeleine Arnot, University of Cambridge, UK

'This book responds to the urgent need for a new vocabulary of the biosocial: emerging in the complex and manifold encounters between a historically situated, critical-affirmative sociology and the new biosciences. Without this new biosocial approach, educators, policymakers, and interdisciplinary researchers will find themselves increasingly at a loss in their decision-making for future educational policies, practices or research endeavors.'

Hillevi Lenz Taguchi, Stockholm University, Sweden

W0009841

BIOSOCIAL EDUCATION

In this groundbreaking text, Youdell and Lindley bring together cutting-edge research from the fields of biology and social science to explore the complex interactions between the diverse processes which impact on education and learning.

Transforming the way we think about our students, our classrooms, teaching and learning, *Biosocial Education* draws on advances in genetics and metabolomics, epigenetics, biochemistry and neuroscience, to illustrate how new understandings of how bodies function can and must inform educational theory, policy and everyday pedagogical practices. Offering detailed insight into new findings in these areas and providing a compelling account of both the implications and limits of this new-found knowledge, the text confronts the mechanisms of interaction between multiple biological and social factors, and explores how educators might mobilize these 'biosocial' influences to enhance learning and enable each child to attain educational success.

By seeking out transdisciplinary and multi-factor answers to the question of how education works and how children learn, this book lays the foundations for a step change in the way we approach learning. It is an essential read for researchers, teachers and practitioners involved in educational policy and practice at any level.

Deborah Youdell is Professor of Sociology of Education at the University of Birmingham, UK.

Martin R. Lindley is Senior Lecturer in Human Biology at Loughborough University, UK.

BIOSOCIAL EDUCATION

The Social and Biological Entanglements of Learning

Deborah Youdell and Martin R. Lindley

Routledge
Taylor & Francis Group

LONDON AND NEW YORK

First published 2019
by Routledge
2 Park Square, Milton Park, Abingdon, Oxon OX14 4RN

and by Routledge
711 Third Avenue, New York, NY 10017

Routledge is an imprint of the Taylor & Francis Group, an informa business

British Library Cataloguing-in-Publication Data
A catalogue record for this book is available from the British Library

Library of Congress Cataloging-in-Publication Data
A catalog record for this book has been requested

ISBN: 978-0-415-78709-3 (hbk)
ISBN: 978-0-415-78710-9 (pbk)
ISBN: 978-1-315-22640-8 (ebk)

Typeset in Bembo
by Apex CoVantage, LLC

to Edith

CONTENTS

List of figures   *x*
List of tables   *xi*
Acknowledgements   *xii*

1   The social and biological entanglements of learning   1

2   When biology and the social meet   14

3   Optimizing humans   35

4   Being human: brain-body-environment entanglements   56

5   Feeling the classroom   77

6   Biosocial assemblage: the case of Attention
    Deficit-Hyperactivity Disorder   94

7   Biosocial learning   124

References   *152*
Index   *169*

FIGURES

2.1   Images of human chromosomes generated through microscopy   18
2.2   Representation of a section of genetic code: the genes
      within the DYX2 locus on chromosome 6p22   19
2.3   Epigenetic mechanisms of gene regulation   21
2.4   Histone modification captured by confocal microscopy   23
2.5   Scales of granularity   33
3.1   Tadpole neurons influenced by Omega-3   46
3.2   Methylation of the oestrogen receptor in offspring of
      low-lick-groom rats   48
4.1   Phrenology and functional areas   65
4.2   Brain region-function relationships   66
5.1   Brain connectivity and emotional states   83
5.2   Volatile organic compounds showing feelings in cinema
      auditorium   85
5.3   Regional brain activation and test-induced stress   87
5.4   Volatile organic compounds in the exhaled breath of children
      undertaking a maths test   88
6.1   A biological model of complexity   119
7.1   Schematic of learning styles   127
7.2   Engerstrom's activity theory of learning   130
7.3   Wenger's learning and 'communities of practice'   130
7.4   Histone methylation as evidence of memory   133
7.5   Brain activation and working memory   135
7.6   Auditory cortex and learning to read   139
7.7   Biosocial influences on learning   148

TABLES

6.1   'Hot genes' associated with ADHD   106
6.2   The brain and ADHD   113

ACKNOWLEDGEMENTS

This book is the product of a more than three-year collaboration. While it started as the typical heated debate between a sociologist and a biologist, we hope that we have managed to transform that into a much more productive dialogue.

Invaluable to the project has been a British Academy Mid-Career Fellowship, awarded to Deborah during 2016 and 2017 (Award number MD140037), which allowed her to undertake much of the exploratory work that underpins this book. Thanks to all of those scholars in the life sciences and social sciences who took the time to meet with Deborah and to participate in the workshops and public events that the British Academy supported as well as the Biosocial Research Workshop supported by the BRIDGE Partnership between the University of Birmingham and the University of Illinois-Urbana Champaign. Thanks in particular to Matthew Bennett, Paul Badenhorst, Stefano de Brito, Adriana Bus, Frances Champagne, Frances Child, Dez Fitzgerald, Samantha Frost, Val Gillies, Usha Goswami, Celia Greenway, Nathan Hughes, Marnius van Ijzendoorn, Amanda Kirby, Maggie Mclure, Ian McGimpsey, Murizio Meloni, Celia Roberts, Nikolas Rose, Kim Shapiro and Sally Tomlinson.

Thanks also to all of those who have participated in seminars and conference sessions at which ideas that are developed in this book have been presented, and to the organisers for the invitations: the Nordic Education Research Association Annual Conference 2017; Experiments in Thinking the Human Seminar, University of Illinois-Urbana Champaign; Gender and Education seminar, UCL Institute of Education; School of Education Research Conference, University of Birmingham; Summer Institute in Qualitative Research 2017, Manchester Metropolitan University; Bio-rationalities Symposium, European Conference for Education Research, Copenhagen 2017; Education seminar at Alberto Hutardo Universidad, Santiago, Chile; Gender Disability and Education Seminar, Umea University, Sweden; Latin American Summer Institute 2018, Universidad Catholica-Villarrica,

Chile; Education and New Materialism Seminar at Simon Fraser University, Vancouver, Canada; Theorising Race Seminar, University of Cambridge; and Bristol Conversations in Education Research, Bristol University.

Our gratitude to our universities, the University of Birmingham and Loughborough University, for sustaining space for new thinking. In particular, thanks to Julie Allan and the School of Education, University of Birmingham for supporting the developing field of Biosocial Education and for supporting this writing project with a semester of study leave.

Thank you to a number of critical friends: John Evans, Alejandra Falabella, David Gillborn, Kalervo Gulson, Claudia Matus, Ian Mcgimpsey, Tim Mickelborough, Jesu Montecino, Laura Teague, Taylor Webb and Pat Thomson. Thanks also to Madeleine Arnot for a great lunch where the idea for this book was first discussed, to Anna Clarkson and Elsbeth Wright at Routledge for their enthusiasm and patience, and to Kate Coss for insisting that surely difference couldn't *all* be social.

Finally, special thanks to the members of the Translational Chemical Biology research group at Loughborough University and the group of colleagues in sociology, political theory, education, biology, analytical chemistry and neuroscience who continue to have the imagination and curiosity to pursue these ideas with us: Sara Assecondi, Andrew Bagshaw, Samantha Frost, Valerie Harwood, Anna Hickey-Moody, Peter Kraftl, Jim Reynolds, Matthew Turner, Sarabjit Mastana and Kim Shapiro. We are delighted to have you to do this work with.

Deborah Youdell and Martin R. Lindley
Woodhouse Eaves, April 2018

1

THE SOCIAL AND BIOLOGICAL ENTANGLEMENTS OF LEARNING

Why we wrote this book

This book brings together the most recent research from the biological and social sciences in order to think differently about education and about learning. The book is unusual because it is written collaboratively by a sociologist of education (Deborah) and a human biologist (Martin). From our first thinking about the book, we wanted to bring the social and the biological together; we wanted to understand, and help readers to understand, how social and biological processes are entangled with each other and the implications of this for how we think about education and learning.

This is a contentious project. Education scholarship carries a longstanding mistrust of biology, due largely to the perception that biology naturalizes and fixes differences (often referred to in critical literature as 'biological determinism') and that this naturalizing and fixing is particularly evident when biological knowledge is mobilized politically in ways that segregate and discriminate on grounds of race, disability gender and so on. This has been seen most starkly in eugenicist accounts of who is fit to be educated and the practices of exclusion, and indeed extermination, that eugenic thinking has been mobilized to justify. This history continues to reverberate in education, with ideas of differentially distributed natural intelligence still widely influential. We will return to this in Chapter 3, *Optimizing humans*.

Yet contemporary education policy is engaged increasingly with the new biological sciences, in particular neuroscience and genetics. And while policy engages biology, the last 20 or 30 years has seen diminishing policy interest in sociologically orientated research – policy concerned with competition and accountability has little or no point of articulation with sociological research concerned with injustices and inequalities in which policy itself is implicated. This sets up a series of alignments and divisions in which biological sciences become more and more central to education and wider public policy, while the sociology of education becomes more divorced from and inconsequential to this policy. The fear amongst critical education scholars is that this turn to neuroscience and genetics will allow education policy to be undergirded by ideas of 'hard wired' brains and genetic intelligence, leaving institutional processes and students' experiences out of the analysis and leading, in turn, to inequalities in education being explained as the biological deficit of particular populations of students and, potentially, not open to intervention.

A key problem for us is that these sorts of accounts of the naturalizing and fixing effects of biology do not reflect the sort of findings that are being presented by research in the new biological sciences. Much of this research is characterized by the recognition of the complex interplay between social, environmental and biological processes and attempts to identify the mechanism of these combined influences. Applied to education, this recognition of the interplay of social, environmental and biological processes suggests that education studies and new biological sciences need to find ways to engage in collaborative scholarship in order to make best use of their respective insights and better understand the biosocial processes at stake in education. Drawing on our own previous research in sociology of education and human biology, and borrowing from cutting-edge developments in epigenetics, nutrigenomics, biochemistry and neuroscience, we want to explore how it is possible to integrate emerging evidence from new biological sciences with evidence from sociology of education, showing how the social and the biological are folded together in an endless exchange of influence and demonstrating how this new insight provides the foundation for a step change in our thinking about and approaches to education and learning. This book is the beginning of this work.

Standardized tests, stress and the biosocial

To begin to illustrate the potential significance of the biosocial approach we are taking, we start by considering Standardized Assessment Tests (SATs), the national standardized assessment tests that children as young as 6 and 7 sit each summer in schools across England. The tests are used to measure the performance of schools and report on the adequacy of progress made by children. As is now common, in the weeks and days leading up to the annual SAT tests, social media and the press carry strings of articles and posts that attest to the limited relevance and usefulness of the tests (Guardian 09/05/17) and the harm done by them to children, and sometimes to teachers (Rosen, 2017).

Educationalists' concerns over the forms of high-stakes testing that are now well established internationally have focused on the way that such tests alter the way that schools and classrooms operate, drive selective practices and make inequalities worse instead of better (Apple, 2006; Gillborn, 2008; Gillborn and Youdell, 2000; Thompson, 2016). More recently, however, popular and educational concern has shifted to the impact of these tests on children's well-being. In England, the national tests that are compulsory in primary schools have come to be discussed in popular and news media in terms of the 'stress' and 'anxiety' they cause children, reported as manifest in a range of ways: from tears and sleeplessness to one teacher's account of a child's eyelashes falling out (Weale, 1 May 2017).

There is a body of critical work in education that engages with the emotional dimensions of education, and foregrounds the importance of the psychic encounter between the teacher, the learner and learning (Bibby, 2011, 2017; Zembylas, 2007), as well as the social nature of feelings as they circulate in classrooms and between students and teachers (Harwood et al., 2017; Hickey-Moody, 2009; Kraftl, 2013; Youdell, 2011). Furthermore, recent research has offered compelling accounts from students and parents of their 'stressful' experiences of contemporary schooling in general and assessment regimes in particular, giving weight to the popular accounts discussed earlier (Youdell et al., 2018). Yet while work of this sort tells us much about the psychosocial dimensions of teachers' and students' encounters with assessment-driven education, it is not able to tell us about what is happening in the bodies of the teachers and children who are living this schooling in the day-to-day; whether this is best considered through the languages of 'stress'; or what the implications – emotional, educational, embodied – of these experiences might be.

Social media and press reports use 'stress' and 'anxiety' as interchangeable popular terms, calling up our common sense notions or experiences of feeling anxious or stressed. 'Stress' and 'anxiety' are referenced as though we know in advance what these are, how to recognize them, and what their implications are for children. Yet in scholarly psychological and biological research, as well as in clinical practice, the terms stress and anxiety have specific meanings that are embedded in the typological, diagnostic and biological parameters of the disciplines. This means that when education commentators claim that children are made stressed or anxious by assessment regimes, this may not be demonstrable in the terms of the disciplines in which stress and anxiety exist as identifiable and diagnosable psychological and/or physiological conditions. Furthermore, when critical sociologically and psychoanalytically orientated work seeks to speak to feelings, their flows and their experiences – in particular difficult feelings or feelings of 'disease' in the classroom (Bibby, 2011, 2017: 2) – this is seldom in terms of 'stress' or 'anxiety' (whether in scientific or lay terms) and so does not map straightforwardly onto life science definitions. Key here is that existing sociologically informed education research provides important insight into the significance of feeling in education, its capacity to speak to the 'more-than-social' is limited (Kraftl, 2013) – it cannot tell us about the physiology, neuroscience or biochemistry of 'stress'.

When we claim that children are made anxious or stressed by SATs, then, do we really know what anxiety and stress are? Are we able to demonstrate anxiety or stress? Do we know what is happening physiologically? Are we clear about the effects? And can we show how this anxiety or stress is generated in the ebb and flow of pedagogic practices and relationships in the everyday of classroom and school life?

We do not pose these questions to refute claims that education dominated by high-stakes tests is stressful for children, or that this stress might be both bad for their health and counterproductive for their education. Instead, we want to, first, hold over the claim until we have properly furnished it with current understandings of the mechanisms and effects of anxiety and stress drawn from the new biological sciences and, second, interlaced this bioscience with nuanced understandings of school processes and pedagogic practices. By doing this, we may begin to see how stressful educational styles and situations become instantiated in the bodies of some children in ways that can affect both their current and future health and well-being and their current and future educational engagement and capacities to learn. The issue of school and stress, then, provides a useful first illustration of how the social and the biological are tied together, and how schools have everything to do with these entanglements. We will return to the look in detail at stress and other feelings in Chapter 5, *Feeling the classroom.*

A love affair with biology

Policy makers, the media and the public can at times seem to be involved in a love affair with new biological sciences. Findings from genetics and neuroscience research, in particular, have been made into mainstream media headlines, are shared widely through social media, and furnish evidence for genetic- and brain-science-based policy making and professional practice – seen in particular in the use in early years policies of epigenetic and neuroscience research on attachment and brain development. We explore this in Chapter 3, *Optimizing humans.* The extent of the popular, policy and professional embrace of these new fields has led neuroscientist and critical policy scholar Nikolas Rose to suggest that a 'new biological age' has been inaugurated (Rose, 2013). In this new biological age technologies such as genome mapping and brain imaging are shifting the scale at which the body is engaged and transforming what we aspire to know about it (Gulson and Webb, 2016).

While policy and the media appear full of optimism, critical social science scholars have raised concerns over the way that ideas from these new biosciences have been taken up and put to work in expert discourse, policy and professional practice. Indeed, as ideas drawn from the new biological sciences are used to shape parenting interventions, early years provision, school education and approaches in the criminal justice system, critical scholars have argued that a set of a new 'bio-rationalities' can be seen to be taking hold (Baker, 2015; Gulson and Webb, 2016). With policy and popular responses to the promise of new biosciences so positive, it is important to understand the misgivings of critical scholars. Exploring these policy directions and the biological research underpinning them is a central task of this book, and we will explore social science misgivings fully in Chapter 3, *Optimizing humans.* Here it is useful to illustrate the disconnection between the popular and policy enthusiasm and the critical sociological concern. For instance, in parenting and children's services, ideas have been taken from bioscience research to inform the way that the quality of parenting is understood and assessed and, in turn, to assert the impact of parenting on child development and promote particular sorts of parenting practice (Allen, 2011; Feinstein, 2003). While for policy makers and practitioners this new evidence helps identify and support better parenting practices, critical scholars have argued that, based on the available scientific evidence, the policy over-claims and even misleads and is intrusive to and demonizing of parents (Wastell and White, 2012; Edwards et al., 2015; Gillies, 2008). Similarly, education policy borrows from behavioural genetics research that uses 'genome wide association studies' to support the notion of 'g' – generalized genetic intelligence (Ashbury and Plomin, 2014), yet this intelligence research has been dismantled in critical sociological work (Gillborn, 2010, 2016).

Despite the emergent nature of research findings, part of the popular and policy love affair with new biological sciences seems to rest on the fantasy of complete insight and understanding. This fantasy seems to imagine that new technologies such as functional Magnetic Resonance Imaging (fMRI) scanners that can image the blood flow of brains while they function, and electron microscopy that can see inside cells and even molecules, enable bioscientists to see into the body across scales to the finest level of granularity – into the cell and on into the DNA itself – and know precisely what the thing seen does. This fantasy, we suggest, is often fuelled by computer-generated images (CGI), which leave unclear the line between seen and imagined, object and function, science and science fiction.

While sociology has tended towards critique of policy uses of new bioscience evidence, we emphasize from the outset that all research in the biosciences is not the same, and that policy makers' and media uses and abuses of work in these fields is not the same as the research itself. Scientists working in frontier fields such as epigenetics, metabolomics and neuroscience emphasize the preliminary nature of their findings, the fact that molecular mechanisms are being identified that are only beginning to be understood (Pappa et al., 2015; Rose and Rose, 2013, van Ijzendoorn et al., 2011), and the need for further research to support translation down the line (Fischer et al., 2010; Mileva-Seitz et al., 2016). Yet it is easy for this to seem lost in the media hype, popular excitement and policy take-up.

In this book we argue that it is unwise as well as inaccurate to dismiss research in these new biological sciences on the basis that they have been or might be badly used or misused in policy and political manoeuvring; that they have no relevance for educationalists; or that they are regressive, conservative or otherwise against progressive or critical social justice agendas. Such a move, we argue, fails to engage the most exciting and potentially important areas of work in the new biological sciences that are exploring the interface between the biological and the social. This work is generating evidence that the social and the biological cannot be thought of as opposites or even distinct, and so misses the radical or unexpected potentialities of biosciences that are now precisely concerned with the ongoing interplay and exchange of influence between the social, environmental and biological. We need, we suggest, to work across these currents or research in order to develop educational understanding and practice that is *biosocial*.

People and bodies

Put simply, sociology is concerned with people in their social milieu and in relation to social institutions, and human biology is concerned with the functioning of the human body. A biosocial approach unsettles this neat distinction between a person who is social and a body, which is biological.

Of course, the social sciences have an abiding interest in the body, in particular people's experiences of embodiment and how the body is made meaningful and how its capacities are socially constrained. Likewise, philosophy has a longstanding concern with the relationship between mind, body, self and brain. Across such engagements with the fundamentally embodied nature of the person, the body remains interpretive, and the interior of the body – from beating hearts to metabolic pathways within cells and movements across membranes – remain out of reach.

In recent humanities and feminist scholarship concerns with embodiment have moved on to consider the human and the relationship between the human and other forms of life, objects, the environment and the planet itself. This posthuman (Braidotti, 2013) work has posited an orientation where the not-human or more-than-human are foregrounded and the distinction between the human and its milieu suspended. This informs much 'new materialist' (Coole and Frost, 2010) work that aims to foreground the materiality of the body and the worlds bodies inhabit and interact with; refusing a special status for the human and insisting on the capacity of the non-human to make things happen (Bennett, 2010) and the productive intra-actions of actants in phenomena (Barad, 2007). Like the scholarship in sociology, however, much of this work does not move to an encounter with the scientific evidence of the porosity and malleability of the body, and so the materiality of the body and its milieu remains a matter of theory or poetics.

There are notable exceptions that offer ideas for how we might go about working biosocially. Catherine Malabou works across feminist theories of gender and neuroscientific assertions of brain plasticity to propose a fundamental transformability of sex and gender (Malabou, 2009). Samantha Frost's work traverses scales and domains of knowledge from the molecular to the cultural builds an account of the human as biocultural creature (Frost, 2016). Elizabeth Wilson's work on the entanglement of social, cultural and economic forces and the central and peripheral nervous system (Wilson, 2015) and Celia Roberts' biopsychosocial investigation of contemporary puberty (Roberts, 2015) both demonstrate the possibility of moving across domains of evidence. We extend these approaches through our engagement with the problem of the relationship between body, brain and person, and what new biosocial accounts mean for understanding the human in Chapter 4, *Being human*.

The new biosciences

The new biosciences that we are interested in throughout this book are those that acknowledge and explore the interaction between the biological and the social, or the environmental as it is more often termed in these sciences. Being concerned with this interaction, these biosciences have particular potential to be articulated with social sciences and, through this articulation, the potential to transform how we think about ourselves, our bodies, and our relationship with our social and material environment, and about education.

Epigenetics is perhaps the most prominent of these and can be thought of as being where work in genetics has moved to since the human genome was mapped. It asks how genes are made to work, how they are regulated and expressed, and importantly, how environments influence how genes work during our lifetimes as well as across generations. Epigenetics findings of environmental influences on how genes are regulated and expressed show that genes and the cellular activities they manage are changeable. This means that genes are not the fixed components of what and who we are, while the social is a separate set of factors that influence just those bits of us that are changeable. Rather, genes and environment are both subject to change and, furthermore, they are enfolded together.

While epigenetics is the area of new biology that has captured headlines and significant engagement from social scientists, it is not the only field in the new biological sciences that recognizes the important entanglement of the biological and social. For instance, nutrigenomics is concerned with the within-generation interaction between diet and the body's genetic code; metabolomics is concerned with the intermediate chemical processes involved in metabolism through which factors such as nutrition and physical activity influence the body at a molecular level; and analytical chemistry is providing new insights into the metabolites of the body and their relationship to environmental as well as molecular processes (Heaney et al., 2016; Mickleborough and Lindley, 2013; Reynolds et al., forthcoming; Turner et al., 2013).

Neuroscience is perhaps the most prominent of the new biological sciences in education, with attention to the brain, its development and its potentialities and limits perhaps self-evident in a field concerned with learning. Yet at present neuroscience offers few certainties about learning as we might conceive of it in education. We explore this in Chapter 7, *Biosocial learning*. Current neuroscience, as we explore through the chapters that follow, discards the 'hard wired', 'computer-processor' and 'filing' and 'storing' accounts of the brain that dominate popular discourse and instead emphasizes the 'plasticity' and 'connectivity' of the brain (Malabou, 2009; Rose and Abi-Rached, 2013). The brain undergoes changes to its structures, networks and functions within and across regions, and inside individual neuronal and glial cells over the life course, and many of these changes occur in interaction with environmental factors. The extent, particularity and effects of brain plasticity continue to be explored within the field, but the fact of plasticity is well established and opens up a broad field of potential interface between the brain and the social world.

Together, this work demands that we recognize that *we are biosocial*. We offer an introduction to these new biological sciences and how they might be articulated with key concepts from sociology of education in Chapter 2, *When biology and the social meet*.

Inequalities, education and the biosocial

Unequal educational experiences and outcomes are a persistent problem faced by societies across the globe. These inequalities disproportionately affect the most economically and socially disadvantaged, including minority race and ethnic groups, those with disabilities and those who have experienced adversity early in life. Educational inequalities translate into poorer employment, economic and health trajectories for these individuals and communities, and enduring welfare responsibilities for states. As such, persistent and entangled health, social and educational disparities are major global social issues. Despite decades of education research concerned with inequalities, we still do not have any consensus on how best education might intervene into or limit these inequalities, or how best to enable all children to learn and attain the sorts of educational and life outcomes that are necessary economically and acceptable socially in advanced democratic nations.

These questions have received much attention from researchers, policy makers and practitioners and, despite important advances, insights and responses remain partial and disjointed. This may seem an unlikely claim given the huge amount of research endeavour in the field of education, and the clear preference amongst politicians and other high-profile advocates for 'evidenced based' educational practice. Yet researchers and politicians and commentators continue to research and debate why education is so unequal. Sociology of education researchers have looked for answers in the relationships between teachers and pupils; in the ways schools organize themselves and are required to act; and in the judgements that teachers make about the children they teach. For sociology of education, these *social* aspects of schooling are important because, being social, *we can change them and make a difference*. With its deep and abiding commitment to social justice, sociology of education is confronted by the suggestion that at least some elements or aspects of inequality are due to instinct or genetics – girls being good at arts, boys liking non-fiction books, poor kids and black kids doing less well than white and well-off kids. The histories of colonization and slavery, of women without property and voting rights, of indigenous children or children with disabilities being deemed unfit to educate, all lead sociologically orientated education research back to the social aspects of schooling, and the ethics that we can use to guide what education is and does.

A key problem underpinning the limited capacity to respond to educational inequality is our partial and fragmented understanding of what constitutes learning, what it is influenced by, and what its mechanisms might be. Yet when we examine what we actually know about learning in education, we find a surprising lack of certainty or completeness and understanding the complex ways in which children's social and educational worlds and their learning are interlinked remains a pressing challenge. And when we look in neuroscience or molecular biology we find that understandings are only now emerging and that work is at a grain size so small that it can be difficult to scale it up to think about how it can inform pedagogy. Central to the work of this book is an exploration of the multiple and interacting social and biological factors that help and hinder children's learning. We bring learning –

understood as a complex biosocial phenomenon – to the forefront of our thinking about biosocial education. We explore this research into learning, its potential intersections and how it might be folded together, developing new understandings of learning and new approaches to pedagogy in Chapter 7, *Biosocial learning*.

Biosocial assemblages

To navigate this terrain of interlinked and multidirectional influences, we use the idea of biosocial assemblages, adopting Deleuze and Guattari's (2008) notion of assemblages in which a whole range of diverse productive forces and factors come together (Youdell, 2015; McGimpsey and Youdell, 2015). We borrow Frost's (2016) account of the human as biocultural creature, traversing scales from the molecular to the cultural, as well as Barad's (2007) notion of the productive intra-actions of actants in phenomena and Wilson's (2015) work on the entanglements of the social and the bodily. As yet there have been few attempts to integrate these insights with applied empirical research – biosocial research is often either theoretical (Meloni, 2016) or focused on large data sets and quantitative measures (Blane, 2013, 2016), missing the nuances offered by qualitative social sciences (Chung et al., 2016). There are significant examples of work of the sort we want to do emerging, such as Celia Robert's (2015) analysis of early sexual development and Elizabeth Wilson's analysis of depression (Wilson, 2015). We draw on these ideas as we explore the potential of the biosocial to transform our understanding of how biological, environmental and social factors interact.

We demonstrate the usefulness as well as some of the vertiginous consequences (Wilson, 2015) of thinking through biosocial assemblages by developing a detailed account of Attention Hyperactivity/Deficit Disorder (ADHD) in Chapter 6, *Biosocial assemblage*. We choose ADHD for this exploration because it has been the focus of much research activity in genetics and neuroscience at the same time as ADHD and other social and emotional diagnoses have been the focus of harsh criticism from inclusive educators and critical researchers. This then, is a case in which the biology/social divide has been cemented, and in which the challenges of taking a biosocial approach are substantial.

The uncomfortable problem of difference

When we being to think about inequality this inevitably raises the issue of the particular groups – differentiated along lines of race, ethnicity, gender, disability etc. – and thinking biosocially in turn raises the spectre of a possible biological or even genetic basis for such differences. The research in the biological sciences that we engage with in this book is rarely concerned with population groups based on categories such as race or gender – the research is working at a scale of granularity much smaller than such gross social categories, and is underpinned by understandings of biological complexity and openness to change, or plasticity, and so ideas such as race or gender – which have little support in these parts of leading-edge biological sciences – do not fit. But this is not to say that ideas of such differences as genetically encoded and fixed do not continue to have powerful productive force.

Gender

It is popularly understood that human sex is the result of a difference in one pair of chromosomes – XX for girls, XY for boys – yet the detail of the process of sex development from this initial embryonic moment is not attended to in popular thinking. Nevertheless, longstanding ideas such as sex differences in brain volume, that brain volume is important for brain function, and the 'sexed brain', where men have a dominant right brain hemisphere which is the site of logic and women have a dominant left brain hemisphere which is creative and emotional, persist. Contemporary neuroscience is interested in sex differences in areas such as gene expression (Trabzuni et al., 2013) and brain function (Ngun et al., 2011). This work remains contentious and contested (Fine, 2011, 2018), and efforts by feminist scientists and science scholars to ensure clarity and care over the reasoning for, as well as the claims made by, research framed by sex difference concerns are having effect (Fine and Jordan-Young, 2017). These are important movements; it is important to note that studies of sex difference can be concerned with nuanced differences at the molecular level, not gross gender differences that we are familiar with from popular media and culture.

One of the ways to navigate this terrain is to concede that sex may have influences on the molecular body, while the social influences gender and is in turn influenced by gender. A biosocial approach to sex-gender, however, should in principle move from an assertion of the intra-acting influences of gender and the sexed body (Roberts, 2013; Wilson, 2015). This suggests a refusal of a sex/gender distinctions. Indeed, it suggests a revisiting and potential reversal of the now established claim in feminist theory that sex-gender are inseparable because the meaningfulness of the sexed body is necessarily discursively accessed (Butler, 1993; Youdell, 2005). A biosocial approach suggests that sex-gender are inseparable not just for this reason, but due to intra-action and influence in both directions. This means acknowledging the reality of biological sex and the possibility that biological sex influences life (including but not restricted to gender). Feminists may well be concerned that this acknowledgment allows a resurrection of biological determinism that puts women back in their 'proper' biological place – the dystopia of the *Handmaids Tale* (Atwood, 1990) once again looms. Yet we want to suggest that this need not be the case.

While acknowledging sex differences might be risky given the pervasiveness and persistence of sex-gender hierarchies, we want to suggest that a molecular biological difference is not in and of itself a site of subjugation – processes of subjugation are social and historical and the time of evolution and the molecular body are at once much slower and much faster than the time of gendered cultures. As second wave maternal feminists argued, reproduction, parenting and empathy do not a priori need to be denigrated as low status capacities and activities. Of course, the science of sex difference is not self-evidently neutral, and arguably embedded socio-political commitments to sex-gender difference cannot be simply extracted from scientific questions and methods (Harding, 1986; Barad, 2007; Fine, 2011, 2018).

This debate continues to unfold and it is unlikely that any easy resolution is forthcoming. In order to proceed, then, we intend to consider sex-gender through the lens of multifactorial complex causality. This means that we are unlikely to encounter the sort of one-to-one causal correspondence, such as sex = reproduction = dependence, that feminism has rejected. It does acknowledge that biological processes are enfolded with social processes and play a part in enfolded biosocial forms of life. Our argument regarding enfolded biosocial processes and influences and the forms of life these instantiate recurs throughout this book and is developed in Chapter 6, *Biosocial assemblage*, as we explore how we might understand and address Attention Deficit-Hyperactivity Disorder (ADHD) biosocially. This argument is discomforting to critical and feminist sociologists and educators. It unseats longstanding political and epistemic commitments – it is a degrounding (Butler et al., 1994) that insists on a metamorphosis (Malabou, 2009) of our conceptual apparatus without offering any assurance of where this will take us. Given this degrounding and anticipated metamorphosis, we take up the 'no place' of an ever-unfolding multifactorial complex causality, the moving assemblage of the forces that our analysis follows.

Race

There is no gene for race, rather the genetics of humans are constantly changing, and genetic research is demonstrating fluidity not fixity (Rotimi, 2004): 'drawing a line around an ephemeral entity like human race is an exercise in futility and idiocy' (Shipman, 2002 cited in Rotimi, 2004). But these facts delivered by the human genome project do not simply make 'race' go away. Rather we see a 'molecularization' (Fullwiley, 2007) of race, played out in particular in the field of genomic health research where investigation of the 'genetics of race for health' is positioned as an 'anodyne ethical obligation' (Fullwiley, 2007: 1). Genetic variation in population groups is a core part of drug development, which identifies group prevalence of genetic polymorphisms associated with disease susceptibility to offer tailored, personalized (racialized) medicine. This work is often supported by African American scientists and clinicians as well as the populations that stand to benefit from these. Yet the genetic variants identified in trials and associated with particular racialized patient groups may well not be restricted to this group and analyses of the ways in which race-based health genomics have played out and the implications of this suggest that it is not so simple to claim or maintain this as an anodyne activity:

> [T]he use of continentally-based ancestry genetics, admixture mapping, and a focus on genes 'to make live' as a means to eradicate health disparities in black and brown populations in the USA run the risk of reinvigorating the dangerous idea that race is bio-genetic.
>
> *(Fullwiley, 2015: 37)*

The use of 'molecular' race is not restricted to health research, but is also seen in police work, where genetics is increasingly used in the identification of racially profiled (constituted) suspects. Yet as already noted, these analyses do not investigate genes that code for race as no such genes exist. Instead they analyse genetic variation in a panel of biomarkers that are taken together to indicate ancestry and so 'race'. These panels of biomarkers include genes that code for proteins associated with e.g. malaria receptors, vitamin D binding, and muscle enzymes (Fullwiley, 2008) as well as genes that code for e.g. hair texture, beard colour and melanin production. It is important to realize that in genetic terms the ancestry being identified is an amalgam of traits. These traits are used to build a phenotype, not a specific 'race' genotype, and many traits are polygenic i.e. they are influenced by the expression of many genes.

These panels of data have also been used to develop a booming ancestry industry which offers analyses of 'ancestry' based on genotyping of saliva samples for less than £100. One such ancestry and health genotyping company, 23andMe, advertises that it uses more than 150 global locations in its ancestry analysis. The detail of the science is embedded in links in the paid-for reports; what the buyer gets is an attractive data visualization of coloured chromosomes and the percentage ancestry from different places e.g. 46.4% European, 41.8% East Asian and Native American, with these then broken down into finer regions e.g. 19.7% Iberian, 34.4% Native American, as well as a time line of 'most recent ancestors' e.g. Iberian 1810–1720 and Native American 1780–1690 (23andMe, n/d).

These analyses do not claim to identify race, but in the transformation of panels of gene variants into geographical locations that are deeply associated with race, they act to reinscribe race as both meaningful and important.

When we add into this racializing mix epigenetics, which analyses how environment influences gene expression and so body functioning, and note that racialized and marginalized groups are historically poor and concentrated in areas where exposures to environmental toxins are highest, social and educational services most limited, and stressors worst, we encounter the sort of array of social factors that become instantiated in the bodies of particular racialized groups. Research at the University of Illinois at Urbana-Champaign is examining the genomics of poverty, stress and resilience amongst African American mothers in one of the most disadvantaged areas of Chicago (Mendenhall et al., n/d).

These lines of research and critique once again take us to analyses of multifactorial complex causality and of the forces of assemblage, including the force of discourse in the face of new facts, and the reach of White Supremacy.

Biosocial possibilities

A key contribution of emerging biosocial research that is informed by understandings of complexity is its development of concepts and methods that reach across domains in order to explore the interactions of diverse influences and processes (Youdell, 2017a). In this book we demonstrate a biosocial approach that can work across domains of study, orders of influencing factors, and grain sizes (from the cell to the socio-economic setting of children's lives) to generate new understanding of these relationships and the processes that underpin them.

As we do this we explore the potential to move beyond approaches that are either able to offer deep interpretation of social, discursive and cultural meaning, or demonstrate statistical associations and modelled causality, or provide tightly demarcated biological mechanisms of action. Instead we develop analyses that integrate interpretive, associational and mechanistic analyses; offer bio-molecular and social mechanisms of influence; and move from linear and one-to-one models of causality to develop analyses of *multifactorial complex causality*. These approaches move well beyond the naïve scientism that underpins the current policy obsession with 'evidence' in the form of randomized control trials (RCTs) (Thomas, 2016) to radically extend what method and analysis might look like.

By seeking out transdisciplinary and multi-factor answers to the question of how education works and how children learn, the book opens up a step change in our understanding of learning and, by extension, helps us to understand how education can enable more children to attain educational success. Furthermore, by thinking through what biosocially informed interventions in homes, schools and classrooms might be, the book offers models for positively limiting inequalities by enhancing learning processes for more children.

2

WHEN BIOLOGY AND THE SOCIAL MEET

What is 'biosocial'?

In this chapter we set out key current thinking in the new biological sciences and social sciences in order to offer the reader a foundation in the ideas, approaches and findings that we work with in the book.

As we said in the previous chapter, the book develops a biosocial approach that spans and integrates the domains of the social and biological.

We are not advertising new findings from biology to an education audience, nor are we convincing scientists that they need to augment their research with elements of social science. Our approach is not about picking bits and pieces from biosciences or sociology and tacking them onto the established ways of thinking and working in the other field. Rather, our approach is about developing a whole new way of thinking about and researching education based on the underpinning premise that *we are biosocial*. Understanding the human as biosocial necessarily means doing biosocial research that is transdisciplinary.

There is an established literature that explores cross- or interdisciplinarity – respectively scholarship that reaches across and creates interaction between disciplines. More recently, transdisciplinarity has come to the fore. This encompasses the idea of traversing not just disciplines but, more fundamentally, domains of knowledge, generating new understandings that are not reducible to a set of discrete, already existing disciplines. The ambition of this book is *transdisciplinary*. We suggest that to understand the enfolded biological and social processes at work in education, knowledge domains need to be integrated so fully that they are transformed – and a new biosocial domain is created, making possible new ways of thinking about and investigating problems that are simultaneously biological, sociological, cultural, political and economic. Feminist scholar Elizabeth Wilson has talked about the interaction of social and biological sciences as a 'mutual rough and tumble' that destabilises the disciplines it draws on; she says that 'the alliances should feel vertiginous' (Wilson, 2015: 171–172). This echoes with work in the humanities and social sciences that takes concepts themselves as the object of study (Evans, 2014) and contemporary philosophy that suggests that we should start from the premise that everything (including people) is 'plastic' or 'transformable' (Malabou, 2009).

Having suggested that we envisage the creation of a new transdisciplinary and plastic biosocial domain, we recognize that, in order to cross, blend, traverse or transform disciplines, it is necessary to have a decent understanding of the fields that are being brought into the mix. And in order for this blending, traversing, transforming and inventing to do something worthwhile – to have the potential to generate new and game-changing analyses and ideas – the components that are brought together need to be drawn from the leading edge of where each contributing discipline or field is working. It is a state-of-the-art generated by bringing together the state-of-the arts from across domains. This is why for us this transdisciplinary work necessarily involves deep collaborations between experts from across fields who are ready to interrogate the premises and concepts that their research questions are built on; who are willing to get involved in Elizabeth Wilson's 'rough and tumble'; who are open to vertigo.

What this demands of the bioscientists and social scientists involved, however, is that we have a working understanding of key ideas and approaches from each other's fields. We cannot all be experts in everything, but we do need to understand enough to be able to engage in rigorous and generative explorations with each other (Frost, 2016; Roberts, 2015). The same is true for the reader of this book. In this chapter, then, we set out some of the fundamentals from biosciences and social sciences that we will be working with and start to identify what happens when we think about these not just as open for integration but as fundamentally intra-acting, as already folded together in the making of the phenomena that we are trying to understand.

The 'new' biosciences

This raises the question of what is happening in the biosciences at the moment that makes it such an interesting and productive time for social science to engage with biosciences. For us, the answer is that in many fields of biology as well as other life sciences research is showing that biology is influenced by the environment. This interest in environment opens up new potential and motivation for social sciences to engage with biosciences. We will look at 'environment' in Chapter 4, *Being human*. For now, we note that as these connexions and influences are shown, it becomes increasingly evident that biosciences need sophisticated and robust understandings of a whole range of social and cultural institutions and practices that come to be clustered together under the term 'environment'. And it becomes clear that social science needs to re-think its aversion to the biological and find ways to engage the biology-social interface. Part of doing this is moving past an image of 'biology' as a monolith of determinism and fixity (contrasted with an image of the social and cultural as fluid) and instead developing a working understanding of a whole range of fields and sub-fields of sciences that speak to the social: genetics, epigenetics, metabolomics, proteomics, neuroscience, analytic chemistry.

Across these fields and sub-fields there are two common premises and concerns that make them of particular interest to us here – one is that the biological is in interaction or exchange with its milieu, making the social or environmental of key importance; another is that mechanisms of action can be identified at the molecular level, even as these molecular functions contribute to the further functioning of a system. These seem central to the potential for a productive biosocial transdiciplinary endeavour. We have bracketing out of our exploration fields such as evolutionary and behavioural genetics that factor the social out of, rather than into, their analysis and so offer little potential for biosocial inquiry. What follows, then, is a somewhat encycolpaedia-style run-through of the key ideas that we use and that we want readers to have some sense of in order that they can make their own assessments of our endeavour.

Gene

A gene is the basic physical and functional unit of heredity. A gene exists as a sequence or region of DNA or RNA that encodes for a molecule that has a function within the human body. In humans genes vary in size from a few hundred DNA bases to more than 2 million bases. However the specific concept of 'gene' is being continually refined as new discoveries are being made in the biosciences about regulation and expression of genetic material.

Genome

This is all the individual genes of human beings grouped into a single collective term. The now famous Human Genome Project mapped the complete genome, that is all the genes of the human being (approx. 20,500) allowing us to identify the specific location of each gene on each chromosome (International Human Genome Sequencing Consortium, 2004).

Genotype and phenotype

An important distinction in genetics is that between a genotype – a person's genetic profile – and their phenotype – a collection of discernible traits, characteristics or vulnerabilities that in classic genetics would be seen to be expressions of the genotype. We say 'classic genetics' because it is the current unsettling of the anticipated correspondence between genotype and phenotype that makes human biology and social science such an interesting and promising coupling at this moment. We explore this in more detail in Chapter 6, *Biosocial assemblage*.

Chromosomes

Threadlike structure of nucleic acids and protein (DNA) which is found in the nucleus of most living cells and which carries genetic information in the form of specific genes. Usually arranged within the cell as a pair, humans have 22 pairs of chromosomes called autosomes which are the same in both male and females (see Figure 2.1). The 23rd chromosomal pair (the sex chromosomes) differ between male and females (females have two X chromosomes while males have one X and one Y).

DNA

Deoxyribonucleic acid (DNA) is the hereditary material found within a cell's nucleus and also in small quantities within the mitochondria (mitochondrial or mtDNA). The genetic material within DNA is stored as a code made up of four chemical bases: A adenine, G guanine, C cytosine and T thymine. There are approximately 3 million bases which are arranged in pairs such that A pairs with T and C pairs with G forming units called 'base pairs'. As well as the actual base itself there is a sugar molecule and a phosphate molecule which are both attached to the base and which form what is called a nucleotide.

Nucleotide

The base, sugar phosphate structure of DNA is in the form of two long strands that form a spiral in the form of a double alpha helix. The traditional image is one of a ladder with the base pairs forming the rungs of the ladder and the sugar and phosphate molecules forming the vertical sides of the ladder.

RNA

Ribonucleic acid is very similar to DNA; however, unlike DNA, which is double stranded (base pairs) RNA is a single stranded molecule and also tends to be much shorter than DNA. RNA contains a hydroxyl group on the pentose ring at the 2nd position which gives it the ribose rather than the deoxyribose of DNA. This leads to RNA being less stable than DNA and prone to hydrolysis (breakdown). RNA also differs from DNA in that T thymine is replaced with U uracil which is a related but unmethylated base. The single stranded and complementary nature of RNA means that it is ideally suited to the process of replication which is one of the major roles of DNA within the cell.

Gene locus

The site on the chromosome where a gene is found; these locations are ordinarily stable across chromosomes, and it is often where locations are transposed that

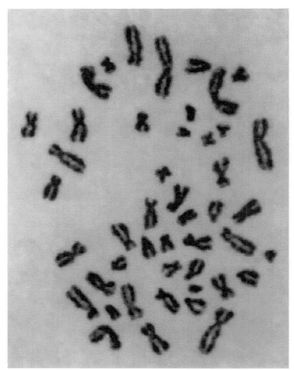

A human metaphase plate (Tjio Joe and Levan 1956/2010 cited by Gartler, 2006)

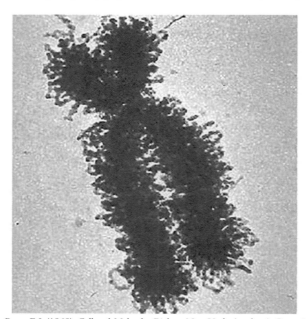

DuPraw, E.J. (1968) *Cell and Molecular Biology*. New York: Academic Press, Inc.

FIGURE 2.1 A AND B   Images of human chromosomes generated through microscopy

Genes in light grey, DCDC2 and KIAA0319, have replicated associations with written and verbal language phenotypes, namely RD and LI. Regions in mid grey mark two functional variants, READ1 in DCDC2 and a risk haplotype containing markers in KIAA0319 and TDP2, which have been functionally associated with RD and LI using animal models and molecular techniques.

FIGURE 2.2 Representation of a section of genetic code: the genes within the DYX2 locus on chromosome 6p22

Source: Eicher et al., 2014.

changes to potential function are also found. For example, for genes that have been related to reading, see Figure 2.2).

Transcription

For DNA to have effects, it has to undergo 'transcription'. Transcription is the process of taking the information from a gene – an enzyme called 'RNA polymerase' does this – and making a copy of it in the form of messenger RNA, or mRNA, so that it can go elsewhere in the cell to produce protein.

Protein

These are large biological molecules (macromolecules) that are made up of one or more long chains of amino acid residues. Proteins perform a huge number of different functions within the human body including but not limited to: DNA replication, catalysing metabolic reactions, transporting molecules and responding to stimuli. Proteins differ from one another in the sequence of their amino acids which in turn is dictated by the nucleotide sequence of their genes. The result is usually a sequence of amino acids that is folded into a very specific three-dimensional structure which then denotes its function.

Gene variants

Genes can have one or more variant, that is, the gene is not the same in all people. The effects these variations have on gene function is a key area of genetic investigation (see Figure 2.2). These variations take a number of forms: *Single nucleotide polymorphisms* (SNPs) are the most common type of genetic variation with each SNP representing a difference in a single DNA building block (nucleotide). An '*allele*' is one of the two possible forms of a gene with most genes possessing a dominant and a recessive allele. Humans are called diploid organisms because they have two alleles at each genetic locus, with one allele inherited from each parent. A gene 'mutation' is a permanent alteration in the DNA sequence that makes up a gene such that the sequence differs from what is found in most people. Mutations range in size from a single DNA building block to a large segment of a chromosome that includes multiple genes.

Missense mutation: This type of mutation is a change in one DNA base pair that results in the substitution of one amino acid for another in the protein made by a gene.

Nonsense mutation: A nonsense mutation is also a change in one DNA base pair. Instead of substituting one amino acid for another, however, the altered DNA sequence prematurely signals the cell to stop building a protein. This type of mutation results in a shortened protein that may function improperly or not at all.

Insertion: An insertion changes the number of DNA bases in a gene by adding a piece of DNA. As a result, the protein made by the gene may not function properly.

Deletion: A deletion changes the number of DNA bases by removing a piece of DNA. Small deletions may remove one or a few base pairs within a gene, while larger deletions can remove an entire gene or several neighbouring genes. The deleted DNA may alter the function of the resulting protein(s).

Duplication: A duplication consists of a piece of DNA that is abnormally copied one or more times. This type of mutation may alter the function of the resulting protein.

Frameshift mutation: This type of mutation occurs when the addition or loss of DNA bases changes a gene's reading frame. A reading frame consists of groups of three bases that each code for one amino acid. A frameshift mutation shifts the grouping of these bases and changes the code for amino acids. The resulting protein is usually nonfunctional. Insertions, deletions and duplications can all be frameshift mutations.

Repeat expansion: Nucleotide repeats are short DNA sequences that are repeated a number of times in a row. For example, a trinucleotide repeat is made up of 3-base-pair sequences, and a tetranucleotide repeat is made up of 4-base-pair sequences. A repeat expansion is a mutation that increases the number of times that the short DNA sequence is repeated. This type of mutation can cause the resulting protein to function improperly.

Where a particular 'candidate gene' is explored in association with a particular disease or trait, it is often particular variants of this already identified candidate gene that are investigated.

Pluripotent cells

Pluripotent cells are ones that are capable of developing into any type of cell or tissue except those that form the placenta of embryo.

Pluripotent genes

These are genes that are thought to be essential for the successful formation of pluripotent cells. These genes have become pivotal to our understanding and characterization of embryonic cell development.

Germ lines

These are cells that form a series and that have descended (or developed) from earlier cells in the series and are therefore regarded as continuing through successive 'generations' of an organism.

Polygeneticity

Multiple genes, potentially each with small effect, being involved in a function or, more often in the literature, associated with a trait. Often explored through *genome wide association studies* which analyse large population data sets containing substantial (but not complete) genetic information from each subject.

Epigenetics

Epigenetics is concerned with the ways that the events and experiences of a life influence and shape the way the body's genetic code is put to work but do not change the genetic code (genome) of a body (Moore, 2015) (See Figure 2.3) There are a range of accounts of epigenetic effects, some which look to persistent effects that endure across the lifetime; some which look to this to extend

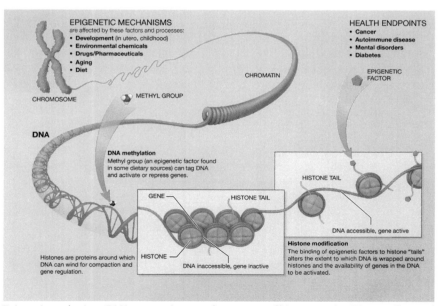

Epigenetic mechanisms. DNA wraps twice around an octamer of histone proteins. Histone tails extend past the coiled DNA. The DNA-wrapped histones continue to coil, compressing the DNA 10,000-fold. Long sections of this compressed DNA form chromosomes. Image courtesy of NIH (public domain).

FIGURE 2.3   Epigenetic mechanisms of gene regulation

Source: Molfese, 2011.

into enduring intra-generational effects; and some which suggest shorter time-frames in which epigenetic changes can be transient, variable and reversible in response to further influences in the environment. Across these accounts, epigenetic changes 'exponentially extend the computational power of the genome' (Molfese, 2011: 2). It is important to keep in mind that epigenetic regulation of gene expression is not inherently good or bad – 'it is an environmentally primed adaptation that may or may not be adaptive to future environments' (van Ijzendoorn et al., 2011: 307). Under the broad umbrella of epigenetics we can locate **nutrigenomics** (interaction between diet and the body's genetic code) and **metabolomics** (intermediate chemical processes involved in metabolism) (Mickleborough and Lindley, 2013).

Chromatin

The material in which DNA (and RNA) is carried. The DNA within the cell nucleus is packaged by special proteins called histones with the formation of protein/DNA complex being termed chromatin. Chromatin's structure is not well understood and therefore the subject of constant investigation.

Histones

Spool type structures within the chromosome around which the DNA- and RNA-bearing chromatin is wound. Without histones the unwound DNA within chromosomes would be very long indeed. While there is a huge catalogue of histone modifications described within the literature, a functional understanding of most is still relatively unknown.

Methylation

Technically this is the addition of a methyl group to a molecule. This can be added to chromatin or histone and the effects of methylation vary (Figure 2.4 shows histone methylation). This methylation process is catalyzed via enzymes and is involved in the regulation of gene expression, protein regulation and RNA processing. DNA methylation in vertebrates typically occurs at CpG sites (cytosine-phosphate-guanine sites – that is, where a cytosine is directly followed by a guanine in the DNA sequence). This methylation results in the conversion of the cytosine to 5-methylcytosine. The formation of Me-CpG is catalyzed by the enzyme DNA methyltransferase. Human DNA has about 80–90% of CpG sites methylated, but there are certain areas, known as CpG islands, that are GC-rich (high guanine and cytosine content, made up of about 65% CG residues), wherein none are methylated.

Acetylation

Simply put this is the addition of an acetyl group to a molecule. Acetylation is an important modification of proteins in cell biology; and proteomics studies have

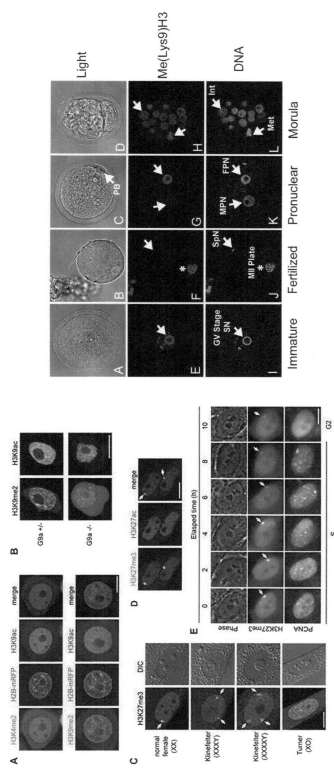

Localization of methylated histone H3 in living cells. (A–D) Confocal microscope images of living cells. (A) H2B-mRFP-expressing HeLa cells loaded with FabH3K4me2-488, or FabH3K9me2-488, together with FabH3K9ac-Cy3. (B) Nuclear concentration of FabH3K9me2 is diminished in G9a knockout ES cells. FabH3K9me2-488 and FabH3K9ac-Cy3 were loaded into conditional G9a knockout ES cells before (top) and after (bottom) the gene deletion. (C) FabH3K27me3 is concentrated in inactive X chromosomes. Arrows indicate FabH3K27me3 foci. (D) Mouse MC12 cells loaded with FabH3K27me3-488 and FabH3K27ac-Cy3. Arrows indicate FabH3K27me3 foci. (E) Behaviour of inactive X chromosomes during S phase. hTERT-RPE1 cells were loaded with FabH3K27me3-488 and PCNA-Cy3, and phase contrast and wide-field fluorescent images were collected every 15 min. Arrows indicate FabH3K27me3-enriched inactive X chromosomes. Bars, 10 μm.

FIGURE 2.4 A AND B   Histone modification captured by confocal microscopy

Source: Hayashi–Takanaka et al., 2011.

identified thousands of acetylated mammalian proteins. Acetylation occurs as a co-translational and post-translational modification of proteins, for example, histones, p53 and tubulins. Among these proteins, chromatin proteins and metabolic enzymes are highly represented, indicating that acetylation has a considerable impact on gene expression and metabolism.

Gene regulation and expression

Regulation of gene expression includes a wide range of mechanisms that are used by cells to increase or decrease the production of specific gene products (proteins or RNA) and is usually referred to as gene regulation.

Genes do control an organism unmediated; rather, genes interact with and respond to the organism's environment. Some genes are constitutive, or always 'on', regardless of environmental conditions. Such genes are among the most important elements of a cell's genome, and they control the ability of DNA to replicate, express itself, and repair itself. These genes also control protein synthesis and much of an organism's central metabolism. In contrast, regulated genes are needed only occasionally and these genes get regulated depending on the environmental stimuli that prevail.

Volatile organic compounds

These are chemicals that contain carbon and are found in all living things, they can easily become gases and can therefore be measured readily. The abundant nature of VOCs mean they are found in a variety of biological samples and are found in large numbers and varieties in exhaled breath.

Cells

A cell is the smallest unit of life that can replicate independently and they are often described as the 'building blocks of life'. The structure of different cells within the body relates to their function within a specific biological system. Human cells consist of an external **cell membrane** which is selectively permeable and so can 'control' what crosses into and out of the cell. This allows compartmentalization to occur within the system and so concentration gradients can be formed. Human cells usually contain organelles (e.g. mitochondria, endoplasmic reticulum, etc.) as well as a nucleus which has its own selectively permeable membrane. However the majority of the cell is made up of cytoplasm and this is where the majority of cellular activity takes place (i.e. enzymatically controlled reactions).

Molecules

A molecule is the smallest particle in a chemical **element** or **compound** that has the chemical properties of that element or compound. Molecules are made up of **atoms** that are held together by chemical bonds. These bonds form as a result of the sharing or exchange of **electrons** among atoms. The atoms of certain elements readily bond with other atoms to form molecules. Examples of such elements are oxygen and chlorine. The atoms of some elements do not easily bond with other atoms. Examples are neon and argon. Molecules can vary greatly in size and complexity. The element helium is a one-atom molecule. Some molecules consist of two atoms of the same element. For example, O_2 is the oxygen molecule most commonly found in the earth's atmosphere; it has two atoms of oxygen. However, under certain circumstances, oxygen atoms bond into triplets (O_3), forming a molecule known as ozone.

Atom

An atom is a particle of matter that uniquely defines a chemical element. An atom consists of a central nucleus that is usually surrounded by one or more electrons. Each **electron** is negatively charged. The nucleus is positively charged, and contains one or more relatively heavy particles known as **protons** and **neutrons**.

Metabolism

This is the collective name given to the chemical processes that occur within a human organism (body) in order to maintain life. It is the series of life-sustaining chemical transformations within the cells that have the explicit purposes of conversion of food to energy, the conversion of food for building blocks of growth and repair and the elimination of waste products within the body. Usually human metabolism is broken down into two categories; **catabolism** which is the breaking down of organic matter (usually producing energy) and **anabolism** which is the building or creation of new substances within the body (usually consuming energy).

Nutrition

This is the science that interprets the interaction of nutrients and other substances in the food that we eat in order to regulate growth, reproduction maintenance and repair of the body.

Neuroscience

Neuroscience is the study of the brain, in particular using new brain imaging technologies such as functional magnetic resonance imaging (fMRI), EEG, and MEG but also using molecular methods to study at the cellular and molecular level the brains of deceased humans (such as the brains donated by the families of deceased US NFL players) or the brains of sacrificed laboratory animals. Epigenetic neuroscience is a significant field of enquiry into the environmental influences on the way that genes within brain cells are regulated and how cells within the brain function. In recent decades there has been something of a convergence between aspects of developmental and cognitive psychology and neuroscience, as new imaging technologies have provided methods to investigate and test psychological theories of development and cognition.

Brain

The brain is the organ of the body that, to a great extent, controls the functions of other parts of the body. Popular accounts often use the computer as analogy for the brain and talk in terms of brains being 'hard wired', 'programmed' and information or memories being 'saved' on the brain as 'hard drive'. Yet contemporary neuroscience has set aside these metaphors, emphasizing that the brain is not like a computer and foregrounding its 'plasticity'. Furthermore, as we explore in Chapter 4, *Being human*, the brain's control of the rest of the body is not as complete as we often imagine.

Brain research spans a broad spectrum of scales, from the whole brain to the molecules within individual brain cells. This span reflects both what is possible with current technologies, what different researchers are seeking to find out, and the underlying theories or hypotheses that inform the approaches they take.

Neurons

These are the cells within the brain that make up the nervous system. Neurons have a cell body or 'soma' and extending nerve fibres called axons and dendrites. These enable neurons to make connexions through electrical impulses or 'synapses'. Together with glial cells and blood supply, these make up the **grey matter** of the brain.

Glial cells

These cells form part of the central nervous system are the cells that make up the **white matter** of the brain. Previously little understood and thought to be relatively unimportant 'glue' or 'insulation' for neurons, glial cells are being increasingly attended to. There are four types of glial cell: microglia, astrocytes, oligodendrocytes and NG2-glia and the specific functions of each of these is the subject of ongoing research (Jakel and Dimou, 2017).

Brain volume

This has long been associated with intelligence and/or efficacy, with larger brains considered to be more efficacious. Recent research has largely refuted this and previous associations between e.g. gender, race, poverty and brain volume and cognitive function have been shown to be unsound.

Brain regions and functions

There has been longstanding expectation that particular regions of the brain will be responsible for particular functions – a region for sight, for hearing, for feeling and so on. Such region to function correspondence does appear to exist to some extent, but this is increasingly being shown to be differentiated, mobile and fine-grained and there is significant caution amongst many neuroscientists over what is termed pejoratively neo-phrenology or 'blobology' (Hruby et al. citing Lieberman, 2006).

Brain activation, networks and connectivity

These are the aspects of the brain that for many neuroscientists are at the forefront of the field. These are researched in the laboratory using experimental set ups and increasingly also in a non-experimental 'natural' state, at rest, or even when asleep and in natural settings using mobile technology. It is possible to research these processes due to developments in brain imaging technologies which make various grain sizes within the brain available across various spans of time. Although in daily life minutes tend to be the smallest grain size that we concern ourselves with, and only then when we have a meeting or a train to catch, in the time of brain activity seconds are massive units.

Functional magnetic resonance imaging (fMRI): measures blood flow taken as a proxy for activity. This works at a temporal grain size of 2–3 seconds, and is, in effect, always slightly behind the brain: activation > blood required > blood flow. An image of the brain with coloured regions is not a picture of one brain and its active areas but a statistical graph, where activity from a number of brains (from as few as 10 or 20 to hundreds) are plotted onto a single 'brain atlas' and colour-coded to make the activity of interest stand out from all of the other activity that would have been picked up during scanning.

Electroencephalography (EEG): measures electrical activity on the surface of the brain by placing sensors on the scalp that pick up millisecond-by-millisecond fluc-tuations in voltage across neurons. These are now available wirelessly and can be used outside the laboratory.

Magnetoencephelography (MEG): measures fluctuation in the magnetic fields that occur in the brain, again through sensors on the scalp and, although more sensitive in some respects than EEG, the related equipment means that it remains high-cost and laboratory based.

Event Related Potential (ERP): can track precisely when activation happens, measured through either EEG or MEG. ERP experiments use a baseline of 'nor-mal' and compare it to a change of state when something changes or something unexpected happens. Typical ERP experiments might involve exposing subjects to a series of predefined images/sounds/words punctuated with an anomaly e.g. the subject expects to see words but intermittently sees a nonsense word.

Brain chemistry

At the cellular level, the changing chemistry of the brain has a significant influence on function. Neurons produce a range of **neurotransmitters** which are chemicals that pass between cells via **receptors** which are proteins in cell membranes that neurotransmitters can bind to allowing ions into the cell. Epigenetic changes to the production of neurotransmitters and/or to receptors, and so to the brain's capacity to up- and down-regulate these neurotransmitters, are a key target of research, as we show in detail in Chapter 6, *Biosocial assemblage*. Key neurotransmitters include:

Glutamate: an 'excitatory' neurotransmitter which stimulates the neuron when it binds with one of its receptors.

Gamma-aminobutyric acid (GABA): an 'inhibitory' neurotransmitter which inhibits activity in the nervous system.

Serotonin: the neurotransmitter associated with mood; variations in the regulation of serotonin have significant effects. A wider range of serotonin receptors exist on neuronal membranes and these mediate the effects of this neurotransmitter.

Dopamine: the neurotransmitter associated with pleasure; regulation of dopamine is associated with pleasure as well as a range of other brain functions, including memory.

Endocrine system

This is the chemical signalling system distributed across the body that releases hormones from endocrine glands to be circulated to target organs. The brain is a key site of endocrine glands and activity of the hormones these secrete. Notable hormones active in the brain include adrenaline, cortisol, melatonin, oxytocin and norepinephrine. We will encounter a number of hormones, their regulation and their functions over the course of this book.

Social sciences and sociology of education

Social sciences and sociology of education approach social processes and practices across a range of scales – from the micro level of the feelings and encounters between people; through discourses and the making of meaning, practices in social settings and institutions; to social and economic structures and systems. It is at points across these scales that we make connexions with and seek out interactions with biological processes in order to generate biosocial insights. While the conceptual resources of the social sciences and sociology of education are likely to be more familiar to many readers than the bioscience ideas outline in the previous section, we set out key sociological concepts here in order to provide an overview of the resources we draw on and to orientate our conception of the social.

Economic and social structures, economy, institutions

The structures of the economy, society and institutions are understood in social sciences to exert significant influence on what is meaningful, possible and impossible within a given society. These structures shape and constrain the social processes and practices of everyday life and the opportunities, experiences and outcomes available to individuals and groups. While critical sociology is often more focused on the fine grain of practices, interactions and subjectivities, these structures and the material conditions they generate continue to be recognized as highly important in social analysis.

Power

Understanding social systems and social relations demands an account of power. Foucault (1991) sets the idea of power that is *productive* alongside the more usual conception of power as something that is held by the powerful and wielded over the powerless. Foucault argues that as well as understanding the power embedded in the law, state or monarch, we should also take account of the power that circulates in the everyday practices of institutions, communities and persons. Foucault calls this disciplinary power. Education researchers who have developed Foucault's ideas to understand contemporary institutions and subjects have made use of the idea of bio-power to explore the ways that expert knowledges create particular sorts of individuals and manage populations. This analysis has been significant in social science critical responses to developments in the new biological sciences (Gulson and Webb, 2016, 2018).

Discourse

Discourses are shifting systems of knowledge that appear to be descriptive but, according to Foucault, are also productive. The content and status of these is variable, shifting across historical moments and milieu – ranging from what is taken as self-evident and valorized (for human biologists, genetics? for feminist theorists, the posthuman?) through to what is unspeakable or ridiculed (for scientists, astrology? for policy makers, feminism?). At a given moment certain discourses may be taken as reflecting the way things are (in the popular imagination, neuroscience?) – they become 'regimes of truth' – and this is the moment and means of the production of these truths. What discourses are circulating, how they come to be taken up and contested, and what they produce and foreclose become essential social and political questions.

Critical/political pedagogy

Pedagogy in our usage infers more than the practical aspects of teaching and includes underpinning understandings of the value and purposes of education, the nature of the teacher, the learner, the processes through which learning takes place, and the significance of relationships in the pedagogic encounter. Critical pedagogies have sought to conceptualise and identify in practice pedagogic approaches and relationships that have the potential to transform education. The goals of these pedagogies vary according to the conceptual framings and political commitments of their advocates, but include transformation of economic relations; exposure and open up of the subjectivities available to students and educators; unsettling enduring knowledges; and undoing educational inequalities and exclusions (Atkinson and DePalma, 2009; Davies, 2003; Grande, 2004; Leonardo, 2005; Teague, 2017; Youdell, 2011).

Perhaps key amongst these are 'inclusive' and 'alternative' education, that have argued for and demonstrated modes of education in which students are not sorted and sifted into the normal and the abnormal, the desirable and the intolerable, the ideal and the impossible (Youdell, 2006a, 2011; Kraftl, 2015). Taking up the ideas of critical pedagogy and transformative education, inclusive educators have advocated a move away from the 'correction' of the child who does not 'fit' schooling and instead advocated for education systems, institutions and practices that change themselves to 'fit' children (Allan, 2008; Armstrong, 2003; Barton, 2001).

Identity

Identity foregrounds social groups understood through classificatory systems such as race, class, gender, disability, sexuality, religion, nationality. Identity politics make claims to recognition of and rights for the people who come under (identify themselves as) particular categories within these classificatory systems.

Subjectivation

The idea of subjectivation, and a subjectivated subject, replaces the idea of identity and instead interrogates the social and discursive processes that allow such categories to exist and operate. Subjectivation suggests that we are simultaneously made subject to power and made a subject, explaining how a sense of self – an 'identity' or 'subjectivity' – is always the product of relations of power and social forces. This means that subjecthood is always situated and constrained – we must be 'recognizable' and we must take up this 'identification' if we want to exist as social subjects (Butler, 1997: 5). Recognition and identification are central to processes of subjectivation and the possibility of particular subject positions being resisted or given new meaning (or 'reinscribed') (Butler, 1997, 2004). Our sense of self, then, is not an awareness of an interior identity that is unique to us. Rather, our 'self' emerges as a partial awareness of the subjectivity (or subjectivities) made possible by the processes of subjectivation, recognition and identification that make us subjects (Youdell, 2006b).

Performativity

Performativity can be seen as an important element of subjectivation. Drawn from linguistic theory of words that make things happen, the effect of a 'performative' is that they make the thing they name. Here, characteristics such as gender, race or intelligence are not understood as biological givens but as performatives. Performatives are often understood as spoken or written, but also work through representations, bodily gestures, clothing and adornments, and what is *not* said or represented. This insists that we are not particular sorts of subjects outside of our subjectivation in particular discourses – while this may seem disorientating it also offers ongoing potential for change.

Embodiment

A central concern of critical social theories has been resisting hierarchies that have been claimed at various moments to be biologically determined, e.g. those based on gender, sexuality, race, disability. Uncoupling the body from the social meanings ascribed to it and challenging a biological basis for difference has been important politically and conceptually; e.g. gender decoupled from sex, race posited as wholly constructed. For instance, feminist philosopher Judith Butler has offered a compelling account of how the sexed body is only accessible to us through the discourse, meaning that an a-political or a-historical body is not accessible (Butler, 1993). Sociological concern with the body, in this framing, is about how the social subject comes to be 'embodied' and experiences her/his 'embodiment' in a particular discursive milieu.

Feeling and affectivities

Social science has an abiding interest in feeling and the significance of feeling in the social world. In thinking about feeling a distinction is made between 'affects' – the visceral, bodily experience – and 'emotion', the meaning attached to these visceral experiences. Feminist and critical scholars have developed Deleuze and Guattari's (1983, 2008) idea of affective intensities that flow in social spaces. Here affectivities are understood as flows of bodily sensation that exceed symbolic orders. The emphasis is not on the self-reflection of a subject concerned with her/his emotions, how the person says they 'feel', but on social flows of affective intensities that circulate and are pre-personal (Hickey-Moody and Malins, 2007; Bolar, 1999; Hickey-Moody, 2009; Zembylas, 2007).

Psychoanalysis

Psychoanalysis makes space for the significance of the unconscious and processes such as recognition, identification, desire and abjection (Britzman, 1998; Henriques et al., 1998). In place of the usual rational lens that is used to think about education, these ideas show how relationships, feelings and desires are important forces in education because 'knowing and learning are bound up in the unconscious emotional flows of relationships' (Bibby, 2009: 52).

Posthuman

Feminist education scholars have taken up the idea of the 'posthuman' which foregrounds the fundamental entanglement of the human with the non-human. Posthuman thinking suggests that the entanglement of nature, culture and technology is now obvious and makes it impossible to think of the human as distinct from or exceptional in its milieu (Braidotti, 2013, 2017). This also brings to the centre of analysis the fundamental entanglements or 'intra-actions' of human and non-human elements (Barad, 2007), and the capacity of non-human 'actants' to make things happen (Bennett, 2010).

New materialism

Recent new materialist approaches in education foreground the 'matter' of the body and what bodies do and feel as well as the productivity or vitality of things that precedes or exceeds representation and meaning (Coole and Frost, 2010). This has supported an invigorated interest in embodiment in sociology of education and a concern for the body itself in education (Evans et al., 2011; Ivinson, 2012; Leahy, 2009; Stolz, 2015).

Assemblage

The idea of the assemblage, developed from Deleuze and Guattari (1983, 2008) suggests that complex social formations or phenomena, such as education of learning, are formed by the coming together of a range of elements which interact to produce them. Components such as the state, policy, social practice, representation, discourse, subjectivities and affectivities interact in such assemblage (Youdell, 2015; McGimpsey and Youdell, 2015). In education studies there is growing engagement with a range of theories of complexity to understanding persistent educational phenomena and issues, and assemblage is a useful tool for conceptualizing the ways that components or productive forces come together in education and has the potential to be further developed by incorporating analyses of the workings of the body and biosocial intra-action.

Working biosocially

New techniques in metabolomics, epigenetics and neuroscience are rapidly advancing our understanding of metabolic mechanisms; gene × environment interaction, and brain function (Khalsa et al., 2016, Kumar et al., 2016) and their implications. Likewise, current social science research provides substantial insight into the social dynamics that influence education and learning (Youdell, 2011). Yet so far these insights remain largely in-discipline and potential transdisciplinary understandings remain underexplored. The current recognition of the significance of environment in biology opens a space for transdisciplinary working. Likewise, moves in social science to find ways of understanding the complexity of phenomena or assemblages, and acknowledgments of the need to engage more meaningfully with affectivities, the 'matter' of the human and its milieu, the vitality of things, and the significant interplay of nature, culture and technology together suggest important openings for a sociology-biology alliance in education.

In thinking about this trans-domain encounter it is useful to note the nature and extent of biosciences engagement with social dimensions and influences. While epigenetics and other areas of the new biosciences recognize the importance of environment and are investigating the influence of environmental factors on the way bodies function, the account of environment remains both restricted and underdeveloped when compared to sociological accounts. Of course this is not surprising given that biologists are having to reach out of their fields of expertise in order to work with environment. As we explore further in the next chapter, it is agreed, by sociologists and bioscientists alike that biosciences need more nuanced and plural accounts of environment. It is also important to avoid approaching biosciences, or

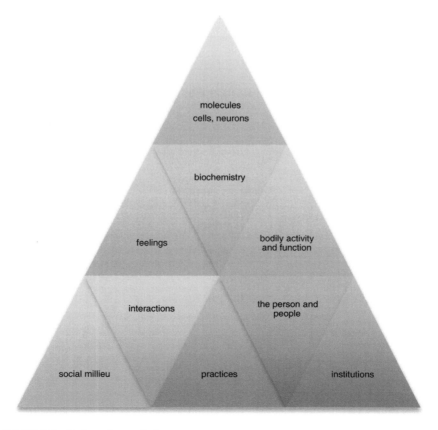

FIGURE 2.5   Scales of granularity

even specific fields amongst these, as a monolith. Evolutionary genetics and analytic chemistry are quite distinct, and neuroscientists range from those interested in gross brain structures and behavioural traits to those interested in the minutiae of neuronal membranes. Each suggests a different encounter with sociology of education.

Throughout our discussion of both biological and social sciences we have moved across grain sizes from the macro or gross e.g. economic structures, the whole brain – to the micro e.g. visceral feelings in encounters, the movements of molecules across cell membranes (see Figure 2.5). These multiple grain sizes, as well as the varied conceptualizations of the terrain and object of study, must be attended to in trans-domain biosocial work.

There is a risk of education scholarship, like policy, becoming infatuated, even intoxicated, by the state of the art of new biosciences, its technologies, and its capacity to 'see' inside the body in new ways and at new levels of granularity. There is a persistent possibility of exporting and translating prematurely or inappropriately, or of overlaying educational questions with bioscience in ways that obscure insights from critical sociological analyses of education. It is, then, important to think about the nature of the encounter. For us, this should not be the integration of biosciences into education, or the incorporation of social science understandings of the social into bioscience accounts of environment. As we emphasized at the beginning of this chapter, we envisage a transformatory, trans-domain encounter in which all fields are changed.

The account that we have offered here provides some introduction and orientation to the concerns, concepts, methods and grain sizes from across social and biological domains that we want biosocial education to bring together. Sociological accounts of the subject may seem at some distance from biological accounts of molecular activity, and they will not be simply synthesized or integrated. Rather, we approach our biosocial project with a willingness to be 'degrounded', get involved in 'rough and tumble' with other domains, and engage in experimental thinking that might go nowhere. The movement to informing education practice needs to be made with caution, and with good evidence, but with considerations we believe there is real potential for biosocial education.

3

OPTIMIZING HUMANS

The hopes and fears of 'optimizing humans'

The relationship between sociology and the life sciences has not been a comfortable one, and scholars within the sociology of education offer sustained critique of biological sciences, calling for caution in engaging with these fields (Evans, 2014; Gillborn, 2016; Gillies, 2008; Gulson and Webb, 2017). We are very mindful of persuasive accounts of the harm done through particular political uses of biological science in the past and policy misuses of scientific evidence in the present. Yet in this book we make a case for biosocial education as a field of research and as a framework for approaching education. This is a risky case to make in the field of education where social justice-orientated educationists point to the ways that science has been deployed to sort and divide and to naturalize a range of hierarchies between learners (and non-learners). We anticipate, then, that some critical educationalists will resist our biosocial project. We anticipate this resistance being offered on a number of grounds: that biosocial education does not recognize the damage that policy can do with scientific evidence (Evans and Davies, 2015; Gillborn, 2016; Rose and Rose, 2013; Wastell and White, 2012); that biosocial education inadvertently contributes to discriminatory accounts of educational (and other) failure that 'blame the victim' of racist and otherwise biased institutions (Gillborn, 2010; Gillies, 2008); and that the sorts of 'interventions' that biosocial education might advocate are inevitably caught up in normal/deficit accounts of learners and so are concerned with 'optimization' towards an 'ideal' (Gillies, 2008; Rose, 2000).

In this chapter we take up this problematic of wanting to use biosocial insights to intervene positively in education to the benefit of children, while being aware of the ethical and political concerns that surround projects for 'optimizing humans'. The task is made more complicated by the trans-national education and early years policy context which is firmly in the mode of identifying a policy 'problem' and responding with a policy 'solution' (Webb, 2013) and which seeks to these solutions in particular forms of quantitative 'evidence' (Sellar and Lingard, 2014; Sparkes, 2013), and leans heavily towards particular pockets of research in the genetic and neurosciences (Gillborn, 2016; Wastell and White, 2012). Indeed, this entrenched policy orientation away from recognition of any structurally or institutionally generated inequalities and towards individualized (universalized/ decontextualized) problems that invite solutions identified and tested through scientific evidence and randomized control trails renders any positive account of biological sciences almost unspeakable in the critical sociology of education.

In considering what it is and is not possible to say, political theorist Judith Butler suggests that '[t]he question is not what it is I will be able to say, but what will constitute the domain of the sayable within which I begin to speak at all' (Butler, 1997: 133 cited by Teague, 2017). In the sociology of education it seems that biosocial education and the potential 'optimization' that its interventions might infer demarcates the outside of the domain of the sayable – the charge of 'optimization' becomes the response (or prior foreclosure) that constitutes the biosocial and the interventions it might suggest as unspeakable in advance. This may well be why for Deborah, but not for Martin, speaking about optimization flowing out of biosocial education insights feels like speaking the unsayable. We will return to this later in the chapter when we discuss the question of 'personalization' in medicine and in education.

The question of whether new biological and biosocial sciences tend towards and/or should be used for 'optimization' provokes both hopeful ambition and anxious critique. In this chapter we consider what it might mean to 'optimize' humans and we look in detail at examples of research and interventions that might be charged with 'optimizing humans'. Through our orientation to biosocial education, we make a case for a careful optimization, showing how this is a longstanding part of what societies do, especially in relation to children; that it is often in the best interest of the child; and that, despite an understandable focus in the critical literature on interventions that might be hierarchizing or discriminatory, in fact biosocial interventions that optimize might be equalizing.

To do this we consider a selection of concrete cases, exploring the state-of-the-art from a range of biosciences to see where the science is actually up to, and what it might be able to offer. Drawing on research on **intelligence, nutrition, relationships and reading**, we show that a single blanket response, either in the affirmative or negative, is inadequate. Instead we show how individual strands of research need to be engaged and assessed independently, and we suggest that when we find ourselves reacting against bioscience in general or against a particular study, line of research, or policy adaptation, we should check carefully the source of that reaction.

Orientations to optimization

Across the fields of biological and social sciences a range of orientations to optimization are evident, orientations echoed and revised in wider popular accounts.

Social science orientations

As we have begun to explore, critical social science tends toward the position that optimization entails embedded value judgements, ethical risks and threats to equality (Gillborn, 2016; Gillies, 2008; Rose and Rose, 2013). In this perspective optimization means not accepting a whole range of cultures, forms of life, modes of parenting, sets of engagements with schooling and education outcomes. The critique is that there is a normative centre (white, middle class/elite, academic attaining) which others must be pushed to emulate (Edwards et al., 2015; Gillies, 2008).

One of the difficulties here is that sociology has something of an obligation to resist biology. In *Political Biology* Maurizio Meloni (2016) offers a compelling account of how sociology emerged out of, and dependent upon, the movement of biology towards a hard heredity concerned with the sealed interiority of the body. Meloni shows how this turn from the interaction of the social, environmental and the biological in the first half of the 20th Century set the conditions for sociology as a discreet field of knowledge positioned as untainted by the alignment of the science of hard heredity and right wing political agendas (Meloni, 2016). In the sociology of education we inherit and are caught up in the multiple re-makings of this nature/nurture divide.

Critical scholars see in optimizing moves a moralizing incitement to 'betterment', to good living, to being a good parent and good child that infers a criticism, from outside and internally. It echoes the pastoral morality of the Christian church, the protestant good life on earth as sign of God's favour. It also stands as a new instance of the self-reflexive, neoliberal subject who is engaged in a project of the self, which has been robustly critiqued by scholars who point out how this subject functions in the interest of global capital, small state free market and self-regulating, individualized and against collective and cooperative forms of politics and daily life. Critical social scientists working with ideas of bio-politics as a mode of simultaneously managing the lives of individuals and populations see in the new biosciences the emergence of a molecular bio-politics, in which the self-managing and self-realizing subject of neoliberalism, called upon to be the best they can be, is supplemented by a 'plastic subject' (McGimpsey et al., 2017) who is permanently changeable, including at the molecular level (Gulson and Webb, 2017). This plasticity at the level of the molecular body provides new sites of governance, new ways in which bio-politics can intervene and manage.

Yet not all social science comes to this position. In feminist science studies in particular, it is possible to find both careful warnings against and careful advocacy of interventions that might amount to 'optimization' of humans. In Celia Roberts' book *Puberty in Crisis* (2015) she gives an account of the well-established critique of contemporary processes of 'medicalisation', 'pharmaceuticalisation' and *'biomedicalisation'* (Roberts, 2015: 200 our emphasis). These processes are charged in the critical literature with 'controlling and manipulating biological life through industrialised science, technology and medicine' and 'actualizing optimal futures' (Clarke et al., 2010: 23–24 cited in Roberts, 2015). This charge of 'actualizing optimal futures' carries with it the suggestion, if not assertion, that to make something (or someone) 'optimal' is almost certainly to relegate others to the position of sub-optimal and to do that thing or person a disservice. Like Roberts, we want to hold open the possibility that to intervene in these ways might not necessarily be to create a 'sub-optimal' or to do a disservice and, indeed, that to make 'optimal' might be a good thing.

Roberts (2015) explores 'puberty blockers' – the use of gonadotropin-releasing hormone (GnRH) analogues – to hold off 'early' puberty in (usually) girls who are considered to be moving into puberty 'too early', as well as to hold off puberty for young people who identify as transgender and who may be anticipating gender reassignment interventions as they reach early adulthood. Of note to Roberts is the fact that feminist accounts tend towards critique of diagnosis of 'abnormal' (untimely) puberty and subsequent hormonal interventions at the same time as parallel feminist accounts promote and support the same hormonal intervention to support transgender identification and, potentially, gender reassignment.

Roberts does not directly rebuke Clarke and colleague's critical account of the biomedical actualization of 'optimal futures', but she does take up Evelyn Fox Keller's claim that 'we are surely committed to trying to maximize the development of human potential' (Keller, 2010: 84 cited in Roberts, 2015: 239). As Roberts contrasts reactions to the different purposes to which GnRH analogues are put, her reader is pushed to recognize that in the terms of contemporary feminism, actualizing an optimal future for a transgender young person may not just be acceptable, it may even be valorized. It is noteworthy that Fox Keller asserts that we are *surely* committed to maximizing (optimizing) human potential because, in much of critical sociology this 'surely' works in the opposite direction: *surely* we have learnt from the history of eugenics that maximizing potential (optimizing humans) inevitably involves sorting, hierarchizing, selecting and rejecting. Roberts' work shows how, when we understand a number of social and biological factors as folded together to make particular phenomena – for instance transgender – we no longer have the option of choosing between 'this' or 'that' cause and therefore 'this' or 'that' response, and must instead think in terms of enfolded influences and responses, some of which may well be in the realm of the biological. It also shows, however, that this brings with it disciplinary, political and ethics demands (and potential costs).

Bioscience orientations

In contrast to the general caution and concern in critical social sciences, in much of the biosciences we find hopeful ambition situated in the fine grain of specific hypotheses and research programmes and often tempered by reminders that in fields such as epigenetics, metabolomics and neuroscience research is in the early stages and much remains to be done and understood.

Despite many reminders from researchers in the biological sciences that findings are preliminary and that in some instances translation to applications is some way off, bioscience research is being put to work in policy and practice in health care, social care and education. In some instances policy appears to focus on the work of high profile vocal advocates in the biosciences (e.g. the work of the Plomin Lab on intelligence), but it is drawing on applied research in educational neuroscience (Fischer et al., 2010), developmental neuroscience (van Ijzendoorn et al., 2011; Noble et al., 2015), and criminology (Hughes and Strong, 2016). The translation of research in these fields into interventions into the lives of particular populations has itself become a policy objective. For instance, the UK Government and the Wellcome Trust recently co-financed a targeted funding stream for research-based interventions in the field of 'Education and Neuroscience' administered through the Education Endowment Fund. The Education Endowment Fund has an express objective of improving outcomes for the most disadvantaged and addressing gaps in achievement, and to testing measurable interventions, often through RCTS, in order to realize this objective. Research supported by the education and neuroscience stream, then, is precisely concerned with using neuroscience research to inform interventions that might optimize educational outcomes for targeted groups. Some critical commentators have suggested that biological optimization appears as the future into which we are now arriving, even where policy and interventions may be pushing further than the science they are built on allows (Rose and Rose, 2013).

Furthermore, 'optimization' is happening quietly anyway – prenatal testing for Down syndrome and other conditions, with these tests informing selective termination of pregnancy, has been the norm in the developed world for some time. Genetic medicine allows embryo selection using pre-implantation genetic diagnosis of conditions such as cystic fibrosis, haemophilia, motor neuron disease, sickle cell, autism and Down syndrome and this has become a regular feature of IVF reproductive services. (see for instance CooperGenomics, 2018; Adamson, 2016). Of course, these are unevenly available, with notable differences in national legislation and availability through free-at-point-of-use/insurance covered health services. Reproductive 'optimization' currently remains a luxury of the wealthy.

However commentator Jamie Metzl, a Senior Fellow of the Atlantic Council and holding a range of senior government advisory positions, has blogged on *Quartz* magazine that *'By the year 2040, embryo selection could replace sex as the way most of us make babies'*. In the piece Metzl suggests '[s]ome embryos will be identified as having a greater than normal chance of being brilliant at math, or super empathetic children' (Metzl, 2016).

Metzl makes clear that he is not advocating this approach, but rather is reporting the state of the science, the range of international practice, and the speed of advances. For Metzl we are heading to this situation no matter what, and in a competitive environment we will be either forced into such selective practices or face leaving naturally born children with lower IQ, shorter stature and so on. It is the world of the sci-fi film *Gatica* come to pass. Of course such predications and related concerns depend on traits such as IQ being 'real' and traits such as height mattering, but of course these are made real and made to matter through the very processes of their selection.

Social science and eugenics

Some of the current practices discussed in the preceding text feed into critical sociological work's concerns over eugenics. It is difficult to address the question of optimization without encountering the pervasive legacy of eugenics. In the first part of the 20th Century eugenics had both 'hard' and 'soft' strands – the latter of which suggested environmental influence and thus mutability, the former which suggested biological heredity and therefore fixity – and it was only in middle of the 20th Century that the alignment of hard heredity and right wing political projects crystalized (Meloni, 2016). During this period eugenics was the proffered scientific basis of selective reproduction – people deemed to be substandard were sterilized while the social elite, who claimed to have achieved their status because they were genetically superior, were encouraged to reproduce amongst their own ranks (a practice they had of course been engaged in for centuries in order to consolidate wealth and power).

Enactments of eugenic principles were not restricted to Nazi Germany and its empire, nor to the outer-reaches of the old colonial empires. Across the Anglo world in the first part of the 20th Century, and sometimes continuing into the 1960s and 70s, people with learning and other disabilities, indigenous people, people of colour, people living in poverty, people in prison, were actively prevented from reproducing. This relatively recent history – within the last 50 years and well within living memory – sets the context for valid concerns amongst contemporary critical sociologists over the way new biological sciences might be put to work. And this is more than just a backdrop; these sorts of historical practices create meaning in the present and they create contemporary societies as ones in which interventions into the person are part of what we do.

Optimization and ethics

This pervasive legacy of eugenics can create intense feelings (revulsion? anger?) and these are potentially bound up in responses to possibilities for interventions drawing on new biosciences. We do not ask readers to set aside such feelings, instead we want to keep these in play, remembering that bodily affectivities and the meanings made with these are a key part of the biosocial terrain and might be part of what we intervene in/with (Turner et al., 2013; Wilson, 2015; Youdell et al., 2017).

One of the issues that this throws up is what 'sorts' of optimization are acceptable, indeed part of normal life, and which provoke deep anxieties. Significant bioethical questions are raised: what is known, what should/can be applied, who defines the good life, the good body, the optimum, who pays, who has access, who profits (Rose and Rose, 2013).

To resist optimization is to resist hierarchical values being placed on humans: some humans are better than others, the lesser ones might be assisted to become more like the better ones, and some might be best. Optimization might also suggest an unspecified range of variation, within each of which there might be an optimum, a 'best'. Again, this is hierarchical and entails a stratification of value. And again it suggests intervention to reach an optimum, within whatever range of possibilities is posited.

However, resisting optimization also seems to resist an idea of mutability, to resist the idea that a body, or a person, can change or, indeed, is in a constant state of change, becoming a new version of themselves as they interact with the world they inhabit. Or resisting optimization might be to suggest that the person may be malleable, but that they should be treated as fixed, or that any intervention into the malleability that may exist is so fraught with moral and ethical problems as to render it unthinkable. The problem with this position is that it may mean that particular bodies and people are left to rot.

Critical accounts seem stuck in something of a double bind. When education systems and schools deploy ideas of intelligence or ability, critical educationists dispute this internalizing and fixing account and call to social, institutional and pedagogic influences on learning and insist that all children are provided with real and ongoing opportunities to learn without being written off as without ability or intelligence. Yet biological science-led arguments for mutability and a biology × environment interface are also met with critical scepticism and concern. Although this makes sense for the reasons we have discussed, it is also puzzling as in the case of a phenomena such as 'ability' or 'intelligence' the critical sociologists and the mutability biologists appear to be making similar case from different ground.

We find, then, that critical readings of the ways that particular forms of governance render us neoliberal self-realizing subjects have been so persuasive that any suggestion of incitement to be 'better' has become taboo. And yet, we want to agree with Fox Keller's suggestion that 'surely' we are 'committed to trying to maximize the development of human potential' (Fox Keller, 2010: 84).

Matters of health, well-being, learning and even subjecthood might provoke different sorts of responses to optimizing intentions – an intervention that enables a vital organ to function is a staple of medicine; an intervention that enables a deaf child to hear is a matter of substantial contestation. On the surface, different substantive issues may be involved in considering health interventions than learning or well-being interventions. Yet, as this example shows, health, well-being, learning and even subjecthood are not easily divisible – whether a child can hear is entangled with how that child might learn, the recognition s/he is offered, and who that child might understand her/himself to be. What a body is, what a body can do, and who a person is are not divisible.

Education and (as) optimization

In the domain of education in particular, optimization, and entanglements such as the ones sketched earlier, seem particularly evident. Indeed, we might suggest that education is inherently optimizing – each time we teach a child a new skill, are we in some way enhancing that child, are interventions that optimize precisely what education does?

We have long intervened to make children 'better' – from the emergence of mass public schooling in the 1800s to current UNESCO sustainable development goals, States and transnational agencies have sought to establish universal education for the betterment of individual children, communities and societies. We have intervened in the health of children's bodies by providing school meals (since the late 1800s) and school milk (since 1946); by fortifying food products such as breakfast cereals and bread with nutrients; by adding fluoride to the water; by immunizing against a range of illnesses; by establishing health visiting programmes and so on. This is not to say that the desirability of each of these interventions is settled, for instance immunization continues to be vigorously contested and food fortification is often an attempt to ameliorate the degradation caused by food processing methods. Nevertheless, intervention into the bodies and lives of children is well-established, both in ways that may well govern, as the bio-politics analyses show, but also in ways that may sustain and enhance. This suggests to us that as researchers concerned to e.g. understand education, enhance learning and promote social justice, we should get past the horror associated with the prospect of optimization and think carefully about it.

'Intelligence'

We begin with perhaps the most contested issue – intelligence.

> *Headteacher:* You can't achieve more than you're capable of, can you?

The Headteacher of a London secondary school said this to Deborah while she was researching school responses to education reforms (Gillborn and Youdell, 2000). At the time David Gillborn and Deborah argued that the teacher's comments laid bare how the idea of intelligence, taken to be an innate and fixed quality of the person, underpinned thinking and practice in education. This idea of fixed intelligence, they said, permeates policy; teaching practice; school life; teachers', pupils' and parents' thinking; and public understanding of ourselves. It frames what we all take to be the task of education – to get people to do the best that they can do, to fulfil their potential. But, as the headteacher states, not to do better than that, that's impossible, isn't it?

This idea of innate and fixed intelligence, alongside ideas of gifts and natural talents, are key ingredients in the meritocratic principle that says you do your best and you get what you deserve. This meritocratic principle remains a core underpinning of education systems and was restated by the UK Prime Minister in her first major speech to her party (May, 2016). Yet the question of ability has continued to fuel debate and controversy in education. Education researchers committed to social justice argue that there is no such thing as innate intelligence, only differential resources, opportunity and treatment. Whereas cognitive psychologists and behavioural geneticists argue that their research shows intelligence is a real, measurable trait and that a large proportion of variation in intelligence is hereditary, that is, passed genetically across generations.

Enter the human genome project – genome mapping and the search for genes that cause particular traits. With the mapping of the human genome, many geneticists and the public at large anticipated that a whole range of traits, conditions and illnesses, including intelligence, would be traced back to a single causative gene. This has not proved to be the case, and no gene or even set of genes have been found for intelligence.

Yet claims to genetic intelligence continue to have significant influence in education policy. Policy in the UK has been particularly sympathetic to the work of Robert Plomin's laboratory which offers the notion of 'g'; generalized genetic intelligence (Ashbury and Plomin, 2014). Much of this work has been based on twin studies, but as genetic science and the technologies to study the genome have moved, this work has expanded into 'evolutionary genetics'. This work draws on genome-wide association studies (GWAS) or genome-wide complex trait analysis which search for many genes that are thought to have small effects on intelligence (making it a 'pleurigenic' trait) using large population genetic samples (but not whole genomes). Findings speak to associations not demonstration of causation or function. Twin studies asserted that around half of variance in intelligence is hereditary (Ashbury and Plomin, 2014), a claim that has been dismantled in critical sociological work (Gillborn, 2010, 2016). Initial genome-wide association studies show a much smaller degree of hereditary variance (just 2%), but this is suggested to be an artefact of the data not an undermining of twin study findings (2014; Ashbury, 2014, Plomin and Deary, 2015) and more recent analysis is returning a higher proportion (6–15%) of variance as hereditary (Selzam et al., 2016).

Yet moving away from the notion of intelligence might lead us to quite different lines of biological research concerned with molecular *function*. This is not just of genes but of molecules within cells (neurons and especially neuronal membranes) and how this function is variously influenced, including by environment. This work shifts to a concern with learning, and memory as a fundamental underlying aspect of learning (Molfese, 2011). This is a very different set of concerns, approaches to research, and much smaller, equivocal and open-ended claims. Furthermore, it provides a different sense of the potential application in education of the knowledge that is emerging in biological sciences, as well as an honest sense of the distance we are from actually knowing how we learn and how genes and environment are involved in this.

This sense that 'intelligence' cannot be easily pinned down; that genes and more importantly their functions change under the influence of a range of environmental factors; and of the ongoing movement of memory under epigenetic influence underlying learning, all move us away from an idea of innate and fixed intelligence. Instead we are moved towards ideas of open and ongoing processes of learning, memory making, membrane renewal and gene function that might mean that 'you *can* do better than you can do', because what you can do is simply that, what you can do today. This is what David Gillborn and Deborah always argued, but now we want to approach this from the direction of the interplay of social, cultural, psychic, emotional, cognitive and chemical processes, all of which are simultaneously and inseparably biosocial. Under the Ashbury and Plomin model of 'g' generalized intelligence and education orientated to 'match' the 'g' of particular (groups of) students, we can only do what we can do – there is little space for making us more intelligent because intelligence is genetic. Under the new biosocial plasticity model, intelligence is not simply genetic and therefore fixed, because genes do not mean fixity, gene function and regulation are mobile over the life course. So even if Ashbury and Plomin's claim to the heritability of variance was right, those many genes would be potentially open to shifts in regulation and expression meaning they could function in different ways. Any notion of 'intelligence' as we have known it seems to sit uncomfortably in such a plastic model where, certainly in principle, learning is open to ongoing optimization.

Food: nutrition, justice and optimization

Food has long been a medium of intervention into the bodies and lives of children in schools (Foucault, 1991; Rose, 2000). International concerns over both obesity and malnutrition have led to interventions targeting fat, sugar and highly processed food in children's diets (International Food Policy Research Institute, 2014. In the UK, high profile media campaigns have also been influential in re-regulating school meal services, with the standard and content of food now mandated (HM Gov, 2016). Yet despite new forms of nutritional knowledge, degrees of understanding of the significance of food for molecular functioning appears uneven and policy and practice is inconsistent across nations, administrative regions and schools.

Sociological analysis of the entanglement of food in schooling points to the workings of bio-power which simultaneously governs individual bodies and populations and constitutes and constrains the embodied subjectivities of children and young people. The food practices of schools are social and political as well as material and bodily (DePian et al., 2014; Leahy, 2009; Wright and Halse, 2014; Rich et al., 2011). Yet these powerful sociological critiques of the healthy body say little of the workings of the body itself.

As longstanding interventions into the diets of school children show, there is a general scientific, medical and popular understanding that we are what we eat. New research in metabolomics is able to demonstrate this in new ways – demonstrating the metabolic function of the metabolites of nutrients. Polyunsaturated fatty acids (PUFAs) and specifically Omega-3 fish oil have been a key focus of research. Omega-3 metabolites docosahexaenoic acid (DHA) and eicosapentaenoic acid (EPA) are found in cell membranes throughout the body, in various types of tissue (including neurons and muscle tissue), and in blood and contribute to complex processes that change cells at the molecular level, including anti-inflammatory and respiratory functions (Groeger et al., 2010; Mickleborough and Lindley, 2013, Shei et al., 2014). DHA is a major component of neurons and speeds up neuronal membrane fluidity and EPA is involved in neural connectivity and reduced stress reactions (Kirby et al., 2010a; Igarashi et al., 2015; Tammam et al., 2015; Tanaka et al., 2012).

Omega-3 has become a research focus because EPA and DHA have important cellular functions and Omega-3 appears to be in short supply in cells fed on contemporary developed world diets in which Omega-3 competes for cellular uptake with overly abundant Omega-6. To give a sense of the extent of the contest for uptake between Omega-6 and Omega-3, it is estimated that the ratio of Omega-6 to Omega-3 in the cells of bodies fed on contemporary Western diets has risen from a ratio of between 1 and 2:1 in the pre-industrial period, to between 15 and 25:1 today (Kirby et al., 2010a, 2010b; 2010c; Mickleborough and Lindley, 2013). Like the epigenetic neuronal effects of nurture, the neuronal effects of Omega-3 deficiency are examined in animals. The Cohen-Cory Laboratory at Irvine has led work in this area, identifying the effects of Omega-3 deficiency on frogs and their offspring. The contrasting neuronal activity of tadpoles with expected and deficient Omega-3 (Figure 3.1) suggests strongly the role of EPA and DHA in neuronal activity. This is an effect that highlights why researchers concerned with brain function in human children look to the effects of Omega-3 (Kirby et al., 2010b; Tammam et al., 2015).

Food and schooling: what can fish oil do here?

The potential effects of Omega-3 in education have undergone some investigation, in particular in relation to general cognitive performance, reading and language learning difficulties, Autism and ADHD. In the main, this research involves randomized control trials in which children are supplemented with Omega-3 and pre- and post-supplementation tests, observations and questionnaires to measure associated effects. In some studies baseline ratios of Omega-6 to Omega-3 are measured, and cheek-cell samples are used to measure uptake of Omega-3 during supplementation.

In relation to general cognitive performance, the research to date is equivocal. A high ratio of Omega-6 to Omega-3 in the central nervous system has been shown to have negative effect on neurotransmission (Tammam et al., 2015). Omega-3 supplementation appears to have a beneficial effect, but this does not show association with cognitive performance when Omega-3 levels are measured in both red blood cells and plasma (Kirby, 2010a, 2010b). Clearer results have been offered in relation to reading and language difficulties, where an association has been shown with deficiency of Omega-3 and with phospholipid metabolism disorder (which inhibits uptake/synthesis of Omega-3) (Kirby, 2010a). Higher levels of Omega-3 have also been associated with higher literacy performance (Kirby et al., 2010c). Similarly, diagnoses of ADHD have been associated with deficiency in Omega-3, as measured through blood plasma (Kirby, 2010b), and supplementation resulting in higher Omega-3 levels, as measured through red blood and plasma cells, are associated with improved parent and teacher scores for attention, hyperactivity and

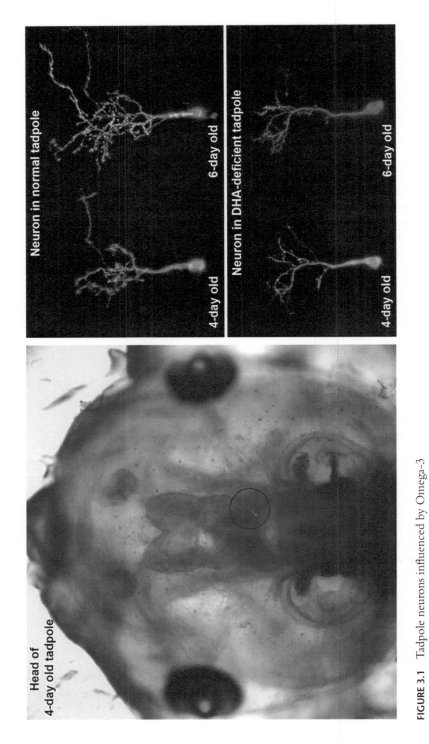

FIGURE 3.1 Tadpole neurons influenced by Omega-3

Source: Vasich (2015), with permission from the Susana Cohen-Cory Laboratory, University of California-Irvine.

antisocial behaviour (Kirby, 2010b). Omega-3 supplementation has been associated with reduced 'behavioural transgression' across student groups (Tammam et al., 2015). Supplementation has not been shown to be beneficial for students with Autism diagnoses (Mankad et al., 2015).

The Omega-3 research in education to date has been conducted within a scientific paradigm in which RCTs and quantifiable outcomes are foregrounded and has suggested associations, not molecular mechanisms or pathways. It has also proceeded from an acceptance of underpinning concepts such as cognitive ability and diagnosed learning and other disorders. A whole range of forces making up the flows of everyday life and of central interest to sociologists remain to be integrated with research into the effects of Omega-6:Omega-3 ratios and their involvement in learning. What we know from the sociology of food is that food practices are social: they are situated in and shaped by milieu; are expressions of and constitutive of culture and subjectivity; that they make, sustain and sometimes break relationships; and they are profoundly influenced by the uneven distribution of financial and other resources – a diet high in oily fish and low in Omega-6-bearing vegetable oils requires financial resources, access to good food sources, the know-why and knowhow to cut out vegetable oils and prepare fish meals, and the desire to do so. While education has long been intervening into the bodies of children through diet (school meals, school milk), at present we suggest that only children whose families are in the know and can afford the substantial cost are receiving Omega-3 supplements. This suggests that not attending to Omega-6 intakes and offering Omega-3 to all children may have real social justice implications.

Relationships: rats, attachment and classroom relationships

Research into the epigenetic effects of early care brings the theory attachment and 'good enough' care together with the effects in rats of maternal care. This field of research takes the variability in rat mothers' (dams) licking and grooming of offspring (and less centrally arch-back i.e. protective nursing) and examines the impact these practices have on the brain and behaviour of offspring, including on the offspring's subsequent rearing of their own young (see Figure 3.2). In these studies maternal rat behaviour is classified as Low, Medium and High lick groom (Low-LG, Medium-LG, High-LG) and comparisons are made across the offspring of these.

One key effect on offspring of Low-LG is on what is known as the 'HPA axis', or 'stress axis'. This axis refers to the confluence of hypothalamic, pituitary and adrenal activity, hence HPA. Rat offspring are subjected to restraint tests intended to provoke stress and therefore allow controlled analysis of reactions in the HPA, as measured by blood or brain tissue analysis. Rats reared by Low-LG dams are found to have higher and longer lasting levels of adrenocorticotropin (ACTH) (a pituitary hormone acting on the adrenal cortex) and corticosterone (an adrenal steroid hormone provoked by ACTH) than offspring of other rats.

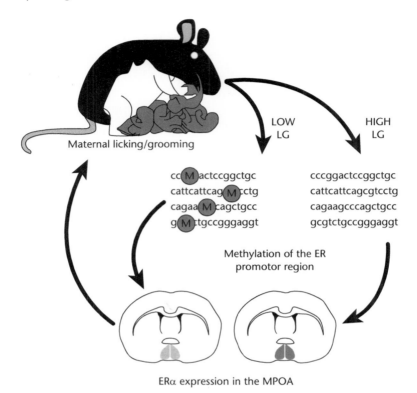

LOW
LG

HIGH
LG

Maternal licking/grooming

cc(M)actccggctgc
cattcattcag(M)cctg
cagaa(M)cagctgcc
g(M)tgccgggaggt

cccggactccggctgc
cattcattcagcgtcctg
cagaagcccagctgcc
gcgtctgccgggaggt

Methylation of the ER
promotor region

ERα expression in the MPOA

FIGURE 3.2 Methylation of the oestrogen receptor in offspring of low–lick–groom rats
Source: Champagne, 2008.

The suggestion here is that Low-LG leads to changes in the functioning of the HPA axis which mean Low-LG offspring have elevated ACTH and CRH because they are less able to 'down-regulate' their release (Champagne, 2008). Down-regulation, in this instance, means there are fewer receptors for the molecule so it has less effect (up-regulation here would mean there are more receptors for the molecule so it has greater effect). Licking and grooming behaviour is also shown to have an effect on particular mRNA, which is crucial to the functioning of cells. In order for DNA to have effects, it has to undergo 'transcription'. Transcription is the process of taking the information from a gene – an enzyme RNA polymerase does this – and making a copy of it in the form of messenger RNA, or mRNA, so that it can go elsewhere in the cell to produce protein. Low-LG offspring have lower hippocampal glucocorticoid receptor (GR) mRNA levels (glucocorticoids are a class of steroid hormones involved in metabolism of carbohydrates, fat and protein) so lower levels of receptors means these are less well down-regulated. Low-LG offspring also have higher levels of mRNA for hypothalamic corticotrophin releasing hormone (CRH) (which is a neurotransmitter involved in stress response), which means there will be more of this hormone. So, because there is less GR (glucocorticoid receptors) mRNA in the hippocampus, and more corticosterone, once the stressful event is over it is harder to down-regulate the corticosterone that has been released with HPA activation (Champagne, 2013a; van Ijzendoorn et al., 2011).

Recent work by Beery et al. (2016) notes the effect of LG on social behaviours, with High-LG offspring identified as more social. This is associated with variability in oxytocin receptor levels and distribution across areas of the brain's limbic system ('social behaviour network' Beery et al., 2016: 43). They note that oxytocin receptor gene (OXTr) methylation associated with Low-LG in rats has been associated with anxiety and depression in humans, however, OXTr methylation is variable over time and over tissue, and they highlight that human studies rely on blood tissue which may or may not reflect brain tissue.

Across this field of animal research, findings suggest that higher levels of licking and grooming behaviours between adult and infant animals optimize a range of capacities in offspring across their life course, and that these capacities can be reinstated through High-LG relationships into the animal's adolescence.

Care, stress and schooling: what rats can teach teachers

Critical sociologists may find somewhat discomforting (even preposterous) the idea that rat dam behaviour and its effects in rat offspring might have some relevance for the education of human children. Yet researchers in the field suggest that the relational and environmental stressors that are introduced to rats under controlled laboratory conditions are indeed reflective of the sort of amalgam of environmental factors that coalesce to create conditions of profound disadvantage for children: '[f] or humans, conditions of chronic poverty may, in fact, be a close approximation of the constant manipulation of the environment used in research with rats or rhesus monkeys' (van Ijzendoorn et al., 2011: 308).

Of great importance in thinking about the implications or practical relevance of this research to humans, is the fact that these epigenetic changes in the brain are not fixed (Tognini et al., 2015) and emphasize the significance of the scope of plasticity in the human brain. In rat studies this is borne out by the effects of positive intervention – where infant and adolescent offspring of Low-LG dams are fostered to High-LG dams, the HPA axis effects are reversed (Champagne, 2008).

Sociology has approached policy predicated on the claim to the effects of mothering on children with extreme caution, rightly noting the tendency for such policy and its enactments to dislocate families from the structural and material conditions that pattern their lives and therefore make mothers singly responsible for their child's poor relative outcomes (Gillies, 2008). But this policy inflexion does not follow necessarily from the epigenetic research, nor is it reflective of the way that the scientists themselves see the work travelling – as we indicated earlier, van Ijzendoorn makes a parallel to poverty, not mothering.

In thinking about humans, relatively straightforward lick groom behaviour must be translated. An established comparison is with attachment theory and the sensitive-responsive mothering that is popular in the early intervention literature (van Ijzendoorn et al., 2011). Yet the plasticity that is demonstrated across infancy and adolescence suggests a concern with a whole range of modes of relationality and relationships spanning childhood into adulthood. This suggests we might look outside the mother-child dyad and the family to include relationships in classrooms with teachers and other adults as well as with peers. This plasticity and the variability of the HPA axis should guard against these research findings being taken up as evidence of organic, albeit epigenetic, causes for diagnosed disorders. Changes to the HPA axis prove to be adaptive for some (Ijzendoorn et al., 2011, Beery et al., 2016).

Furthermore, such epigenetic adaptations may well be susceptible to the everyday processes, practices and feelings of the classroom and school, just as they are to early experiences of nurture. This highlights the potential significance of this research for understanding, facilitating and maximizing learning. There is longstanding psychoanalytic work in education that emphasizes psychic processes in the classroom and the profound importance of the teacher's relational capacities – to love, after Bion, and to hold the child in mind, after Winicott (Bibby, 2011; Britzman, 1998; Teague, 2015). Attending to the biosocial nature of relationality and learning, then, has the perhaps counter intuitive potential to move difficulties in the classroom *out* of the child, pursuing instead an array of interacting influences in the environment, including the classroom, and the ways in which these become embodied in order to optimize children's capacities to learn.

Reading

Being able to read might, we hope, be a relatively uncontentious goal to posit for all children. Certainly at the level of policy making and educational institutions, literacy is understood as an incontrovertible good for all. That said, the reasons why children enter formal education differently prepared to read, and why some learn to read readily and others do not, opens up a range of intersecting social, cultural and biological debates about parenting, early years education, the differential availability of language- and reading-learning resources in the home, diagnosable language and reading difficulties and dyslexia, and the neural mechanisms of reading. Intervening in reading, then, might entail optimization. Learning, it seems, is seldom uncontentious.

Professor of Education Neuroscience at Cambridge University, Usha Goswami, is a leading reading researcher and her lab is at the forefront of neuroscience in education. The work of her lab stands out because of its sustained core focus on language and reading learning, and because of its emerging work that is suggesting mechanisms, not just structure-function associations, for learning to read. Education neuroscientists themselves say that the quality of applications of neuroscience in education have been 'variable', 'premature' and even 'overexuberant' (Hruby and Goswami, 2011: 156) but that reading is the best site of application (Hruby and Goswami, 2011 citing Varma et al., 2008). The point of such work is not to capture images of the brain reading for its own sake, but to support reading acquisition and 'remediate severe instances of dysfunction' (Hruby and Goswami, 2011: 158).

Specifically, this work is concerned first, with understanding the brain regions, networks and activities involved in language and reading learning, and second, with developing interventions based on this understanding that can support and accelerate the language and reading learning of children who are struggling compared to their age peers and/or who have a diagnosis of a language or reading impairment. This 'remediation' of 'dysfunction' suggests a project of 'optimization' at the centre of reading research. This, then, is neuroscience using new bio-technologies to look to the interiority the brain and its functioning across a range of grain sizes in order to understand and intervene to improve the capacity to read.

Of course what happens in the brain as we learn to read may be of general interest to educators, and perhaps to all of us with an experience of learning to read. It might tell us about how reading might be better taught, what skills are needed to build reading on, and when best we might start preparing children to read and then start formal reading instruction. But emerging evidence of neural mechanisms of learning to read may be of particular interest because it also tells us what might be happening in the brain when reading or language learning is difficult or blocked (in the psychological parlance 'impaired') and it might tell us what mechanisms might be intervened into, provoked or supported in order to facilitate the reading of children, and adults, struggling to read.

Engaging with this work requires us to take on a number of proceeding ideas: that language and reading learning can be developmentally 'normal' or it can be 'impaired'; that while learning to speak happens ordinarily and is universal, learning to read is an actively acquired skill and requires concerted and structured instruction/effort; that language and reading may be impaired by specific disorders, a key one of which is diagnosed dyslexia; that children might be identified as at risk of dyslexia through family history i.e. others in the family diagnosed as having dyslexia; and that dyslexia and other conditions can be identified and intervened into.

This begins to suggest why critical education researchers might be averse to researching the functioning of children's brains as they learn to speak and read, and then intervening to improve the language and reading of children doing the least well. It demands teacher assessments and judgements transformed into hierarchies and normative frames in which the children of interest are those not performing as they might – identified by teachers as 'struggling readers' or having reading 'dysfunction'. These frames of judgement are themselves orientated by notions of age and development and 'right' times, and a concomitant fixed temporal pacing of schooling in which children get 'left behind'. This temporal fixing is concretized in the neuroscience research which mobilizes controls based on chorological age and reading level matching.

Disability Studies in education contests such diagnoses, presenting instead an account of the social and institutional constitution of disorders and responding with a politics of difference (Allan, 2008). Special Educational Needs, on the other hand, works with a model of impairments, disorders and related diagnoses, delineating conditions to then be intervened into. In sum the issues exercising the interface between education psychology, special educational needs and disability studies have long been, is there a problem? If there is, what sort of problem is this? Is it organic, social, or emotional? Is it interior to the child to be intervened in and ameliorated? Or is the problem the institutional and societal incapacity to accommodate difference? With schooling in the critical sociology of education as it overlaps with inclusive education and disability studies, Deborah would previously have eschewed the language of disorder and diagnosis and instead sought to think in terms of emergent language practices, dispositions, skills.

With this critical orientation we may wish in principle to accommodate a difference which is not reading. But in the context of an education system that wants all children to have learnt to read by the age of 6 and which is intent on comparing them with each other in order to assert a norm, is such an open orientation to non-reading realistic, pragmatic, fair? Do non-readers wish to not read?

The findings of the neuroscience research conducted by Goswami's lab informs interventions that have the potential to enable those children who have struggled to learn to read and fallen behind their age peers to catch up. In the terms of critical education, ideas like 'falling behind' and 'catching up' are part of the problem of competitive, hierarchical and differentiating education system and institutions and part of what critics of 'optimization' are objecting to. We may well prefer a model such as that adopted in Montessori schools or in the Finnish system where teaching children to read and write is left until they are six or seven, when most children pick it up very rapidly. Indeed, the interventions demonstrated by Goswami are also effective in contexts where reading teaching is left later and prereaders are age 6 (Clark cited by Goswami, 2015). Nevertheless, in the face of many education systems in the highly developed post-industrial west as they stand today, reading interventions that enable children to 'catch up' have the potential to make a number of important things happen: they might actually improve the reading skills of the children doing least well; give children a chance of doing well; help to close gaps (Plak et al., 2016); and shift teachers' (everyone's) attachments to notions of fixed talents and abilities and their obverse – school failure.

The neuroscience of reading

In order to think about the usefulness and implications of education neuroscience reading research, it is necessary to understand it within its own paradigm dialogue with other domains that have an interest in children's reading and their educational experience more widely. Education neuroscience does not treat reading as a technical skill, but as a complex process of meaning making:

> [T]he more complex sub-processes in readers' meaning construction seem to tap areas that process word meaning, syntax, semantics, text and narrative structure, tone, prior knowledge, emotion, and more in a multidirectional fashion and with great variability between subjects and readings.
>
> *(Hruby and Goswami, 2011: 158)*

This means that brain imaging does not 'show' brain areas for reading, rather it shows anatomical and activational differences. This means that 'we cannot immediately determine from these [brain image] data alone whether the difference is neurological/genetic or environmental/instructional' (Hruby and Goswami, 2011: 159). There are, it appears, likely to be multiple influences on reading within and across individuals.

Goswami and colleagues make clear that, if there is region to function correspondence, it is complex – multiple brain regions activate during an activity such as reading, there are disparities across studies and readers, and data are correlational, not evidence of what the activity in a brain region or network actually means, or what a brain is actually doing (Bhide et al., 2013; Fischer et al., 2010). The timeframe of activity to function correlation is important. Hruby and colleagues suggest that in relation to reading, the most promising correlational imaging studies are able to 'localize functional brain activity anatomically' and show 'neural activity that localize it in the time course of a reading event' (Hruby and Goswami, 2011: 157). Nevertheless, in relation to reading, 'we cannot yet dependably match specific brain areas to categories of function that may be impaired in a struggling decoder' (Hruby and Goswami, 2011: 157).

The limits to neuroscience knowledge of reading leaves open the question *what does the brain do when it reads?* There are a range of current theories, with various types of neuroscience evidence and claiming different sorts of proofs, from theoretical, to correlation to potential mechanisms. A popular and widely researched field of inquiry has focused on activity in a part of the brain that has come to be known as the Visual Word Form Area, or VWFA, and EEG research has measured activity in the VWFA during word recognition tasks and identified patterned differences in struggling readers. A novel emerging approach has investigated impaired auditory and may have moved on from correlations between brain regions and reading and begun to identify a neural mechanism of reading and reading difficulty. Research focusing on auditory processing has explored rhythmic processing; exploring rapid auditory processing and sensitivity to intensity and pitch of rise times (amplitude modulation) in onset-rime and phoneme. Findings suggest that rise time sensitivity and rhythmic processing are affected in children with dyslexia, and persist over the primary school years, and that pre-reading children's awareness of music rhythm is a better predictor of reading than letter and phoneme sound awareness (Goswami, 2015). We examine the auditory processes involved in detail in Chapter 7, *Biosocial learning*; here we focus on the interventions that this research has informed.

Reading interventions: 'GraphoGame Phoneme' & 'GraphoGame Rime'

Insights into the mechanisms of reading have been used to develop computer assisted reading interventions that are showing cross-language effectiveness.

Education neuroscience studies do not suggest that the efficacy of these interventions is because they are computer assisted reading intervention, however they do note positively that being computer assisted means interventions can be closely tailored (Kyle et al., 2013) and, for struggling readers who also struggle with attention the computer may facilitate a focus and minimize distraction (Plak et al., 2016). It is noteworthy that this capacity to tailor in real time as a child responds has been the focus of specific criticism in relation to their use in testing regimes, where it is suggested that the responsiveness of the testing programme in fact closes down what it is possible for a child to encounter, via algorithms based on norms but which proliferate the norm based on their own functioning (Thompson, 2016). Once again, we confront the polar orientations of sociology and neuroscience in education.

Graphogame was developed in Finnish, a 'transparent' language where letter and sound correspondence is direct, but has been deployed in 20 international languages, including languages with various degrees of correspondence, as well as ideogram (picture) based languages such as Chinese. Across language types, Graphogame has shown improvements in reading for those struggling before the intervention. The work on English language reading tends to talk about both 'struggling' readers and those 'at risk' of having reading problems. Elsewhere two struggling cohorts – one with dyslexia diagnoses and one with 'delayed' reading have been used (Plak et al., 2016).

In the UK, English language study a 'normal cohort' was compared with a cohort identified as 'at-risk of developing reading difficulties due to their low pre-reading skills'(this is not 'family risk' of dyslexia) (Kyle et al., 2013: 8). Cohorts were subdivided with some using Graphogame Phoneme and some using Graphogame Rime. As synthetic phonics is mandated in primary schools in England, it was anticipated that Graphogame Phoneme would simply supplement general phonics instruction, while Graphogame Rime would add a further area of learning, informed by auditory neuroscience understanding of rime in reading learning (Goswami, 2014). Graphogame Rime did indeed produce stronger results than Phoneme, with both showing improvement over a control group, but gains were not statistically significant.

> [A]pproximately 16 months after the intervention ended, the reading accuracy, fluency and spelling skills of the at-risk children who played Grapho-Game were commensurate with those in the mainstream classroom whereas the children who received the traditional intervention still exhibited delays.
>
> *(Kyle et al., 2013: 8)*

Education neuroscientists are clear on the potential value of such interventions, in particular when these are based on accurate understandings of the mechanisms of language learning difficulties:

> Identifying the correct cause (or causes) of dyslexia would benefit the education of millions of children, enabling early environmental enrichment. In

the future, accurately targeted enrichment may even allow this academically limiting disorder of learning to be eradicated.

(Goswami, 2015: 52)

With an emerging appreciation of mechanisms researchers and educators can begin to think very precisely about interventions such as Graphogame Rime which specifically works to entrain rise time discrimination in struggling readers, with apparent success. This success of a mechanism-informed intervention begins to suggest that the reading of all children might be optimized.

Cautious optimization

A biosocial orientation releases us from a (false) moral dilemma over whether we ought to or can engage the biological and the optimizing interventions its knowledges might inform, because we see how the biological is already folded together with the social, psychological, and cultural, and how optimizing humans, ourselves and others, is part of living. The moralizing approach that can overshadow proper concerns about eugenics is problematic in the contemporary moment when it is increasingly evident that the biological and the social are inescapably entangled and that plasticity is at the centre of the human condition. Not all interventions are 'bad', indeed not all activities that might be named as modes of bio-politics are undesirable. We need to consider individual cases, and engage their productive as well as their governing force, and not persist in a polarized (and unrealistic) debate over 'optimization'. It is also important that we keep sight of the fact that optimization is not only biological – the social can also be a site of optimization. The entanglement in positions, including this one, needs to be set out. We should be using the knowledges we have with care, but we should be using them, especially to give resources/skills/capacities to those currently most disadvantaged. We are optimizing humans.

4

BEING HUMAN

Brain-body-environment entanglements

Introduction

The purpose of this chapter is to think about the person that each of us is, to explore how that person comes into being and how that person is related to the brain, body and environment. This relationship might seem self-evident – we all have bodies, of which brains are a part, and the workings of these brains and bodies and the contexts and experiences of our lives are all part of the person we become. But as we show in this chapter, things are not so straightforward.

In thinking about a person 'coming into being' we are making use of sociological ideas about the person as emergent through social processes of 'embodiment' and 'subjectivation' and putting these ideas alongside biological work on the 'plasticity' of the brain and body. That is, we want to understand 'being human' through brain-body-environment relationships at the level of the cell, the organ, the whole organism, the whole person and the milieu. As we attempt to understand being human we map out brain-body-environment relationships and influences that run in a variety of directions and include the interactions of a number of factors at once. We explore how the brain, the body and the environment relate to each other as well as how they contribute to making the person. We would like to forego a brain/body distinction completely, keeping the brain in its place as an organ of the body. But, its popular, elevated special status means we need to attend to it separately, even if this is only to then go on to resituate it as an integrated part of the body.

We find the idea of *entanglements* particularly useful here as it conveys for us multiple factors and directions of influence in a way that the idea of interaction can sometimes lose. This is not to say that we are willing to stop at an assertion of multiple influences, messiness, or complexity. As we investigate being human through body-brain-environment entanglements, we seek to detail some of the precise relationships and lines (mechanisms) of influence that are involved in these and through which the environment becomes instantiated in the brain and body and shapes and constrains the being of the person. This may seem like a convoluted set of relationships, but we want to understand the precise character of these crisscrossed and porous entanglements – across membranes, across zones and networks in the body, across body and environment, and across bodily and social forces.

Environment

In thinking with the idea of 'environment' we take up the lexicon of those biological sciences that are concerned with the interaction of the biological and the environmental. Reflecting back on the epigenetics schematic that we looked at in Chapter 2, we note again the short list of environmental factors that affect epigenetics mechanisms that is offered in the image: 'development (in utero, childhood); environmental chemicals; drugs/pharmaceuticals; aging; diet' (Molfese, 2011). Condensed into single words on a schematic, these environmental factors seem broad and disconnected from the social or cultural. We know that there is a rich sociological literature exploring the ways that social forces – from macro structures and institutions to the mundane practices of daily life – are at play in these, each shaped by and shaping social experiences of e.g. poverty, citizen status, age, geographic/spatial location, social class, race and ethnicity, disability status, and so on. Indeed, it is the persistent association of such factors with particular marginalization and disadvantage that makes us look for ways of understanding the complex array of biosocial forces that produce these patterns, including in the bodies of particular groups of people.

Social sciences, and perhaps sociology and cultural studies in particular, can offer a significant expansion of 'environment' to epigenetic and other bioscience work that is interested in the interaction of body and environment.

This is recognized by social scientists who identify a key challenge as:

> [C]reat[ing] adequate accounts of lived, everyday complexity as it emerges through the social *epigenome*, that is myriad miniscule interactions that are at once socioculturally and materially, relationally and biologically situated.
>
> *(Chung et al., 2016: 171)*

This is also recognized by bioscientists working in epigenetics. Leading researchers in developmental epigenetics say that scientists need to be as careful and precise with their definitions and uses of environmental factors as they are with their epigenetics: 'many correlational G × E studies assess genes in a very precise way but fail to measure the environmental component in an equally precise manner' (Belsky and van Ijzendoorn, 2015: 1).

In the spirit of this recognition of the nuance and complexity of environment, we extend that notion of environment in order to allow a more nuanced encounter between the biological and the sociological, including in our thinking about environment all sorts of things, practices, relationships, ideas and institutions. In this sense the notion of 'milieu' may be a better sociological fit to the sorts of factors we want to include in our thinking about environment, but given that the notion of environment is already established in biological and social biology literatures we will carry this notion forward, albeit in our expanded way.

Being human

A person does not pre-exist her/his encounters with the world, nor is she/he the realization of a set of internal biologically encoded potentials that unfold through a process of development. The sociological and biological ideas that we draw on and bring together can be used to instead understand being human as an ongoing process, what Deleuzians might call 'becoming'. From this starting point we are seeking to tease out the trans-domain entanglements of the brain, body, environment and person.

In this chapter and throughout the book we use the language of the person, rather than the more abstract and technical language of the 'subject'. Even though, as we detailed in Chapter 2, conceptually we suggest that we are subjectivated as social subjects, for the most part we each experience ourselves, and those around us, as people, as human beings. Recognition or identification has failed or been refused when the person or the human is not recognizable as such – these are the limits and politics of subjectivation.

As has become a regular refrain in this book, across disciplines the body, brain, environment and person are each treated very differently, with divergent understandings, disparate conceptual framings, and starkly different problems, questions and techniques. To state the obvious: social theory and research foreground the person and life contexts; human biology foregrounds the workings of the body, both healthy and unhealthy; and neuroscience foregrounds the structures, activities and functions of the brain (which is often not the same as the 'mind' of philosophy). It is easy, then, for ideas generated in each of these domains to be at cross purposes with ideas generated in other domains, or for researchers in each domain to simply be oblivious to the work and ideas of those in others. One of the tasks of this chapter is to map the state-of-the-art and limits of discipline knowledge and explore points of connexion and incompatibility across fields. From this we explore the potential for new possibilities to be generated through trans-domain encounters. In this chapter, then, we map accounts from sociology, biology and neuroscience in an attempt to offer a picture of what we know and do not know, and how these different knowledges might be joined up. We do this anticipating 'degrounding' (Butler, 1993) and destabilization as we try to establish 'dissonant alliances' (Wilson, 2015: 172) across these domains. Indeed, these encounters may lead to the 'metamorphosis' of concepts (Malabou, 2009) as meanings from different disciplines collide – metamorphoses that could begin transforming disciplines and even our notions of knowledge domains.

Person 1 – the social (sociological) subject

Who the person is, where the person emanates from, and where the person is located are longstanding social, psychological, philosophical and theological questions that bring to the fore questions of self-identity, development, social relationships and power as well as the soul, vitality, consciousness and self-knowing.

We find scholars grappling with the nature of and relationship between the body, the mind, the person and the soul or vital life force in writing dating back, for example, to Augustine's early Christian writing on the will (Sheed, 1978); early modern religious work on the body and sinfulness (Kempe, 1990) and the possibility of knowing God (Hodgson, 1944); and Spinoza's philosophical work on the life force or 'conatus' that is neither rational will nor soul but desire for life itself (Spinoza, 1996). This latter concern with the life force persists into turn of the twentieth century 'vitalism', separating matter from a secularized 'vitality' (Bergson, 1998) and on into contemporary new materialist work on the agentic force of matter (Coole and Frost, 2010) and posthuman work on the entanglement of human and non-human things (Braidotti, 2013). Yet despite these new forays into vitalism and posthumanism, taking the long view we find that 'rationality' assured by a mind-body split has dominated.

Descartes represents a key moment in the separation of the (rational) mind from the (excessive and potentially sinful) body. Descartes asserts the capacity for rationality and self-mastery, establishing a 'rational man' that has persisted into contemporary scholarly and common-sense accounts of the person. Foucault's critical intervention into this line of thought has shown how this version of the thinking person has been sedimented as a regime of truth and the crucial role of European colonialism in proliferating this account globally has been demonstrated (Foucault, 1991, 1990; Said, 1997, 2003). Critical studies of science have built a compelling account of the way that this understanding of rationality becomes embedded in science and how scientific enquiry becomes the effort to corral the body, and nature more widely, by knowing and intervening into it (Foucault, 2002; Fox Keller, 2010; Franklin, 2007, 2013). Whether this critical characterization of science continues to be either a good or useful account of work at the leading edge of new biological sciences is something we will turn to shortly. For now we note the persistent productivity of the exchange between human exceptionalism and modern science.

Against the rational man of modernity, a range of critical social, political and psychoanalytic theories have posited a 'decentred' subject. As we began to show in Chapter 2, in place of Cartesian man (sic), we find a subject who is contingent and in the making. The 'decentring' of the subject has made a number of moves and reconfigured the subject along multiple lines:

- a subject who does not endure but is continually made (Butler, 1990, 1997; Derrida, 1978, 1988; Lyotard, 1984)
- a subject who cannot know him/herself or be fully known (Butler, 2005; Grosz, 1990, 1995)

- a subject who is fundamentally dependent on relationality with and recognition from another (Butler, 1997, 2004) and made in relations of power (Foucault, 1990, 1991)
- a subject who is no longer at the centre of history as its driving force and who is not exceptional relative to other living creatures and non-living elements (Braidotti, 2013)
- a subject who is perhaps not even a subject, but is a nomadic person 'of the line' and 'becoming' (Deleuze and Guattari, 2008).

This decentering of the subject and assertion of the subject's fundamental dependence and incompleteness also suggests a 'precariousness' – being a person is not a given and may be at risk. Explorations of this precarity have taken place in the context of a recent shift in social and political theory to a focus on the 'human'. Judith Butler's *Precarious Life* (2004) offers an important starting point, as it explores the status of the human in the post 9–11 context of the 'war on terror' and associated global dislocations and migrations. Butler shows powerfully how some lives are human and therefore both liveable and grieve-able, and other are less-than-human, each constituted through persistent processes of subjectivation.

This decentering also foregrounds human entanglements with the natural and technological non-human. Rosie Braidotti, a leading thinker of the 'posthuman' (2013), stresses the intense mediation of the contemporary human by technology and, following Spinoza, suggests that there is no difference between the natural and manufactured non-human. The non-human, she suggests, bridges the gap between nature and culture and establishes a 'monistic' view of the human and non-human, all made of the same matter (Braidotti, 2016). With this framing, 'the posthuman knowing subject' is seen in process 'to singular becoming' (Braidotti, 2017) and the ethical and political implications of human/non-human entanglements come to the fore.

The person, or human, is not self-evident, and the status of being human is not about the rational mind's conquering of the animal body – power, culture and meaning as well as biology are tied up in who we are and who we can be.

Embodiment and materiality

The fact of the body of these socially conceptualized persons has not gone unnoticed in sociological work. Feminist theory and research in particular has a persistent concern with the way that meaning comes to be attached to bodies and how bodies are experienced and seem to constrain what and who it is possible to do and be.

In earlier accounts of feminism we see a move to separate sex and gender and disrupt any linear relationship in which the biological could be said to determine the social. Here the focus is on the social (Fuss, 1990) and discursive (Butler, 1990). Yet this does not necessarily disregard the body and experiences of embodiment (Grosz, 1995). Indeed, the most compelling 'poststructural' feminist work on gender has a strong recognition of the significance of the materiality of the body and seeks to engage this without returning to a sex-gender causal correspondence. In response to criticisms that understanding the performativity of gender was to erase the embodiment of gender, in *Bodies that Matter* Judith Butler writes:

> Is there a way to link the question of the materiality of the body to the performativity of gender? And how does the category of 'sex' figure within such a relationship? Consider first that sexual difference is often invoked as an issue of material differences. Sexual difference, however, is never simply a function of material differences which are not is some way both marked and formed by discursive practices. Further, to claim that sexual differences are indissociable from discursive demarcations is not the same as claiming that discourse causes sexual difference. The category of 'sex' is, from the start, normative: it is what Foucault has called a 'regulatory ideal'. In this sense, then, 'sex' not only functions as a norm, but is part of a regulatory practice that produces the bodies it governs, that is, whose regulatory force is made clear as a kind of productive power, the power to produce – demarcate, circulate, differentiate – the bodies it controls.
>
> *(Butler, 1993: xi–xii)*

Mobilizing such an orientation, in her work on the way that social categories of gender adhere to particular bodies in ways that are difficult to escape, Mary Lou Rasmussen writes about how women police the use of women's public toilets, moving to eject those who, while self-evidently women, are embodied in ways that do not fit the normative criteria of women (Rasmussen, 2009). Reflecting on her own embodiment, Rasmussen notes that the vigour with which women persistently attempt to expel those bodies that do not match gender norms exposes the inseparability of sex and gender – the body and the social – and the endurance of normative identity categories that, ironically, make any easy call to jettison either biology or identity and move on to other forms of politics a luxury of those who fit readily within these classifications. Similarly, in Deborah's work positing the inseparability of sex-gender-sexuality, the demand that bodies adhere to normative modes that are at once social, discursive and embodied is demonstrated in the mundane but powerful practices of boys and girls sitting on a school assembly hall floor and respectively displaying and concealing genital regions (Youdell, 2005).

Concerns of this sort are extended further by Braidotti's move to bring back into the centre of analysis the 'biomateriality' of the body (Braidotti, 2017), and this is a concern that spans what might be referred to as feminist new materialism (e.g. Bennett, 2010; Coole and Frost, 2010; Frost, 2016). In particular relation to new biological sciences, Braidotti draws on a Deleuzian reading of capital as producing knowledge and capitalizing on it: 'knowledge about life becomes the codes of genetics and the algorithms of computational systems'. But while there is extensive science and technology studies literature on the force and effects of biosciences, new materialist feminism and posthumanism have only recently begun to engage the biological in productive ways. For instance, Elizabeth Bennett (2010) has begun to consider Omega-3 fish oil as a component in assemblage; Celia Roberts (2015) has explored the biopsychosocial influences on sexual development; and Elizabeth Wilson (2015) has traced the relationship between the social, the neurological and the enteric (the gut) in the production of depression.

Person 2 – biologies of the brain and body

The fields of human biology (and we include neuroscience here) divide the body up into zones and functions. For example, at the level of the organ: the brain, the lungs, the gut – cognition, respiration, digestion; or at the level of the cell: the membrane, DNA – compartmentalization, protein instruction.

Fields within the biosciences have developed according to such division and deep knowledge has come to require such specialization. Furthermore, scientific method demands hypothesis, experiment and observation, analysis and causal relationships/mechanisms at grain sizes smaller than the person or body as a whole – indeed these relationships/mechanisms are increasingly being understood at the level of the cell, membrane, molecule or gene. The price paid for this precision has been an apparent fracturing of the body, interrogated and understood in parts, not as a whole. This has led critics in sociology of science or science and technology studies to charge biosciences with reductivism – reducing the complexity of the whole person to a single part, and mechanisms and functions to one-to-one relationships, and failing to engage with the dynamic multiplicity of influences on the body and how it works. For instance, a field of research may know the mechanism of a molecule, but may not know how that mechanism relates to another.

However, in developing understanding of a molecular mechanism, bioscience recognizes the significance of this mechanism to the functioning of the organism as a whole and the complexity of biological processes and mechanisms and their interaction. Hence the burgeoning of translational science and the research focus on understanding the impact of focused cellular mechanisms. Likewise, work on complexity in the biosciences: which recognizes the organism as emerging from many interconnecting mechanisms; systems biology, which models complex biological systems; fields such as nutrition, environmental physiology and exercise physiology, each concerned with the interaction of the body and specific elements of its milieu; and epigenetics, which examines environmental influence on gene regulation and expression. Each of these contemporary fields in biology rebuts criticisms of reductionism and suggests a new orientation to study in the biosciences.

As we engage carefully and productively with new biological sciences we begin to find that some of our conceptions of science are indeed just that – popular (mis-) conception or critical accounts that no longer reflect the fields of study as they currently operate.

Brain as body

Contemporary bioscience challenges established critical accounts that suggest that science works with a brain/body split that echoes the series of mind/body, rational/irrational, human/non-human binaries that emanate from the model of Cartesian man. In contemporary bioscience the brain is not positioned as the 'boss' of the body in any straightforward or universal way, rather, the brain is recognized as an integral part of the body. To think of the brain as the boss of the body is to anthropomorphise the brain and body: at the level of molecular function neither brain or body has intent or forward insight – brain and body have multiple, interacting mechanisms that are themselves interacting with environmental factors, including the conscious and semi-conscious desires of the person of whom these are constituent parts.

Research into the brain over the last few decades has seen a shift from the social science of psychology to the life science of neuroscience, and the development of brain imaging technologies and analytic methods, and the ongoing refinement of these, have been significant drivers in the emergence of this science of the brain. And these rapid developments in neuroscience, in particular brain imaging, have seen a burgeoning of popular media interest in the workings of the brain and how the brain relates to body and person. Nevertheless, in prevailing popular accounts, as well as the enduring enlightenment thinking these popular accounts echo, the brain continues to be positioned as the executive organ 'in charge' of the rest of the body (even if there is then 'consciousness', 'mind' or 'will' that 'oversees' the brain-as-organ).

A neuroscientist or molecular biologist confronted with the question of the relationship between the brain and the body is likely to respond that they are the same thing, the brain is part of the body and the brain and other parts of the body function in interaction. While some psychology and neuroscience might appear to take a 'brain in a jar' approach which disconnects the brain from rest of the body, the brain is indivisible from the rest of the body – it needs its cardiovascular and respiration systems, etc., to live and to function.

From a biological perspective the relationship between the organ of the brain and other parts/functions of the body can be summarized in the following range of ways:

- The brain has executive control over some functions e.g. respiration, in which the brain controls respiration through the respiratory centre in the brain.
- The brain does not have control over other important functions e.g. the reflex arc for touching heat or the diving reflex which works through the peripheral nervous system without involving the brain.
- The brain as organ is in constant interplay with other organs e.g. the central, peripheral and enteric nervous systems (CNS, PNS, ENS respectively, see more on these later).

- At a finer-grain size the interplay of brain and body is also clear, e.g. the endocrine organs delivering hormones to cells – the brain stimulates release of x from the endocrine organs (glands) next to brain, those hormones act on another endocrine organ, which release into the bloodstream and so on.
- The brain as organ has a degree of separation from the rest of the body through the blood-brain barrier.

Brain science

While neuroscience fully recognizes the brain as body, in practice neuroscience is a highly specialised set of sub-fields concerned with understanding the brain, and so exists as distinct from human biology. This science of the brain has been concerned with a range of issues, in particular structure, development, function, region-function relations, activity, networks and connectivity. At the leading edge of neuroscience is brain imaging research that investigates the brain through MRI which captures blood flow into regions of the brain; EEG which captures electrical activity, mainly on the surface of the brain; MEG which captures magnetic fields produced by electrical activity in the brain; and, increasingly, through combinations of these methods.

Interest in the relationships between structures and functions of the brain are longstanding. For instance, phrenology in the nineteenth century located a whole array of capacities and traits to particular locations in (on) the brain, associations generated through observation of impairment resulting from brain surgery (see Figure 4.1). While the effects of injury and surgery continued to be a key source of insight into region-function relationships through the twentieth century, twenty-first century brain science has mapped functions to brain regions using imaging technology and many broad region-function relationships have become established (see Figure 4.2).

However, advances in technology, and the increasing sophistication of MRI, EEG and MEG brain imaging makes previously established, straightforward region-function relationships difficult to maintain. Indeed, in a 2013 review essay examining evidence of 'localisation' of function across the frontal cortex, Miller and colleagues suggest that '[t]he appeal of simple, sweeping portraits of large-scale brain mechanisms relevant to psychological phenomena competes with a rich, complex research base' (Miller et al., 2013: 1).

Miller and colleagues show how the most up-to-date EEG techniques combined with MRI make the localization of activity much more precise and offer evidence of differentiation and specificity to regions and functions. Furthermore, they indicate that localization of function can be traced to areas of less than a centimetre through combined use of densely placed EEG sensors and MRI scanning (and smaller areas still with MEG), raising the question of the levels of granularity at which 'functional units' might be considered. Importantly, Miller and colleagues stress the potential diversity of scales of functional units as well as the adaptability of region-function. They say:

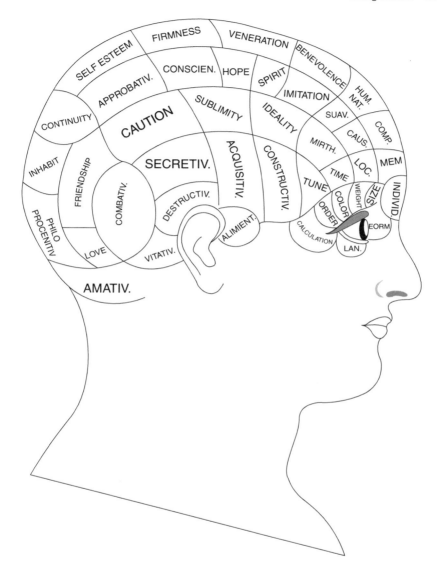

FIGURE 4.1 Phrenology and functional areas

> Much good work lies ahead, with the proviso that localization is of brain
> activity, not psychological function, and that the psychological and biological
> phenomena we pursue need to be understood across multiple scales in parallel.
> *(Miller et al., 2013: 7)*

The distinction that Miller and colleagues make between brain activity and psychological function is an important one as it underscores that what activity in the

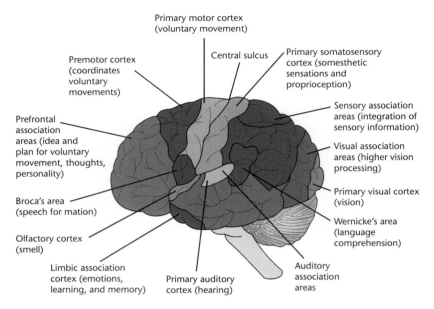

Primary motor cortex
(voluntary movement)

Central sulcus

Primary somatosensory
cortex (somesthetic
sensations and
proprioception)

Premotor cortex
(coordinates
voluntary
movements)

Prefrontal
association
areas (idea and
plan for voluntary
movement, thoughts,
personality)

Sensory association
areas (integration of
sensory information)

Visual association
areas (higher vision
processing)

Broca's area
(speech for mation)

Primary visual cortex
(vision)

Olfactory cortex
(smell)

Wernicke's area
(language
comprehension)

Limbic association
cortex (emotions,
learning, and memory)

Primary auditory
cortex (hearing)

Auditory
association
areas

FIGURE 4.2 Brain region–function relationships

brain *makes happen* often remains uncertain. This uncertainty connects with their emphasis on multiple scales – activity in and across neurons is of a quite different order and scale to something we might identify as a psychological function e.g. empathy or mathematical competence. This non- correspondence underscores the potentially non-linear relationship between scales and orders e.g. the epigenetics of neuronal and glial cells; neuronal connectivity; traits, capacities and orientations; and subjective experiences – and the challenge of moving across these.

This emphasis on the multi-scalar draws attention to brain research outside non-invasive brain imaging, in particular the study of brain chemistry and neuro-epigenetics. These fields of research often use model animals and in some instances human donor brains and offer insights into brain mechanisms and plasticity at an extremely small grain size – within individual neuronal and glial cells. Important features of this work are its demonstration of epigenetic change within brain cells and the ongoing openness of brain cells to change, including under epigenetic influence. That is, at the finest grain size of gene regulation and expression within brain cells, we find significant plasticity resulting from interaction with factors in the environment.

> The brain has an exceptional and unique epigenetic feature with respect to all other tissues in our body, both referring to the abundance of epigenetic marks [. . .] and to an extremely plastic epigenetic landscape due to the con-tinuous stimulation from the environment.
>
> *(Tognini et al., 2015)*

This plasticity in relation to environmental influence suggests both that the world outside the body is instantiated in the brain in ways that influence how it works and that any conception of the person we have needs to include this brain-milieu entanglement.

Brain-mind-person

As we have seen, 'localization' or 'functional specialization' is being demonstrated to be fine-grained and complex, and with comprehensive models of region-function relationship no longer compelling in the face of research evidence there is an emphasis on brain activity over psychological function. Nevertheless, imaging research does continue to identify brain regions that are associated with functions, capacities and affective states. Whether these functions, capacities and affective states amount to either mind or person continues to be struggled over, but in social neuroscience the 'social brain' is at the centre of 'self' (Heatherton, 2011; Walker and McGlone, 2013).

In social neuroscience group membership is taken as necessary for human survival and 'having a "self"' is taken as 'necessary for maintaining effective relations with group members' (Heatherton, 2011: 2). A 'social brain' is said to form and maintain this group membership through its capacity for self-awareness, mentalizing others' minds, detecting threat and regulating the self. In addition, memory, self-memory and emotion are identified as key aspects of self (we will say more about memory later). These brain-based elements of self are explored through fMRI which shows particular regional activation in relation to information about the self as well as inferential and mentalizing tasks (in the medial prefrontal cortex or MPFC) and in relation to emotion and social judgement (in the ventral anterior cingulate cortex or vACC, sometimes referred to as the subgenual anterior cingulate). While this suggests patterns of particular regional activation in relation to 'self', it does not amount to an assertion of the MPFC (or indeed vACC) as the 'location' of the self:

> Although research has consistently demonstrated increased MPFC for conditions that involve some aspect of self, this is not to suggest that the MPFC reflects the physical location of the 'self' or that other areas are not vital for the phenomenological experiences associated with the self. Rather, the experience of the self involves various sensory, affective, and motor processes contributed by disparate brain regions outside the cortical midline area.
>
> *(Heatherton, 2011 7)*

The suggestion here, then, is that the 'self' cannot be traced to a single brain region (i.e. MPFC) because the region-function-self relationship is complex: a range of brain-based processes (sensory, motor, affective) across a range of brain regions are together involved in producing the capacity for and experience of 'self'. Despite this complexity, however, in social neuroscience the brain appears as the locus of this 'self'.

Philosophy of mind

Philosophy of mind, which has a tradition of engagement with brain science, does not accept such a view of the 'social brain' based 'self' which foregrounds brain region-function relationships. The work of David Bakhurst, a leading philosopher of mind, is useful to consider as it pursues a social and historical account of mind as the product of 'initiation into culture' (Bakhurst, 2011: xiii) and so offers a significant counter to the brain-base self we have just discussed. For Bakhurst, the close connexion of reason and mind and the break between brain and person are central. Drawing on Soviet Philosopher Evald Ilyenkov, Bakhurst outlines the position that self is *person* not brain, and that thinking is the property/activity of the person, 'with the help of her brain' (Ilyenkov cited in Bakhurst, 2008). Here the brain is in the service of the person, but the person is not reducible to the brain.

Bakhurst explores Ilyenkov's distinction between 'brainism', which identifies the self as the product of the brain, and 'personalism', which suggests that 'psychological attributes' should be to persons, not brains, and that mental phenomena do not occur 'inside' the brain but are aspects of a person's 'mode of engagement with the world' (Bakhurst, 2008: 416). This, then, is a phenomenological rebuttal of the brain as mind, and especially as identified through the sort of brain imaging work we have just been discussing:

> The subjective dimension, which some claim to be an essential character-istic of conscious mental states, goes missing in any third-personal, physical description of brain states. Hence, we might conclude, all that is observable are the neural correlates of mental activity, not mental activity itself.
>
> *(Bakhurst, 2008: 422)*

We see here a disconnection between neuroscientific and philosophical accounts of what Bakhurst calls 'psychological attributes', raising questions of whether thinking is an activity of the brain or person, whether mental states exist in or emerge from the brain, and whether the brain causes consciousness. Bakhurst does not refute neuroscience and the new knowledge of brain activity it is producing, but he does argue that brain states should be understood as networked in a unified person who has relations in and orientations to the world. Asserting 'the unity of a mental life', Bakhurst suggests that 'we have to think of the person, rather than any of her parts, as the legitimate subject of psychological ascription' (Bakhurst, 2008: 422).

Despite the foregrounding of relations in and orientation to the social world, this account does not sit comfortably with our sociological account of the person because it demands that we accept the existence or at least experience of a unified person. In a post-structurally orientated sociology that decentres the unified person, the need for an enduring self and 'the unity of mental life' recedes, as does the demand for person to be superordinate to brain. In this sense the neuroscience of brain activity and connectivity and mobile region-function relationships may be more compatible than personalism with the poststructural subject or posthuman.

Personalism holds a distinction between brain activity and mental states, and holds this distinction by locating mental states in 'the space of reasons'. Rationality thus becomes central to the account of mind – rationality is posited as the feature of mind that exceeds the physical mechanisms of brain. For Bakhurst this allows 'psychological talk' to be 'a fundamentally different discourse from talk of the brain' and to have 'fundamentally different subjects' (Bakhurst, 2008: 425). Yet this assertion demands that the person is equated with a 'rational agent' which, as we have already noted, sits uncomfortably with a decentred subject of poststructuralism and posthumanism. Furthermore, throughout this personalism, 'psychological attributes' seem to be figured as 'possessions' of a rational and self-knowing person. Yet this person seems to appear post-hoc. The possibility that apparent 'psychological attributes' might be effects of multiple intra-acting processes – including but not restricted to neural processes – that come to appear as the whole and coherent attributes of a person only as they emerge, is a possibility that is not encountered in this philosophy of mind.

Neither brainism nor personalism

As we have already seen, there is a strong movement in neuroscience that foregrounds brain activity and connectivity rather than region-function relationships. This foregrounding does not line up neatly with a claim to brain-as-person, suggesting instead 'brain-as-organ' and so begins to step around a brainism/personalism split. While it may seem odd for sociology to align itself with brain (be it organ or person), thinking about the brain-as-organ and temporarily setting aside the question of 'where' the person might be located or emerge from (brain, rationality, history, culture), allows us to take a different orientation to the person which seems to sit well with poststructural and posthuman accounts of the subject (or person) becoming. This moving on from a brainism/personalism debate is helped by Pierre Pernu's bioscience-informed philosophy of mind (2013). Pernu emphasizes a move away from investigating causality and towards 'functional relationships between variables and data-points'. With this orientation Pernu suggests that '[c]hanges in physical systems are not due to different factors being in causal interaction so much as to *the system as a whole unfolding*' (Pernu, 2013: 22 my emphasis). This unfolding might be brought into a framing of becoming and thought of as rhizomatic – as moving, multifactorial, multi-scalar and trans-order entanglement.

In Pernu's account mental states have a neural physical basis but do not have a one-to-one correspondence with this physical basis, and are bound up in social meaning:

> [A]lthough mental states do not exist on their own, independently of any physical basis, they are not type-identical with some such basis. What makes a mental state the particular mental state it is, is its semantic content, not the fact that it happens to be physically realized in a certain way. In consequence, different physical states could realize one and the same mental state.
>
> *(Pernu, 2013: 26)*

Pernu makes this case without engaging with the detail of what various fields of neuroscience know, and do not know, about e.g neural activity and connectivity, endocrine systems, neural methylation etc. In this sense the workings of mind or mental states in Pernu, like in Bakhurst, remain a struggle of philosophy over science. All the same, Pernu usefully moves us towards a reading of mental states, and a person who experiences, is locus of, and is in part constituted through these mental states, as emergent and involving the intra-action of neuronal and social forces.

Person 3 – body-brain-person

Despite our initial suggestion that biologists and neuroscientists would start from the recognition of the brain as an organ of the body, this discussion demonstrates that in practice the brain and the mind or person seem to remain detached from the body.

Elizabeth Wilson, a leading feminist theorist who has engaged extensively with science, makes an important intervention into this brain/body split and the enduring sense of the brain as the 'boss' of the body. In her book *Gut Feminism* (2015), she explores the significant role of the gut in depression. She does this by examining the exchange between (entanglement of) the gut and the mind, that is, the central, peripheral and enteric nervous systems.

A core part of Wilson's argument is that the functioning of the gut plays a part in depression that is not simply a response to activity in the brain, but rather is an independent feature of depression. This is perhaps most powerfully demonstrated in Wilson's consideration of selective seretonin reuptake inhibitors (SSRIs) used to pharmacologically manage depression. Through careful examination of the dispersal of the action of these drugs throughout the body and in particular within the gut, Wilson shows that depression and its treatment is not as simple as neurons or neurotransmitters, raising important challenges to the assumption of mind as coextensive with or located in the brain and leading Wilson to suggest that the gut is 'minded'. She suggests that the bodiliness of mind is something we are already familiar with but forget, reminding us that in childhood 'body and world and mood remain more intensely affiliated than many adults remember' (Wilson, 2015: 156). It may be that the idea of the gut as minded goes too far (in terms of science or sociology), but the assertion makes an important intervention into the continuing brain/body split and insists that mind is not simply equivalent to brain.

Research in neurobiology is also pursuing the ways that brain systems interact with body systems, how both of these interact with environment, and how these together might impact both behaviour and risk of ill-health. The work in neuro-immunology of Staci Bilbo (2013a, 2013b) is a good illustration of this, underscoring the inseparability of brain and body systems. They use model animals to explore the relationship between the brain and immune system, looking in particular at the effects of early activation of the immune system e.g. in pre-term infants, in response to e.g. exposure to infection, toxins or stress. Using rats as model animals, their research shows that when the immune system is provoked just once by an infant bacterial infection, maze learning in the adult rat is the same as that of other rats. Yet if the immune is provoked again – that is, it has a 'second hit' – the adult rat shows profound memory impairments. Bilbo and colleagues suggest that this reveals that the double activation of the immune system early in life has epigenetic effects that permanently change the microglia (the brain's immune cells). Autism as well as Parkinsons and Alzheimers are suggested as potentially starting in early life/in utero in response to a double immune hit. This epigenetic alteration to the microglia in model rats takes the form of over-response, with too many inflammatory factors produced. This over-sensitization increases with each infection.

These microglia are not just involved in inflammatory immune response, but are also involved in synaptic pruning which happens in particular during early childhood. It is not yet known how the synaptic pruning undertaken by the microglia is provoked and directed, but it appears that if more than one environmental event coincides with this process then the inflammatory response provoked impacts synaptic pruning with implications for brain development. The importance of the 'second hit' is further evidenced in relation to air pollutants. These do not appear to affect the brain on their own, however, when a developing rat is also exposed to a mild stressor, that has substantial impact on the outcomes of that rat's offspring. This suggests that a psychological stressor is interacting with an environmental toxin to produce epigenetic effects that lead to impaired cognitive function, anxiety and increased inflammation and therefore disease susceptibility. This raises important 'environmental justice' issues as populations are differentially affected by both environmental toxins and stress. Bilbo and colleagues' work, then, shows the experience-dependent plasticity of all cells in the body, including the microglia, and the mutual involvement of the developing brain and the immune system.

Holobiont

Recognition of the entanglement of the person, or at least body, and the environment is underscored further by work on the human as 'holobiont' – 'well-functioning wholes that emerge in community with a host of others' (Schneider and Winslow, 2014: 209). The notion of the 'holobiont', which Lynn Margulis (1998) used when raising concern over attempts to clear microbes from the human body and building her argument for the important role of bacteria for human health, is underpinned the idea that biological systems are symbiotic. This idea of multiplicity and symbiosis is taken up by Schneider and Winslow (2014) to explore the implications for thinking about humans of the Human Microbiome Project (HMP), an international collaboration that is mapping genetic material from the trillions of microbial organisms on and in the human body (using e.g. saliva, faeces, throat swabs). The HMP represents a shift in emphasis from the Human Genome Project's (HGP) early anticipation that decoding the human genome would explain the person, to an emphasis on both human and microbial genes and their interactions – the human as holobiont. For Schneider and Winslow, the HMP 'raises profound questions about what it means to be an individual organism, human or otherwise' (Schneider and Winslow, 2014: 208).

HMP findings show that microbial cells outnumber parental germ-line cells by 10 to 1, and that these microbial cells have far greater genetic variety than the germ cells – with a ratio in the region of 130 to 1. These findings, Schneider and Winslow suggest, mean that the human 'is also a community of multiple species of microscopic organisms' (Schneider and Winslow, 2014: 210), transforming what it means to think about the human as an individual. Approaching the human microbiome as symbiotic community, the HMP explores the 'complex population' (Schneider and Winslow, 2014 citing Cho and Blaser, 2012: 210) of human and microbial genetic material. Within a 'metagenome' comprised of microbes, the host and the milieu, the 'second genome' supplied by the microbiota is, according to Schneider and Winslow, particularly diverse and plastic. The HMP has so far offered a range of insights into the function of the microbiome and, in turn, the metagenome. Microbial DNA and RNA provides functions within the genome of the host, assisting in adaptation to environments, contributing traits and functions, and, importantly, affecting expression and inheritance of human DNA and RNA (Pflughoeft and Versalovic, 2012).

The microbiome also appears to invite an extension to Wilson's 'minded gut', suggesting another line of connexion and influence between the gut and the brain. It is suggested that the extensive microbiota within the gut may influence the brain and 'modulate behaviour' (Schneider and Winslow, 2014: 215), an entanglement that leads Schneider and Winslow to suggest, not unlike Wilson, that the 'holobiant human-microbiome' might 'think' (Schneider and Winslow, 2014: 216). These findings suggest that the substance of the human is shaped by microbiota which 'regulate, generate and inhibit a number of metabolic functions' in the human body (Schneider and Winslow, 2014: 215), thereby modulating human development, health and illness. Furthermore, the microbiome has particular functions in regard to metabolic processes that do not appear dependent on the specific species of microbe (Gevers et al., 2012). This leads to moves in the HMP away from a taxonomy of species of microbiota and towards a focus on the functions of the microbiome.

The work of the HMP suggests the human (person) not as a unity, but as simultaneously whole and plural – human cells and microbial cells. Saying that we are (viscerally, functionally, psychically) our microbiota, our viruses, food, environment, relationships, etc., makes a unitary self, such as the one we find in modernist accounts of the person impossible to claim. Nevertheless, Schneider and Winslow retain concerns that the holobiont still implies wholeness or consistency of symbiotic community. They argue that the shift from classification to activity and function in the HMP can be extended to think about the human as 'an unfolding verb-like process of ever composing activity and function' (Schneider and Winslow, 2014: 218).

Person 4 – bio-psycho-socio-cultural human

As we work our way through these various accounts of the brain, body, environment and person, we are compelled increasingly to develop an account of the human who is at once biological, psychological, sociological and cultural. Furthermore, this account needs to be able to engage with how these influences are simultaneous and entangled, interacting with and influencing each other in ways that make them indivisible.

Whereas there is now quite a strong recognition of this need in the social and biological sciences, there is only limited research that works through analyses in these terms. Our previous encounter with Elizabeth Wilson's *Gut Feminism* begins to indicate how this might be done. Wilson's work is an important resource for Celia Roberts' 'bio-psycho-social' (Roberts, 2015: 26) interrogation of the phenomena of 'early sexual development', as this is defined and enacted in the medical and psychological literature and practice, and as it is entangled in and deployed through popular policy, advocacy and feminist concerns both with puberty and with the sexualization of girls. Roberts uses the ideas of intra-action and phenomena (Barad, 2007), and the fold (Deleuze, 2006) and infolding (Haraway, 2008) to engage scientific data and offer a 'folded reading of science' (Roberts, 2015: 194) in which the biological, psychological and social intra-act. As she does this she examines:

> [F]oldings of personal histories (of care in particular), of material bodily encounters with the world (exposure to chemicals, nutrition and sunlight), and of broader social meanings and histories (what it means to be a girl or a woman). [. . .] none of these elements should be posited as independent.
> *(Roberts, 2015: 194)*

Across medical, scientific and psychological data, Roberts sustains a reading of infolding, resisting a slide into either a sociological/feminist critique of science or a seduction by science and its data. The work insists on both the material and the tradition of critique.

By examining the biological, psychological and social dimensions of early sexual development, Roberts shows how sexual development and sexuality are entangled in ways that fold early sexual development into concerns over the sexualization of girls and biomedical concerns into moral concerns. She also offers a conceptual and methodological approach that demonstrates the possibility and usefulness of understanding the person as biopsychosocial.

The usefulness of a reading of the infolding of biological, psychological and social is well illustrated in relation to the prescription of synthetic gonadotropin regulating hormone (GnHR analogues) which are used to override a young person's own GnHR and turn off puberty. What Roberts' analysis shows powerfully is that the effects of this biomedical intervention are infolded with experiences and social meanings such that it has contradictory effects – often experienced negatively by girls treated for early sexual development but positively by transgender young people prescribed it to allay puberty until they are old enough to begin pharmaceutical gender reassignment. Roberts underscores how, in the uncertain but very active field of prescribing GnRH analogues to children and young people, the 'normal' sexed-gendered body is constituted and fixed. Across her analysis of 'early sexual development' Roberts shows the interaction of the biological and the environment:

> [P]ubertal bodies are enacted across and between scientific, biomedical, environmental, social scientific, news media, educational and feminist texts. [. . .] I have articulated a version of science that interpenetrates with related cultural discourses, parental practices, commercial activities and historical figurations of bodies, sex and sexuality.
>
> *(Roberts, 2015: 194)*

What Roberts offers, then, is a demonstration of how a 'biopsychosocial' analysis of a complex and contested phenomena such as 'early sexual development' might proceed. More importantly for us, she shows the infolding of the biological, psychological and social in early sexual development – it is not possible to disentangle these influences or understand the phenomena without this entanglement.

Another very helpful demonstration of this entanglement is offered by Samantha Frost's (2016) *Biocultural Creatures*, which aims to develop an 'affirmative alternative' understanding of the human that enables us to analyse the human and its habitat and think about how we might live inseparably from our habitats. Frost suggests that thinking of humans as biocultural creatures:

> [N]udges us to take into consideration not just dimensions of our living habitats that shape and giving meaning to living bodies and deeply complex forms of social and political subjectivity but also to those dimensions that materially compose living bodies.
>
> *(Frost, 2016: 15)*

This working across habitats' influence on *and part in* the human is an important move, bringing Frost's political theory into direct contact with the biology of the body in a way that resonates with the work of Wilson, Roberts and Schneider and Winslow that I have explored already. We find again an approach that puts theories of the person into contact with biological science, and epigenetics in particular, demonstrating that the human cannot be sealed off from the world s/he inhabits. Instead we find an account of porosity, movement and activity in which there is endless 'traffic' between the body and its milieu. In a similar vein to Roberts, Frost states: 'humans are constituted through a matrix of biological and cultural processes that shape one another over various time scales in such a way that neither one nor the other can be conceived as distinct' (Frost, 2016: 34).

The porosity and activity that Frost foregrounds is demonstrated though accounts of key biological elements and actions that are part of the human. Central to her case is the claim that 'energy takes form as substance or matter through its constrained self-relation' (Frost, 2016: 52). Frost shows that movement and (some) stability come to be simultaneous features of the human by tracing the movements of neutrons, electrons and protons, the bonds that make atoms become molecules, and the fundamental place of carbon in life. She also explores the activity at the molecular level that constitutes cell membranes, showing that any notion of an inside/outside demarcation between the human and its environment is impossible to maintain. In place of this binary Frost demonstrates 'the porous body' whose distinction rests on *activity* rather than a boundary and is 'unavoidably and ineluctably a biocultural creature' (Frost, 2016: 114). Frost is also concerned to move away from thinking in terms of purpose and intent. The activity of proteins involved in the making of cells, and the scope and limits for action that are encoded in/through these, is important for understanding the distinctions between activity and purpose, and direction and intent:

> [W]e can apprehend the specificity of molecular and cellular activity without having to make recourse to notions of purpose and we can understand how a process can have direction without having to make recourse to notions of intention.
>
> *(Frost, 2016: 124)*

Frost argues that considering the porosity and activity of the molecular body enables us to think of creatures as 'energy-in-transition' (Frost, 2016: 147) rather than as 'stuff-built-or-composed' (Frost, 2016: 152), leaving untenable a notion of the human as fixed and self-contained and highlighting instead the critical dependence that living creatures have on their environment, not simply as habitat but 'filtering into and out of their cells' (Frost, 2016: 148).

This work, then, moves us past a human subject who is either wholly social or wholly agentic, and past a biology of causation and hard heredity. Instead we have a biocultural creature of 'energy-in-transition', 'activity-in-response', and 'productivity-in-constraint':

> [T]the concept of biocultural creatures enables us to think of humans as perceptually responsive at cellular, organic, regional and organismic levels, in ways that include neurological stimulation by social and material phenomena (i.e. sense perception and imagination) and in ways that also include more diffuse hormonal or biochemical responses to the ingestion and absorption of the material dimensions of habitats.
>
> *(Frost, 2016: 212)*

We are biosocial: body-brain-environment-person

Across the fields of sociology, molecular biology, brain science, philosophy and political theory we find evidence, often in quite different guises, that compels us to think of a person that is simultaneously brain, body, culture, environment and even microbe. This person might well be sexed, raced, gendered, classed, (dis)abled, but these sorts of categories of identity or social groups are not foregrounded in these accounts. Rather, the accounts emphasize activity, productivity, porosity, interaction and entanglements – movements that flow across membranes and zones in the body, across bodies and milieu, and across bodily and social forces. Here, social forces from economic structures to processes of subjectivation continue to assert themselves on and through the subject and make some things possible and other unimaginable. But these are not the only, and potentially not the most important, lines of possibility and constraint. This has important implications for the relationship between our biosocial approach and various forms of identity politics that have been fundamental to exposing inequalities in education and developing social justice-orientated responses to these inequalities. We explore this in Chapter 6, *Biosocial assemblage*.

As we bring together the interacting forces of culture and biology and engage the multiple interacting factors that make humans and their habitats, we are witnessing and contributing to an important expansion. This is an expansion that adds to, and potentially shifts, theories of identity, identity politics and social and subjectivated subjects. It does this by foregrounding how phenomena (rather than types of people) are made; interrogating creature-milieu entanglements; understanding environmental factors as instantiated in the creature in dispersed and potentially irreconcilable ways – from the microbiota of the holobiont, to molecular functions, to processes of subjectivation.

This means recognizing the limits of our discipline knowledge and being open to uncomfortable knowledge from other disciplines. We advocate working in a transdisciplinary way, not just working across or between disciplines but constantly trying out possibilities for integrating, tethering, articulating the orientations, knowledges, methods and data of disciplines and accepting that disciplines will be transformed by this intimate encounter. Our subject, as far as we have one, is a transdisciplinary Frankenstein's monster of a body-brain-environment-person.

This approach also means bringing a whole range of factors and processes to analyses of education that have been outside its purview, or, like eugenics, considered dangerous and reactionary. Features of education that have been understood previously as wholly social are opened up to re-appraisal. This leads us to a series of pressing questions for biosocial education:

- How does a holobiont, biocultural creature help us to understand the people, children and adults, and processes of schooling?
- How do we make this thinking useful for educationists?
- Where does it leave our older concerns for educational justice that orientate around group identities such as race, ethnicity, gender, disability and social class?
- Does a biosocial orientation replace or augment interest in gender, race, disability, queer theory and politics?
- Can a biosocial approach improve education and educational justice?

We attend to these questions in the following chapters.

5

FEELING THE CLASSROOM

What feeling offers education

In this chapter we bring social theories of feeling and biological science of feeling together to develop an understanding of feelings as simultaneously social and biological and demonstrate the importance of feelings in the classroom. Building on thinking about feeling inspired by Deleuze (Hickey-Moody and Malins, 2007) – which understands feelings as pre-personal social flows and asks 'what can a body do here?' – we examine key processes involved in the production and flows of feelings in the classroom and draw these together to explore what bodies do and can feel, what feelings flow and what is made possible and foreclosed by feeling inside classrooms. Importantly, we extend this notion of feeling as social flow to also incorporate the biological, considering the intra-action of social and biological processes in the production and flow of feeling. We engage with the biochemistry of the brain, brain activation and connectivity, and the volatile organic compounds generated by the body's metabolic processes and exhaled in the breath. This leads us to the brain chemistry of the endocrine system, dopamine and the brain's stress axis, but it also leads us to happiness and pleasure and the feeling of relationships in classrooms.

In developing an account of how entangled social and biological dimensions of feelings might support or inhibit learning, we consider the implications of this new insight for pedagogic practices, classroom relationships, and policy enactments that may invoke particular sorts of feelings inside classrooms and make a case for relationships to be foregrounded in learning and for pleasure to be instated as a key feeling of the classroom. We show how a transdisciplinary approach that works across social and biological dimensions can extend and transform our capacity to conceptualise, access and analyse feeling, offering key concepts, such as 'feeling', 'affect', 'emotional signature' and 'pedagogy' up for metamorphosis, produce a step change in understanding the significance of feelings in classrooms and wider learning situations.

Feeling education

The 21st century policy took a new interest in the unpredictability of education consumers' choice-making (Exley, 2013); this was driven by a desire to make consumers 'choose better'. Attempts to find strategies and tools that could guide or 'nudge' these choices (Bradbury et al., 2013) were not a new policy engagement with consumers' feelings, but an attempt to navigate, influence and domesticate these. And most recently, a turn to 'mindfulness' in education has sought to ensure that children can manage any difficult feelings that they might have in the classroom (Kuyken et al., 2013; Woods, 2014), but this leaves unaltered the systemic factors, such as high-stakes tests, that may provoke the difficult feelings in the first place.

Yet while policy has sought to corral or erase emotional worlds, in the social sciences an 'affective turn' has explored the importance of both the subjective experience of feelings and the ways in which feelings make things happen (Ahmed, 2004; Bolar, 1999; Deleuze and Guattari, 2008). Education scholarship has in the last decade or so returned to feeling and the social nature of feelings as they circulate in classrooms and between students and teachers.

As part of this body of work, feeling is being recognized as an important component of school processes and effects. Sociology and childhood studies have made particular ground in understanding feelings in the context of classrooms, developing methods for researching feeling in real-life settings and delivering detailed accounts of feeling in schools. Recent sociological work has sought to identify how affect, and particularly the sociality of affect that flows between bodies and across school sites, produces particular teacher, learner and abject bodies (Harwood, 2017; Hickey-Moody, 2009, 2014; Kenway and Youdell, 2011; Youdell, 2010; Youdell and Armstrong, 2011; Zembylas, 2007). The importance of feeling has also been examined from a psychoanalytic perspective foregrounding the importance of the psychic encounter between the teacher and the learner and exploring how learning becomes blocked in difficult educational encounters (Bibby, 2011, 2017). Drawing on research based in a London primary school and in a climate of testing, Bibby's (2011) work describes both children's and teachers' difficult experiences of education, such as the 'disease' provoked even by 'being in the top or middle group since the prospect of 'moving down' loomed generating a climate of fear' (Bibby, 2011: 51). Drawing on Winnicott (1971), Bibby asks '[w]hat kind of mirror do assessments hold up? In what ways were the teachers able to "be there" to feed, and enable, playful and creative responses to ideas?' (Bibby, 2011: 46).

Children's capacity for emotional self-regulation in the classroom has been associated with effective learning (Bomber and Hughes, 2013). Yet the theoretical work drawn on in sociology and childhood studies suggests that feelings do not simply exist inside a person who is variably able to regulate these, but are social phenomena (Ahmed, 2004; Bolar, 1999). Ethnographic research in education seeks to show through observation how feelings circulate as affective intensities, including in learning situations and in classrooms, and the social and educational effects that these have (Kenway and Youdell, 2011; Youdell and Armstrong, 2011; Mayes, 2013). Furthermore, current research in the sociology of education is exploring the relationship between the body and learning; the place of the body in pedagogy (Evans et al., 2011; Ivinson, 2012; Lingard, 2014); and the importance of flows of feelings in pedagogic encounters (Hickey-Moody, 2013; Leahy, 2009; Youdell, 2011; Zembylas, 2013); physiological processes are absent from these analyses. It investigates the way that a healthy/unhealthy body is produced and mobilized in education, interrogating how 'normal' and 'abnormal' student bodies are generated through pedagogies of disgust and shame (Leahy, 2009) – providing powerful insight into the monitoring, normalizing and correcting of normalizing the monitoring and correction of child bodies judged to be overweight/obese or sedentary (Rich et al., 2011; Dagkas and Burrows, 2016; Wright and Harwood, 2009). These critiques foreground the problematic nature of evidence from bioscience and the pervasive high-status ascribed to this knowledge. As a result, the possible insights offered by bioscience evidence, or ways of working across the social and biological, remain unexplored. Across sociological engagements with the fundamentally embodied nature of learning our encounter with the body remains interpretive, and the interior of the body – from beating hearts to metabolic pathways within cells and movements across membranes – remain out of reach.

The possibility that biological processes might be embroiled with social processes is important for critical education scholarship to contemplate. In his 2013 paper, Peter Kraftl explores the possibility of understanding the emotional geographies of children's lives through an encounter with the 'more-than-social' (Kraftl, 2013). He suggests we deploy 'hybrid' conceptions of childhood that move beyond a biology/sociology dualism and instead considers their entanglements. Kraftl's assertion is that the fields of childhood studies and education do not understand childhood emotion well enough, and his aim is thus to 'stretch' our conceptions of 'the relationality of children with adults and, indeed, the relationality of children's emotions' (Kraftl, 2013). Key here is that existing sociologically informed education research provides important insight into the significance of feeling in education, its capacity to speak to the 'more-than-social' is limited (Kraftl, 2013) – it cannot tell us about the physiology, neuroscience or biochemistry of feeling.

As we move on, we work across divergent ways of encountering and understanding what is described as feeling, engaging with current understandings of feeling drawn from the new biological sciences and interlacing this bioscience with nuanced social understandings of school processes, practices and relationships. As we pursue this transdisciplinary engagement, we anticipate that the concept of 'feeling' itself might undergo a sort of 'metamorphosis' (Malabou, 2009).

Encountering affect

Leading-edge new materialist-informed critical education research concerned with feeling has detailed the distinctions between *affectus*, *affection* and *affect* and advocated for social science methods that can attend to these. Here, after Spinoza, *affectus* refers to changes in the body's capacities, while *affection* refers to the sensations of the body and *affect* is between affection and *affectus* – it 'moves us', it is 'a visceral prompt' (Hickey-Moody, 2014).

Hickey-Moody suggests that as we try to understand the feelings of education settings we focus on the 'affective assemblage', considering 'the smells, sounds, aesthetics economies' and 'indirect discourses' as ways of encountering the 'affect of our everyday lives' (Hickey-Moody, 2014: 93). Hickey-Moody explores the idea of 'affective pedagogies' in which pedagogy is designed in order to be directed at, provoke or be aware of affectivites and how children are taught to 'feel and respond' to particular types of learning experience or encounter and/or in which affect, the feeling itself, is the pedagogic device. Attending to 'embodied responses and the ways in which contexts make feelings' is central to this work (Hickey-Moody, 2014: 94).Yet while Hickey-Moody offers a nuanced approach to exploring feeling in classrooms, research that can tell us about the biology of affectus and affection and the affect they provoke in relation to and resulting from experiences of education, in particular the ebb and flow of pedagogic practices and relationships and the everyday of classroom and school life, is yet to emerge.

What sociology can tell us about feelings and what they make happen

To illustrate how sociological work is attempting to encounter and understand feeling in school encounters, we revisit here data generated through a research project undertaken by Deborah in a 'special school' for boys diagnosed as having 'Social Emotional and Behavioural Difficulties'.

Running the line

It is mid-afternoon and students and teachers have returned to lessons as I leave Bay Tree School, an English 'special school' for boys designated as having 'social emotional and behavioral difficulties' [SEBD]. As my car bumps slowly over the speed humps that straddle the school's long tree-lined drive, I notice two teachers moving at a scurry's pace along the drive in front of me. Moving faster, they slip between two trees onto the little-used expanse of playing field beyond. I crawl on, pausing at gaps in the trees to watch as the teachers break into a slow run, calling out as they go. I scan the shaded grass in front of them looking for the object of their pursuit. I spot a small, fair, cropped-haired boy, perhaps 12-years-old, running in the direction of the school's perimeter along which mature trees are interspersed with low and sparse immature shrubs. [. . .] I smile inwardly as I watch the teachers flagging, slowing to a defeated adult-paced jog-cum-walk while the boy drops long leaps and high jumps into his easy running. I crawl to the junction with the road as the boy makes the tree and shrub line. But instead of breaching it, which an easy charge through the gaps in the shrubbery would achieve,

he turns hard left and continues to run full pelt along a trajectory that tracks
a line just inside the school perimeter. [. . .] In my rearview mirror I see the
teachers change direction – now simply walking, they head diagonally across
the field toward a point where their trajectory and the boy's might intersect.
I drive home, made exhilarated and sad by the boy's running the line (Deborah Youdell, fieldnotes).

(Kenway and Youdell, 2011: 131)

In analysing this data episode, Jane Kenway and Deborah focus on the subjectivating force of these events – how these practices make particular sorts of
subjects – and the place that feeling might have in these processes. We suggest that
the boy, who is subjectivated through prior constitutions (not least through his
trajectory into this school) as an 'impossible' or 'abject' learner, can be seen in two
ways – as being made again in these terms by his running away from teachers, and
as somehow exceeding or escaping, albeit momentarily, these terms through his
running. The role that feelings play in these constitutions and exceeding them is
also foregrounded:

The affective intensities that drive the boy's flight and the teachers' pursuit
are simultaneously produced in this moment. They flow between the bodies that navigate this school field and its boundary, including the body of
the researcher [. . .]. Throughout this scene the meanings of these spaces and
their constitutive force is evident. We see the capacity of the line to make the
school and the street; to make the 'SEBD' boy who has, or has not 'crossed
the line' of the school's disciplinary regulations; to make the teachers' whose
authority may or may not be able to prevent its breach and to make the
researcher-turned-turkey-necker who cruises by, eyes off the road.

(Kenway and Youdell, 2011: 131–132)

This data episode was written in response to observations in the field that the
research perceived as being shot through with affective intensities, including
for the researcher, and was written in a way that hoped to capture and convey
and perhaps evoke these affectivities. Yet it is unclear whether the data or the
researcher can say very much beyond conjecture about 'what' the boy and the
teachers might have 'felt'. Work of this sort speaks to the psychosocial dimensions
of teachers' and students' encounters within education, and is very clear about
the interpretive burden that data and analysis carry when it begins to analyse
those things that are outside of conscious reflection or language. This is not to
undermine such analyses but to identify a limit. This sort of analysis is not able to
tell us about what is happening in the bodies of the teachers and children who
are living this schooling in the day-to-day or what the implications – emotional,
educational, embodied – of these experiences might be. As the data shows us the
boy running, the biochemistry that changes the affectus, produces the affection,
and generates the 'visceral prompt' of this running are all out of reach. As we look

back on this data, we wonder whether the 'long leaps' and 'high jumps' are suggestive of the pleasure, the jouissance, the desire for life that the researcher hoped they were. Perhaps, instead, the running is just flight, suggesting rage, panic or dread. We are led to ask what more we would be able to say about this running if we knew something about what is happening at different scales in these running bodies e.g. blood flow, heart rate, endocrine flows, brain chemistry, endorphins, the brain's stress axis.

The biology of feeling

We are not alone in noticing the absence of the body in social science and humanities' encounters with feeling. Human geographers are beginning to integrate electrodermal sensing technologies with qualitative methods to capture the biological elements of individuals' emotional responses (Osborne and Jones, 2017). In education, techniques from molecular biology have been used to demonstrate a significant rise in stress, as evidenced by measurements of the stress hormone cortisol in hair samples, as children move from nursery (kindergarten) into school (Groeneveld et al., 2013), but this is a broad marker captured over a relatively long timeframe and so has limited capacity to speak to the specificities of this stressful transition.

Experimental animal work also speaks to the biological significance of feeling. For instance, rats exposed to electric shock (experimentally coded as trauma) in novel environments show on autopsy that this induces patterns of DNA methylation and histone acetylation in specific brain regions that are associated with memory (a common neuroscience proxy for learning) (Molfese, 2011). Studies of the epigenetic effects of early care in rats similarly show the negative impact of stress on learning and sociality (Champagne, 2013b; Gudsnuk and Champagne, 2012). And work that introduces rats to novel objects shows that also inducing stress in these novel object encounters impedes memory (Bevins and Besheer, 2006; Leger et al., 2013). While extrapolating to human children from these animal studies must be done with caution, this distinction between 'trauma' and 'stress' may be important for education, inviting us to consider how stress-inducing educational practice may have neurological effects that block learning. Working across sociology and such epigenetic research is made more complicated by the fact that while sociology of education generally focuses on educational settings, much epigenetic work with humans focuses on the home, and more precisely the mother-child relationship, as the key driver of certain epigenetic changes (Bakermans-Kranenburg and van Ijzendoorn, 2015). Developmental epigenetics is beginning to explore the effects of other key relationships, in particular with the father (Lucassen et al., 2015), but the multitude of compounding variables make it difficult to envisage such research into the epigenetics effects of other key relationships, e.g. with teachers, within an experimental framework. Kraftl (2013) highlights the 'more-than-social care relations' between children and educators, and this too begins to suggest the possibility that non-nurturing relationships beyond the parent-child dyad could have effects at a cellular level, and that these might impact children's capacities to engage and to learn inside classrooms.

Work in neuroscience into feeling underscores affect as an integral part of the brain, arguing that brain physiology is a part of feeling and not result of it (Miller et al., 2013).

Research into the nature of brain connectivity in relation to particular affective states has demonstrated distinct patterns of connectivity at different wave lengths. Using EEG to monitor brain waves of subjects watching film clips selected to provoke specific feelings – 'negative-neutral', 'negative-positive' and 'positive-neutral' – Lee and colleagues demonstrate patterns of connectivity across wave lengths (alpha, beta, theta) as well as across modes of analysis (Figure 5.1). This work demonstrates that brains function differently in relation to different affects.

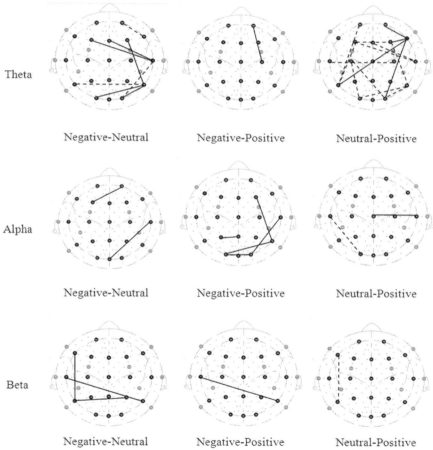

Brain maps of coherence. The lines connecting electrode sites indicate significant higher (solid) and lower (dashed) coherence values or condition listed on left side.

FIGURE 5.1   Brain connectivity and emotional states

Source: Lee, Y.-Y., & Hsieh, S. (2014). Classifying different emotional states by means of EEG-based functional connectivity patterns. *PloS One, 9*(4), e95415. doi:10.1371/journal.pone.0095415.

Mass spectrometry and feeling

Of particular interest to us is metabolomics research, which considers the body's meta-bolic responses to stimuli and draws on analysis of volatile organic compounds (VOCs) in exhaled breath (Turner et al., 2013; Heaney et al., 2016). This is an emerging as an important approach that has not been applied in classrooms but may reveal meta-bolic processes that coincide with pedagogic and wider school experiences, including learning. This approach has the potential to provide new orientations to and insights into affect by identifying 'emotional signaling molecules' (Williams et al., 2016: 1). In education, this could allow us to identify non-invasively biomarkers for feeling, or 'emotional signatures' in the atmosphere of the classroom as well as the exhaled breath of the individual. In order to think carefully about this potential, we detail analysis of VOCs in exhaled breath and what this has (and has not) been able to say.

Williams and colleagues (2016) undertook atmospheric mass spectrometry anal-ysis of VOCs in exhaled breath from a cinema auditorium. This was repeated over an extended period of time and while films of a range of genres were screening. By coding the content of each film and sampling to coded segments, the team was able to predict what masses would be evident in particular samples. Williams and col-leagues do not necessarily know what each VOC is, but they can predict that it will consistently be present during a segment of film, from 'injury', 'hiding' and 'blood (violence)' to 'running', 'kissing' and 'laughter' – emotional signalling molecules that suggest social flows of VOCs in response to particular events on screen (Figure 5.2).

Williams and colleagues' study, then, offers a starting point for atmospheric anal-ysis inside school settings for education researchers concerned with the ways that schooling practices might produce environments that are biochemically laden with feeling in particular ways, and the ways that these VOCs might flow across spaces and bodies and in turn be folded back into the processes, practices and subjectiva-tions of schooling.

School feelings – the example of stress

Much biological work concerned with feelings focuses on states of disease, that is, feelings that have potentially problematic impacts on health, well-being, relation-ships and possibly learning. In a recent paper with our colleague Valerie Harwood, we offered a biosocial examination of 'stress' in education, in order to show how experiences of education stress might be instantiated in the bodies of children (Youdell et al., 2017). We consider some of the issues raised there here.

Epigenetic neuroscience argues that sustained stress, understood neurochemi-cally, results in a 'conserved transcriptional response to adversity' (CTRA) (Cole, 2014: 2) – the way in which cells transcribe DNA information and so function – which increases inflammatory responses and diminishes antiviral responses and so has persistent detrimental health effects (Cole, 2014). Experimental studies in humans suggest that exposure to 'stressors' inhibits future biological capacities to cope with stress, with extreme or 'toxic' 'stress' said to impair stress responses

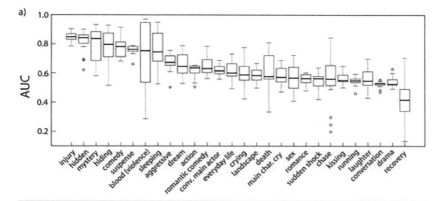

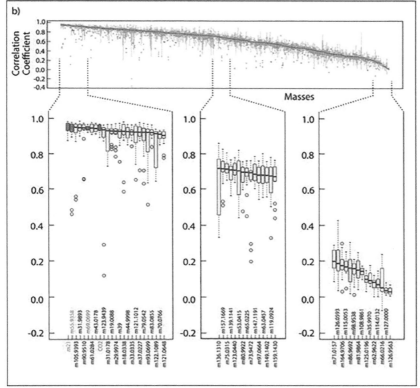

VOC mass spectrums in cinema auditorium during types of film segment

The boxes indicate the extent of 25% of the data either side of the median (solid line). The dashed vertical line represents the lowest/highest datapoints that are still in the 1.5 interquartile range while the circles are outliers. (a) shows AUC which expresses the ratio between true positives (when the model correctly predicted labels based on mass decision trees) and false positives (backward prediction). A random prediction produces an AUC value of 0.5. (b) shows the ability of an individual mass to be predicted by the labels (forward prediction). The performance of this prediction versus the real value for VOC mixing ratios is given as the Pearson's correlation coefficient (r). High correlation coefficients indicate the predictive model was successful for that particular species, and not that all species with high correlation coefficients are inter-correlated.

FIGURE 5.2 Volatile organic compounds showing feelings in cinema auditorium

Source: Williams et al., 2016.

through 'dysregulation of the HPA axis' (Romens et al., 2015: 304). These findings may seem compelling, but it is important to recognize that they 'cannot directly address causality or the cellular processes occurring within the brains of living children' (Romens et al., 2015: 307) – mechanisms remain unproven. Despite proven mechanisms, these studies show that biochemical responses to stressors provoke changes to how cells function that become persistent and that impair a person's future cellular capacity to cope with stress (as well as inflammatory and viral responses). These studies also give credence to educators' and parents' concerns about the stress experiences by children in relation to high-stakes tests and other school practices.

The impact on the human brain of exposure to stressors is also explored by imaging neuroscience using fMRI to map patterns of brain activation as it is exposed to stressors inside the scanner. One approach to inducing stress is to ask subjects to undertake tests, such as time-pressured arithmetic, often with an associated 'social evaluation threat', for example, that the results of the test will be made known to peers. The Montreal Imaging Stress Task (MiST) is one such test, and has been used to map brain activation patterns associated with stress (Dedovic et al., 2005) (Figure 5.3).

Studies have also brought inflammatory and neural responses to stressors together, showing markers for inflammation in blood plasma and under fMRI activation of the amygdala – a brain region involved in responding to threat, including by the sympathetic nervous system (SNS) – and of the dorsomedial prefrontal cortex (DMPFC) – a brain region involved in 'mentalizing' others' thoughts/feelings – in response to negative social evaluation (Muscatell et al., 2016). In this and other studies, brain activation varies across those who perceive themselves to have higher and lower social status, with those with lower self-ranking social status showing greater DMPFC (mentalizing) activity and greater inflammatory responses ('proinflammatory cytokine IL-6') (Muscatell et al., 2016: 918). Thinking about social status and evaluation in the classroom, this brain imaging work suggests that children who perceive themselves to have low social status (e.g. assessed by teachers as being of 'low ability' or 'badly behaved') are likely to be more focused on evaluators' negative feedback and the reasons for it (DMPFC activation) and be more affected by this negative evaluation than children who perceive themselves to have higher social status (e.g. those assessed and treated as 'bright', 'popular' and 'well-behaved'). Again, the brain imaging work concurs with sociological work detailing the effects of the subjectivation of students and the sorting and selecting practices that this is embroiled with. Yet, like animal models and non-tissue specific epigenetic studies, extrapolating from composite brain images generated from multiple subjects during scanner tasks to complex social situations is problematic, as is moving from brain activity to function (Fischer Goswami and Geake, 2010), and especially function in complex and mobile fields of multiple influences such as classrooms (Howard-Jones, 2014; Youdell, 2017a).

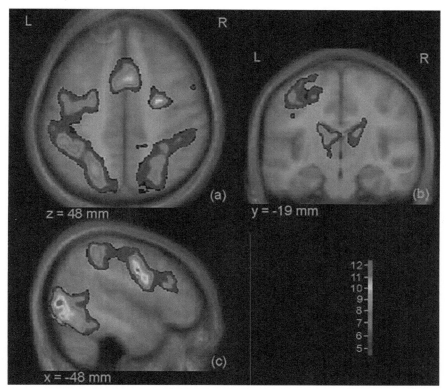

Statistical parametric map displaying significant activations with blood oxygenation level-dependent (BOLD) signal as a result of performing the MiST in study 3 (n = 22). Areas significantly activated as a result of performing the MiST include the visual association cortex, the sensory and motor cortices, the angular gyrus, the thalamus and the cingulate gyrus, as shown here in (a) horizontal, (b) coronal and (c) sagittal slices. All areas shown exceed the threshold for statistical significance of $t > 4.5$.

FIGURE 5.3   Regional brain activation and test-induced stress

Source: Dedovic et al., 2005: 325.

Volatile organic compounds and learning

To consider further the potential to understand feeling, and in particular the place of feeling in learning and the affect invoked by high-stakes testing, we turn again to leading-edge research in analytical chemistry that measures the mass of volatile organic compounds (VOCs) in exhaled breath. Turner et al. (2013) demonstrate the impact of stress on children's VOC profiles in test environments. Turner and colleagues exposed participants to a stressor in the form of a paced auditory serial addition test, along with the social threat of public results, much like in Dedovic's brain imaging work discussed earlier. Importantly, Turner's participants undertook the test (and controls) in a classroom environment providing pre- and post-exhaled breath samples which were analysed using gas chromatographic-mass spectrometry

(GC-MS). This allows the VOCs in the exhaled breath sample to be mapped and matched against known compounds. It is important to understand that this technology and method is emergent and it is not known what all the compounds evident in a mass spectrum are. Turner and colleagues identified six components that were sensitive to the invoked stress (see Figure 5.4). Four of these were shown to be indole, 2-hydroxy-1-phenylethanone, benzaldehyde and 2-ethylhexan-1-ol, while the remaining two components were not identified with certainty. The most

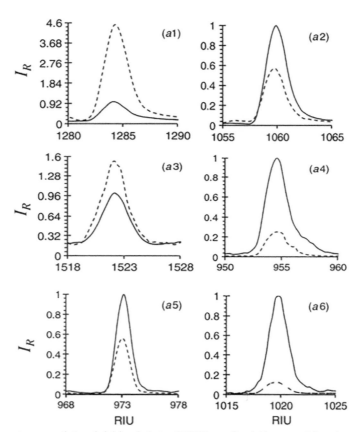

Volatile organic compounds in exhaled breath during PASAT test. Overlaid extracted ion chromatograms (XIC) responses for stressed experimental session (dashed line) and neutral experimental session (solid line) for stress-sensitive breath components: indole (α1), 2-hydroxy-1-phenylethanone (α2), 2-methyl-pentadecane (α3), unknown terpene (α4), benzaldehyde (α5) and 2-ethylhexan-1-ol (α6) from a single male participant. The intensities (IR) displayed have been normalized with respect to the neutral experimental session to indicate those components that have been up-regulated and down-regulated as a result of undertaking the PASAT.

FIGURE 5.4   Volatile organic compounds in the exhaled breath of children undertaking a maths test

Source: Turner et al., 2013.

potentially significant of these compounds is indole, because this is 'associated with the production of the essential amino acid tryptophan, which in turn is part of the pathway that produces serotonin' (Turner et al., 2013: 7) which in this literature is itself associated with cardiovascular and psychological stress.

This mass spectrometry analysis of VOCs in exhaled breath reveals traces of stress in response to testing at the molecular level. These results are extremely pertinent to schooling systems in which testing is embedded as a core practice, and might open a new lens onto the feelings and experiences of the students who are tested and the teachers who do the testing. Turner and colleagues emphasize that having identified VOCs it is not straightforward to assign causes to or from them, and suggest the need for further verification – 'it is perhaps too soon to postulate biological origins and roles for these VOCs as part of a stress-sensitive response in breath' (Turner et al., 2013).

In the light of Turner and colleagues' findings and caution, we suggest that mass spectrometry of VOCs may have the potential to provide new access to the visceral prompts (affect), flows of feeling (affection), and changes in bodily capacities (affectus) that education researchers have been concerned to explore but which have remained out of reach to sociological methods. William's methodology from the cinema auditorium, which attends to the atmosphere rather than individuals, could be adapted to attend to the social flows of feeling in school settings. This might enable analyses of VOCs in the classroom to be embedded in classroom ethnography and so identify those moments when institutional practice provokes peaks in stress or, conversely, peaks in happiness.

Together, these VOC studies demonstrate that a single body and collected bodies do different things – produce different volatile organic compounds – in response to different stimuli, that this is patterned and meaningful, and that we may be able to map between particular practices, VOCs, affects, affections, affectus and self-expressed feelings. This is not to not suggest an individual normative versus pathological VOCs responses. Embedded in critical ethnography VOC analysis has the potential to show mutability and flows, and the folding together (Roberts, 2015) of bodies, feelings, subjects, settings, artefacts, interactions, systems, structures, experiences, pedagogies and relationships. Atmospheric and individual analysis of VOCs in exhaled breath could speak to the collective and individual feeling evoked by particular sorts of teacher-student encounters, pedagogic situations, assessment modes and conditions, creativity and play. That is, VOCs in exhaled breath could offer us new insight into what sort of education is good for children and for learning, and what sort of education might actually work against itself and the well-being of children.

Neuroscience of happiness

Our discussion of the VOC profiles of stress in Turner and colleagues' work and (proxies for) a range of feelings in Williams and colleagues' research leads us away from the disease of stress in classrooms to an encounter with the possibilities of understanding happiness, pleasure and perhaps even *jouissance* in classroom encounters.

Neuroscience is concerned with brain states associated with happiness, and the relationship of this to well-being. Kringelbach and Berridge (2010) demonstrate a 'functional neuroanatomy of pleasure' (Kringelbach and Berridge, 2010: 659) that links pleasure to happiness and happiness to well-being. Building on a classical account of happiness as comprised of both pleasure and a 'good life', Kringelbach and Berridge suggests these two elements cohere in happy people and make sensory pleasure, which is amenable to neurobiological investigation, a powerful indicator for happiness in general. They also emphasis that sensory pleasure is 'liking' but also involves 'wanting' and 'learning' (Kringelbach and Berridge, 2010: 661) and seek to distinguish between affective states that have substrates in brain and affective feelings that are the reported experience of the person. They show that pleasure provokes networks that are extensive and widespread in the brain. The brain's coding of pleasure – the brain's activity in response to stimulus – is distributed, but pleasure-reaction mechanisms are concentrated in a limited number of brain 'hotspots' that form connected circuits. They suggest:

> From sensory pleasures and drugs of abuse to monetary, aesthetic and musical delights, all pleasures seem to involve the same hedonic brain systems, even when linked to anticipation and memory. Pleasures important to happiness, such as socializing with friends, and related traits of positive hedonic mood are thus all likely to draw upon the same neurobiological roots that evolved for sensory pleasures.
>
> *(Kringelbach and Berridge, 2010: 662)*

Psychoanalysis meets neuroscience in Bazan and Detandt's (2013) analysis of *jouissance*. *Jouissance* is understood in a range of ways across strains of psychoanalysis, but it is understood as more than pleasure. *Jouissance* involves drive, aim, object and impetus; it is the satisfaction of desire; the impossible gaining of the longed for lost object – the mother; the satiation of hunger; a motor action and release of tension. It is at once visceral and of the unconscious.

Bazan and Detandt (2013) suggest 'the central dopaminergic system as the "physiological architecture" of Freud's concept of the drive' (p. 5). These central dopaminergic systems 'are connected with paths which convey information of the internal homeostatic situation of the body' and so respond to drive stimuli with dopamine release. Bazan and Detandt emphasize that consummatory pleasure and drive pleasure are distinct, with drive pleasure being anticipatory or expectant. Like Kringelbach and Berridge, they draw on the distinction between wanting and liking, emphasizing that dopamine mediates wanting, but not liking and thereby provides a neurochemistry for the *jouissance*/pleasure distinction. Bazan and Detandt locate *jouissance* within the 'NAS-DA' or 'SEEKING system' of the brain:

> In the striatum, dopamine (DA) serves as a critical motor action signal; increases in DA are associated with increases in motor output, and decreases in DA with inhibition of behavior. In the case of the mesolimbic pathway, the

ventral tegmental area (VTA) innervates the nucleus accumbens shell (NAS), which is part of the corpus striata (basal ganglia); this system is therefore referred to as NAS-DA. This is also the so-called SEEKING system.

(Bazan and Detandt, 2013: 5)

The affect that in psychoanalysis is '*jouissance*', then, is suggested by neuroscience to be dopaminergic systems interaction with the brain's SEEKING system. A neuroscience of pleasure, happiness and the slippery notion of *jouissance* is becoming available. What this might mean for education and classrooms is as yet unclear. It may well mean that we pay attention not just to the difficult feelings that raise concern amongst educators and parents, but also to feelings of pleasure and happiness in the classroom. It may even mean that the visceral prompts that move learners to seek *jouissance*, as well as its drives, objects and impetus, come to be recognized as important forces in classrooms and for learning.

Biosocial feeling in the classroom

[W]hat is it that we seek to gain from knowing, and intervening in, how children feel? in what ways can our fine-grained analyses of the multiple workings of emotion in children's lives 'speak back' to both prevailing orthodoxies and counter-narratives about the deployment of emotion in mainstream or alternative schools, youth work settings, health settings, et cetera?

—(Kraftl, 2013: 21)

Biosocial understanding of feeling in classrooms has the potential to change education at a system level, from policy and directives, accountability measures, curriculum and assessment strategies, to classroom organization, pedagogies and relationships. Attending to the biosocial and its implications for children's well-being and learning demands we prioritise understanding when 'school stress' becomes harmful, the efforts to eradicate 'harmful stress', the promotion of care relationships, and the potentialities of happiness, pleasure and *joussiance* in learning contexts.

Evidencing the significance of feeling in the classroom has the potential to shift pedagogic and assessment practices and classroom relationships. Anticipating that empirical biosocial study will confirm that high-stakes tests and their attendant institutional and pedagogic practices provoke 'stress' in children that has lasting detrimental effects, we envisage a major driver for a shift in policy away from high-stakes testing and towards alternative forms of assessment. Such a shift is profoundly indicated by existing research discussed here and, we anticipate, will be evidenced through critical biosocial research in education settings in the near future. Different forms of relationality, pedagogy and assessment can emerge. A biosocial approach to feeling in the classroom, then, is not a move away from analysis of structures, systems and institutional practices towards the remedying of 'individual disease' – mindfulness on its own will not do, and in fact only reinforces an individualized framing that fails to recognize systemic problems as they play out in classrooms. In the absence of significant policy change, we suggest that educators might explore 'spaces in between' where education might be done differently in pursuit of the feeling school and the feeling classroom where children are 'held in mind' as they encounter the challenges of learning. Teachers might foreground relationality in their classrooms and prioritise this over tests or the regimental production of docility and managed behaviour. Headteachers might do likewise, allowing the pursuit of ever-higher results in high-stakes tests to become secondary to relationality in the feeling classroom.

Identifying the 'emotional signalling molecules' of children's feelings from the air in the classroom and non-invasive breath samples at different times of day and after different kinds of activities e.g. maths, art, sport, break time, a struggle between friends, a disciplinary infraction and intervention, would allow us to analyse the biochemical effects that particular feelings have as children learn and interact. Embedding this biochemical data collection as part of biosocial classroom ethnography opens up the potential to match these emotional signalling molecules with detailed accounts of what happens inside learning situations, demonstrating that feelings are complex, multifactorial biosocial phenomena which are a central part of everyday life inside classrooms and, indeed, of learning.

Understanding feeling in classrooms in this way has implications for policy makers' and educators' approaches to curriculum, pedagogy, assessment and classroom relationships and has the potential to inform transformations in practice in these areas. This could lead to a step change in our understanding of the functioning and importance of how we feel for learning, and, by extension, a step change in our understanding of the functioning and importance of feeling across fields of social life.

By looking at feeling in the classroom through multiple lenses – including those offered by a range of biosciences – we bring back into the frame of potential thinking, analysis and practice the possibility that difficult feelings are not the disease of the maladapted individual, but are affects that flow through social spaces, produced through interacting social and biological forces, and possible to apprehend across scales from the distribution of outcomes in high-stakes tests, and children's self-reports of well-being to the flows of volatile organic compounds in breath. Our understanding of the enfolded production and products of affect becomes simultaneously concerned with social structures, institutional practices, representation and meaning, subjectivities, relationships, feeling, neural networks, metabolic processes and molecular functions. It is not just the case that social processes and biological mechanisms flow together, rather they are enfolded together in the dynamic production of feeling.

Offering a nuanced account of how feelings work as biosocial phenomena has the potential to transform policy and professional practice in education and wider services. Attending biosocially to feeling in classrooms can transform how policy makers, educators and the public understand feelings, how these impact and are felt by individual bodies, how they flow between people, and how they can aid or block learning. Understanding the significance of feeling has the potential in the short term to transform how classrooms are organized, the sorts of relationships that educators pursue with children and promote between children, and the sorts of learning activities that children are encouraged to engage in. In the longer term this understanding of how feelings affect learning has the potential to transform education policy, e.g. in relation to school transitions, setting practices, assessment or in relation to behaviour where relationships between adults and children are a central feature. Extending this learning to wider fields such as children and family services, social care, or youth criminal justice, attention to biosocial feeling has the potential to transform understandings and professional practices by informing practitioners, leaders and policy makers about the importance of incorporating an appreciation of the biosocial nature and effects of feelings into the organization and delivery of interventions and services.

What happens if we revisit the '*running the line*' ethnographic data biosocially? We are confronted with the visceral bodiliness and plasticity of the running body and subject, now understood within biochemical as well as discursive limits. The force that moves the events of the episode, its players and readers can be seen as the locus of affect, affect that is produced through and productive of biochemical and social and discursive entanglements. If the boy, the teachers and the researcher all blew into the mass-spectrometer at that moment might it change what we understood this running to mean, what a body could do, and what it could make happen? Might it transform the concepts of feeling, learning, or 'SEBD'?

6

BIOSOCIAL ASSEMBLAGE

The case of Attention Deficit-Hyperactivity Disorder

This chapter offers a detailed interrogation of what it means to engage the biological and the social together. To do this we engage the field of special educational needs and the highly contentious diagnosis of 'attention deficit-hyperactivity disorder' (ADHD). There has been much research activity in relation to ADHD. One major thread is critical sociological work within disability studies and inclusive education that disputes the voracity of the diagnosis at the same time as it details the damage done to children and their education by such a diagnosis. Another major thread is genetic work that examines genes associated with ADHD and their possible functions. And a final major thread is brain imaging work that examines brain structure, function and connectivity for associations to ADHD. While there is some articulation across neurogenetics and neuro-imaging, sociological work in the field has been highly critical of the endeavour of genetics and neuroscience in relation to ADHD.

In this chapter we suspend sociological objections in order to work across these domains. In order to do this we identify key sociological concerns over ADHD and then go on to map current genetic and brain imaging research into ADHD. We do this to consider together the range of expert knowledges about ADHD that currently circulate and inform understandings of and responses to ADHD in education. We also do this in order to illustrate our accounts of the partial, diverse and fast-moving character of research in the biosciences.

Through this trans-domain mapping of ADHD knowledges, we consider the biological and social productive forces involved in the making of ADHD, and use this to consider the utility of approaching ADHD (and special educational needs more widely) as a complex social formation that might be understood as a biosocial assemblage that spans the macro and micro, from economic flows to movements across the membranes of molecules in bodies (Youdell, 2015; Youdell & McGimpsey, 2015).

The sociology of special educational needs

A dominant idea in inclusive education has, until recently, been that 'special educational needs' (SEN) is a social construct, not a fact of life. Following from this
is the claim that a whole range of educational exclusions of students identified as
having 'special education needs' – from being overlooked or hyper-managed in the
classroom, moved out of the classroom into a range of interventions, or moved out
of mainstream school into 'special' provision – are the result of institutional failures
to work with an idea of the student and learner that is flexible enough to include
all children. This approach argues that children come to be identified, and possibly
formally diagnosed, as having a special educational need by repeatedly being seen
by education institutions and professionals as 'outside' normal expectations of the
student and learner. When recognition as student and learner fails, or becomes
'impossible', alternative ways of understanding a child begin to circulate – e.g. they
are 'developmentally delayed', exhibit 'behavioural difficulties', or have a diagnosable disorder, such as 'attention deficit-hyperactivity disorder'.

Such an approach might seem to overlook the real differences and challenges of
real bodies (and brains) – the point is not to deny such differences and challenges,
but to think critically about their existence, sources and meanings. That is, inclusive
education calls on us to pause to ask whether difference is really present and significant, and if so, whether the challenges associated with this difference are located in
the child or are the result of the (unrealized) demands of a rigid and unresponsive
approach to schooling. In turn inclusive educators are likely to advocate a shift from
deficit accounts of difference to an approach that is able to engage with difference
without a normative framing (Allan, 2008).

In disability activism and scholarship, a distinction has been made between the
impairment of a body and the *disability* that becomes attached to particular sorts
of bodies through institutional, social and discursive practices. This distinction has
been successful in separating out exclusionary and discriminatory social and institutional factors from the bodies of the people impacted by these. Yet, this impair-
ment/disability distinction has sometimes proved difficult to hold, particularly as it
comes under pressure from some of the more contentious 'social' difficulties or disorders that are housed under the category of special educational needs. For instance,
inclusive educators advocating for children identified as having 'behavioural difficulties' are likely to insist that there is no impairment 'beneath' the behaviours
being identified as problematic, but rather that these behaviours are either being
mis-recognized by schools or are manifestations of unrealizable institutional or relational demands.

At the same time as inclusive education and disability studies have sought to
uncouple impairment from disability and promote an open-ended approach to
difference, within the mainstream of special educational needs the naming and
diagnosis of special needs has continued to be seen as the best way to respond to
these needs and the case for 'special' educational provision has continued to be
made. While there have been attempts led by researchers, policy and practitioners

to make a distinction between approaches that foreground diagnoses and those that foreground recognition of additional needs, the notion that particular difficulties or blocks are internal to the individual child persists.

The field of education, then, offers a number of conflicting ways of understanding and responding to special education needs. This fragmented field is facing increasing challenges from knowledges emerging outside education, in particular in the new biological sciences. Furthermore, the persistence of experiences of difference – for children and their teachers – means that often embodied differences continue to need to be accounted for and engaged with.

Inclusive education and disability studies argue for a suspension of diagnoses and more open and inclusive ways of thinking about schooling, learning and learners; education psychology develops increasingly nuanced ways of measuring specific learning difficulties and intervening in these; education neuroscience uses leading-edge technology to investigate the potential neuronal basis for such difficulties; genetics explores genes or combinations of genes and their variants that might underpin diagnosed conditions; and epigenetics and metabolomics explore the interaction of environment, nutrition and gene regulation and expression in the making of diagnosed conditions.

Deborah's work has, until recently, been firmly in the tradition of inclusive education and disability studies. In her 2011 book she states:

> Designations such as 'boy' and '[Social, Emotional, and Behavioural Difficulties]' . . . can be understood as performative – they *create* the gendered and diagnosed subject that they name, and they do this while appearing to be just *descriptive*. By appearing to be descriptive they create the *illusion* of the *prior* existence of gender and of educational disorders. So while it appears that the subject expresses a gender or a disorder, this is actually a performative *effect* of the respective categories and their use.
>
> *(Youdell, 2011: 81)*

But in the light of the new research possibilities emerging from biological sciences and the biosocial approaches we are developing in this book, we begin to question whether this assertion can still stand. Indeed, this very question was put to Deborah recently by a colleague at a biosocial education research seminar. The short answer seems to be no, it cannot. Rather, while we might continue to regard particular special educational needs diagnoses as simultaneously modes and effects of subjectivation that rely on normative accounts of the child and the person, there are other forces in play, including biological and biosocial forces.

The case of ADHD

In the remainder of this chapter we explore the potential to work across the range of educational, activist and biological knowledges sketched in the previous section in order to understand special educational needs as biosocial assemblage. In order to demonstrate the potential and pitfalls for such an approach, we focus in on ADHD, a pronounced and growing diagnosis in education and a site of particular activity in bioscience research.

We begin by presenting the formal diagnostic criteria in full from the latest version of the Diagnostic and Statistical Manual (DSM 5). This is not to privilege the DSM 5 account but to show the diagnostic foundation of ADHD in a collection of observed behaviours (what psychologists and geneticists would call a phenotype).

Attention-Deficit/Hyperactivity Disorder

Diagnostic criteria

A persistent pattern of inattention and/or hyperactivity-impulsivity that interferes with functioning or development, as characterized by (1) and/or (2):

1. Inattention:

Six (or more) of the following symptoms have persisted for at least 6 months to a degree that is inconsistent with developmental level and that negatively impacts directly on social and academic/occupational activities: Note: The symptoms are not solely a manifestation of oppositional behavior, defiance, hostility, or failure to understand tasks or instructions. For older adolescents and adults (age 17 and older), at least five symptoms are required.

a. Often fails to give close attention to details or makes careless mistakes in schoolwork, at work, or during other activities (e.g. overlooks or misses details, work is inaccurate).

b. Often has difficulty sustaining attention in tasks or play activities (e.g. has difficulty remaining focused during lectures, conversations, or lengthy reading).

c. Often does not seem to listen when spoken to directly (e.g. mind seems elsewhere, even in the absence of any obvious distraction).

d. Often does not follow through on instructions and fails to finish schoolwork, chores, or duties in the workplace (e.g. starts tasks but quickly loses focus and is easily sidetracked).

e. Often has difficulty organizing tasks and activities (e.g. difficulty managing sequential tasks; difficulty keeping materials and belongings in order; messy, disorganized work; has poor time management; fails to meet deadlines).

f. Often avoids, dislikes, or is reluctant to engage in tasks that require sustained mental effort (e.g. schoolwork or homework; for older adolescents and adults, preparing reports, completing forms, reviewing lengthy papers).

g. Often loses things necessary for tasks or activities (e.g. school materials, pencils, books, tools, wallets, keys, paperwork, eyeglasses, mobile telephones).

h. Is often easily distracted by extraneous stimuli (for older adolescents and adults, may include unrelated thoughts).

i. Is often forgetful in daily activities (e.g. doing chores, running errands; for older adolescents and adults, returning calls, paying bills, keeping appointments).

2. Hyperactivity and impulsivity:

Six (or more) of the following symptoms have persisted for at least 6 months to a degree that is inconsistent with developmental level and that negatively impacts directly on social and academic/occupational activities: Note: The symptoms are not solely a manifestation of oppositional behavior, defiance, hostility, or a failure to understand tasks or instructions. For older adolescents and adults (age 17 and older), at least five symptoms are required.

a. Often fidgets with or taps hands or feet or squirms in seat.

b. Often leaves seat in situations when remaining seated is expected (e.g. leaves his or her place in the classroom, in the office or other workplace, or in other situations that require remaining in place).

c. Often runs about or climbs in situations where it is inappropriate. (Note: In adolescents or adults, may be limited to feeling restless.)

d. Often unable to play or engage in leisure activities quietly.

e. Is often 'on the go', acting as if 'driven by a motor' (e.g. is unable to be or uncomfortable being still for extended time, as in restaurants, meetings; may be experienced by others as being restless or difficult to keep up with).

f. Often talks excessively.

g. Often blurts out an answer before a question has been completed (e.g. completes people's sentences; cannot wait for turn in conversation).

h. Often has difficulty waiting his or her turn (e.g. while waiting in line).

i. Often interrupts or intrudes on others (e.g. butts into conversations, games, or activities; may start using other people's things without asking or receiving permission; for adolescents and adults, may intrude into or take over what others are doing).

(American Psychiatry Association, 2013)

What is striking about these criteria is their behavioural character and embeddedness in established social expectations about how one should attend, hold one's body, engage in conversation and so on. As we will explore as we move on, bioscience researchers will indicate potential biological underpinnings to these forms of engagement and embodiment. Nevertheless, DSM 5 offers an individualized and individualizing account of practices that sit outside a normative framing of appropriate childhood behaviours. Such accounts are based on the observations of adult experts trained in the identification and treatment of ADHD. But even as this expertise ensures proper diagnosis and guards against the diagnosis of a child that teachers or others find difficult, these experts are nonetheless steeped in the norms of the sites and cultures in which they work, including the norms of ADHD itself. ADHD in DSM 5 is a phenotype – the collection of traits that together constitute a disorder. Phenotype certainly sounds more scientific and objective than behaviour that has been observed, but as we will see, the critical sociological literature suggests this is dressing for hierarchical observation and judgement, and ultimately exclusion (Graham, 2010; Harwood and Allan, 2014; Slee, 2011).

This DSM includes an important diagnostic note that follows the diagnostic criteria, which states that the behaviours identified must co-exist, must appear at particular points in childhood and persist over time, and must interfere with daily life:

> Several inattentive or hyperactive-impulsive symptoms were present prior to age 12 years.
>
> Several inattentive or hyperactive-impulsive symptoms are present in two or more settings (e.g. at home, school, or work; with friends or relatives; in other activities).
>
> There is clear evidence that the symptoms interfere with, or reduce the quality of, social, academic, or occupational functioning.
>
> *(American Psychiatry Association, 2013)*

The requirement for a substantial degree of persistent across time and contexts of the behaviours that become the symptoms of ADHD may be designed to lend consistency and rigour to diagnosis and ensure that one difficult period or relationship does not lead to a diagnosis of ADHD. Yet at the same time, this requirement locates ADHD firmly inside the child and erases the possibility that difficult encounters – with other children or adults, or with particular settings and requirements – might be implicated in the manifestation of behaviours that lead to diagnosis, much less that the behaviours of others or the processes and demands of settings (e.g. formal education) might be culpable either for being unable to accommodate behaviours or for provoking them. Institutions, social milieu and relationships all come to be outside ADHD. This locating of ADHD inside the child simultaneously demands biological explanations for it and renders it a 'problem' amenable to biological 'solutions'.

Sociology of ADHD

Writing about the limiting effect on education and pedagogy of medicalized understandings of and approaches to ADHD, Linda Graham (2010) notes an apparent 'everything and nothing' approach in which educational systems and institutions as well as teachers and clinicians treat ADHD as though it was a well-understood neurological disorder at the same time as neuroscience researchers acknowledge the very preliminary nature of understanding being generated in that field. Graham (2010) cites Riccio et al. who in 1993 wrote: '[i]n the absence of clear neurological evidence for the diagnosis, clinicians will continue to make diagnoses based on behavioural observation' (Riccio et al., 1993: 122 cited by Graham, 2010: 2). The intervening 25 years has seen much further research and a deepening of understanding of genetic variation, gene regulation and expression, and brain connectivity and function. Yet, as the current DSM 5 shows, it remains the case that ADHD is diagnosed through observation of behaviours. As we have said at a number of points in this book, the more bioscience knows, the more evident it becomes how much it does not know. Graham suggests that:

> Far from liberating the 'neurologically dysfunctional' child, the ascendency of the medical model actually leads to premature foreclosure of the critical reflection and ownership that we know is intrinsic to good teacher practice.
>
> *(Graham, 2010: 9)*

Valerie Harwood and Julie Allan's 2014 book *Psychopathology at School* provides a confronting encounter with a whole series of flows through which 'mental disorder', including ADHD, comes to be attached to infants, children and young people. At the centre of their analysis is a reading of the shift in professional and policy expert knowledge from an educational understanding of special educational needs to a medical account of psychopathology – and their own counter assertion that these 'mental disorders' are not psychopathological afflictions, but the products of the entrenched certainties of professionals and the policies, practices and techniques that follow from and persistently reconfirm these.

By tracing the making of 'mental disorder' from the unborn infant, through the early years, to primary school, secondary school and on to tertiary education, Harwood and Allan's analysis shows how psychopathology works on different bodies and how it works differently as bodies grow. In particular, they show how, within the normative frameworks of the education, welfare and health professionals involved, the possibility for 'treatment' recedes as children age, with the professional call to intervene early and correction giving way to an increasingly urgent demand to identify and manage 'threat'. They say:

> The newborn, as well as the prenatal (or antenatal), are critical sites because they are viewed as the points of life holding the most potential. These are the life-points where there is greatest possibility for the potential of mental health problems to be avoided, detected or corrected. On a downward sliding scale, where potentiality decreases as age increases, the unborn, newborns, infants, toddlers and preschoolers have an 'inherent' potentiality for optimization. [. . .] According to this logic, the longer existence continues the less potential there is for intervention and correction.
>
> *(Harwood and Allan, 2014: 67)*

Harwood and Allan identify a deployment of the plasticity that biological science is demonstrating, but it is a plasticity that is time-limited and which solidifies by the time adolescence is reached. Echoing policy commitments to 'early intervention' (Allen, 2011), this renders early life the time during which 'optimization' can happen.

The infant and even prenatal baby is framed in this model by the policy use of neuroscience to inform 'early intervention' before it is 'too late'. Where a 'risk' of 'mental disorder' is identified, Harwood and Allen show, the 'problem' is located by the policy and professional discourse and practice in the materiality of the foetus and infant that is impacted by the genetic codes of its parents and subsequently by the prenatal and postnatal practice of its mother. In the use and misuse of brain science in education and mental health, ideas about 'hard-wiring' and attachment (or specifically poor attachment) come to mean that 'the movements and actions of caregivers can be understood to directly link with the neural connexions/non-connections in the infants brain' (Harwood and Allan, 2014: 81). As the infant grows into a preschool child, Harwood and Allan show how child care workers are expected to be watchful for signs of 'mental ill-health' which early years interventions might assuage. In this model there is 'hope' for the unborn child, the infant and the preschooler; 'early intervention' promises to halt if not wholly undo the neural damage caused by parents' genetic and epigenetic influences. Harwood and Allan trace a shift in understanding and approach as the child moves to primary school. At this age and in this setting the child of 'mental disorder' and her/his parent are 'exalted in their capabilities in exhibiting abnormality' and teachers are exalted in their 'capacity for *noticing* abnormality in their classrooms' (Harwood and Allan, 2014: 87–88) in order to 'rescue' 'from the grip of abnormality' (Harwood and Allan, 2014: 102). At secondary school age the professional intervention and goal becomes 'palliative' (Harwood and Allan, 2014: 119) as abnormality becomes sedimented as a behavioural problem, antisocial behaviour and criminality and the focus becomes managing the impact the mental disordered child has on the normal child. Harwood and Allan demonstrate in fine detail the crushing movement of 'a shift away from efforts to understand and address the abnormal behaviour and towards control, containment and governance' (Harwood and Allan, 2014: 108). This leading sociological research into health, social care and school practices surrounding ADHD traces the age-specific particularities of these practices and the ways that these are informed by policy take-up of aspects of neuroscience. Their analysis extends Deborah's own 2011 claim that diagnoses of special educational needs are performative. This is underscored by their question 'could ADHD in children and young people exist if schools did not exist?' Their answer: 'we suggest not' (Harwood and Allan, 2014).

The bioscience of ADHD

In their 2015 article in *Frontiers in Psychiatry* Schuch and colleagues state that '[t]here is no biological marker for ADHD' (Schuch et al., 2015: 1). This might seem to concur with Harwood and Allan's claim that ADHD would not exist without a schooling (or health and social care services) industry that demands a definitive medical account of children who did not 'fit'. But it is not that simple. While there is no single marker for ADHD, there is significant activity across genetics and brain imaging that is identifying a range of potential biological influences on ADHD.

Back in 2002 the psychiatric community published a *Consensus Statement on ADHD* (Barkley et al., 2002) in which they attempt to quell popular, media and educator concerns over rising ADHD diagnoses by asserting its biological underpinnings and the voracity of treatment interventions. This consensus statement drew on a large pool of research evidence based mainly in brain imaging and twin studies. We should note that the Human Genome Project had not finally reported at this time and the sort of epigenetic and metabolomics research we have explored in this book had not yet begun to develop. The publication was followed by a rebuttal (Timimi, 2004) by a diverse group of scholars and professionals spanning psychiatry, health sciences and community services, who offered an alternative reading of the state of the science, foregrounded social influences including early experiences of trauma and parenting and schooling practices, and expressed concern over the expansion of psychostimulant treatment. Barkley and colleagues produced a swift response (Barkley, 2004) restating their findings as dominant, challenging the evidence base for any social influence on ADHD and reasserting the value of (drug) interventions. The **either** biology **or** society approach to ADHD manifest in this row from the early 2000s has not abated. Genetic, epigenetic and brain imaging research has continued to amass evidence of a biological basis for ADHD, and sociological research has continued to demonstrate how the diagnosis is constructed as the outside to a normative definition of the child and emerges in particular social and historical conditions.

The current state of scientific knowledge

As we move on to explore the current science of ADHD it is crucial to recognize that what we report and consider here is the current knowledge as of the time of the writing of this book – note that this is already out of date as the book is published and read. The fields of genetics, epigenetics, genetic neuroscience, and brain imaging all expand in complexity and detail on a weekly basis. In the current body of scientific research into ADHD, work tends to seek out **associations** between ADHD and particular gene variants, or the activity of particular neurotransmitter in particular brain regions, or particular pathways or connexions in the brain. The associational nature of these gene or brain features to ADHD traits cannot be stressed enough as we begin, as non-experts, to engage the genetic and neuroscience of ADHD. The leading-edge research that we find reported and reviewed in top journals over that last few years is overwhelmingly not reporting finding specific mechanisms that lead to ADHD, it is reporting associations between pre-existing diagnoses of ADHD (diagnoses that have been made based on the observed behavioural criteria (phenotype) set out in the DSM 5) and particular genetic or neurological features. What we present, then, is a body of research identifying a complex series of associations, with no clear mechanistic pathways identified. Geneticists and neuroscientists continue to look for these mechanistic pathways, in order to understand what might cause the traits that are currently bundled together as ADHD. But the search for mechanisms does not correspondence in any direct way to the criteria offered by DSM 5. The commitment in the life sciences to finding causal mechanisms is as deep as the commitment to resisting diagnosis in critical sociology.

ADHD: genetic and heritable or 'missing heritability'?

It is argued in the behavioural genetics literature that child and adult ADHD are genetic and highly heritable (Franke et al., 2012). Family studies, including twin and adoption studies, suggest a heritability of between 30 and 80% across studies (Cortese et al., 2011; Franke et al., 2012). Yet current GWAS do not show statistically significant associations between ADHD and genetic factors (Schuch et al., 2015: 2) and so strong heritability does not imply a specific genetic inheritance (Li et al., 2014) or genetic determinism (Cortese, 2011: 514).

This has led to the questioning of the 'missing heritability' of ADHD in GWAS. Franke suggests that this is 'potentially due to small effect sizes of individual variants, disease heterogeneity and gene – environment interactions' (Franke et al., 2012: 975). In response Franke suggests a different approach which conceives of gene variation influencing a broad phenotype rather than a specific diagnosed 'disorder'. He suggests that 'common variants might influence disorders on the dimensional, syndromic level – for example, emotional dysregulation – while not being associated with a specific disorder *per se*' (Franke et al., 2012: 975). This ties into work targeting the endophenotype to bridge the gap between the genotype and the phenotype.

> Heritability estimates range between 70 and 90% (Faraone and Mick, 2010; Larsson et al., 2013b). Despite this substantial heritability, identification of ADHD risk genes has been challenging (Franke et al., 2009; Gizer et al., 2009). One reason for this may be that ADHD has a complex, polygenic genetic background, in which multiple genetic variants (many of them with small effects) contribute to the etiology of the disorder in most patients. Although a substantial fraction of ADHD etiology is due to genes, many environmental risk factors and potential gene-environment interactions are also linked with an increased risk for the disorder
>
> *(Klein et al., 2017: 116)*

Genotypes and phenotypes (and endophenotypes)

In our introduction to the biology that underpins genetics (Chapter 2), we explained that a genotype is a particular genetic profile, as identified through an analysis of a selection of genes present, and potentially their specific variants. We move from a genetic profile to a genotype when that particular set of gene variants are associated with a disease or trait(s). A **phenotype** is a distinct set of traits understood to be found together in a patterned and meaningful way, and which often serves as the basis for diagnosis. That is, a phenotype is not a genotype – a phenotype may have no clear or demonstrable link to a genotype. This is the case in ADHD where there is not a set of genes that are known to cause these patterned traits. This is underscored when we look at the criteria for formal diagnosis in DSM 5. The distance between a gene variant or a collection of gene variants – a genotype – and a set of manifest behaviours – a phenotype – is substantial. Indeed, making a move across this distance continues to be the major challenge facing neurobiological research into ADHD.

Bioscience responses to the challenge of the distance between phenotype and genotype have included attempts to identify **intermediate phenotypes** and **endophenotypes**. Endophenotypes are biomarkers that function as 'intermediaries between gene and behavioural phenotype' (Klein et al., 2017: 138). To qualify, and to be useful in identifying pathways from gene variant to trait, the endophenotype must be a mediator, and not a separate marker of the trait. Klein et al. (2017) note in a rare paper that assesses the mediation of risk across geneotype, brain phenotype and clinical phenotype, only a subgroup of the intermediate brain phenotypes were actually linked to ADHD (van der Meer, 2015 cited by Klein et al., 2017). Franke et al. (2012) make a slightly different distinction, where intermediate phenotypes are 'mediating pathways' that may be identifiable 'once one or more genetic markers are found that show association to both the clinical disorder and the endophenotype'. From here 'the additional step of demonstrating mediation between genes and disorder' can be taken (Franke et al., 2012: 276).

What is underscored is the goal of moving to the use of endophenotypes instead of 'clinical phenotype' or 'categorical diagnosis' to identify disease/disorder, using intermediate phenotypes to identify relevant processes. For instance, for ADHD 'neuropsychological phenotypes' such as 'response inhibition, vigilance, working memory and planning' are suggested (Franke et al., 2012: 796). Whether research into these mediators will be fruitful in identifying pathways from gene variants to phenotypes based on behaviours or clinical criteria remains to be seen. The focus on them demonstrates a recognition by neuro- and genetic scientists of the need to deal with the gap between genes and traits. Noteworthy is the way in which the search for these intermediaries is part of a wider shift to a concern with complex systems that may be involved in multiple traits (e.g. similar diagnosed conditions) rather than single genes with singular causal effects (see Franke et al., 2012: 976).

'Hot genes'

In a 2014 meta-analysis of genes associated with ADHD, Li and colleagues make use of the notion of 'hot genes' – the genes that researchers keep returning to in their investigation of the genes and their specific variants that might be involved in the manifestation of the traits identified as part of ADHD (Li et al., 2014). This body of research takes a number or forms and includes studies of 'candidate genes' that are thought (through their association with potentially similar trait) to be likely 'candidates' for involvement in ADHD; 'linkage' and GWAS that explore the statistical association with ADHD of multiple genes with small effects; the mapping of gene expression to brain regions; and studies of specific variations of the genes, e.g. copy number variations (CNVs), single neucleotide polymorphisms (SNPs) or allele variations, that appear to be involved in ADHD.

Li et al. note that over the course of ADHD genetic research (dating back in their analysis to the 1990s), over 300 genes have been identified as being associated with ADHD. But when they look at those that are recurrent across at least 5 studies just 24 genes recur:

> Most of these genes are involved in biological process related to monoamine neurotransmitter, including monoamine metabolic biosynthesis and mono- amine transmission (transporter and receptor).
>
> *(Li et al., 2014: 16)*

Li highlights that the interest in these particular genes reflects thinking in drug, imaging and animal work that focuses on associations between ADHD and imbal- ances in dopamine, serotonin and noradrenaline neurotransmission.

Important to note here is the identification of genes' *involvement* in biological processes that are *related* to synthesizing, transporting and receiving monoamines – the neurotransmitters and neuromodulators dopamine, serotonin and noradrena- line. That is, these are not mechanisms through which a gene or gene variant leads to ADHD, but statistical associations between the occurrence of a gene or gene variant and the traits identified as ADHD.

In order to offer a sense of the genes and their variants that are currently under investigation, the known or anticipated function of these gene, and the ways in which they are thought to be associated with ADHD, we offer some detail of a selection of these 'hot genes' in Table 6.1.

Genetic mechanisms for ADHD?

The 'hot genes' under investigation have in common their demonstrated associa- tion with ADHD in the absence of substantial progress in identifying the genetic mechanisms or pathways through which particular genes or gene variants might contribute to the manifestation of traits identified as ADHD.

Li and colleagues note that genome-wide association studies of common gene variants are underway but stress that 'no locus has yet been identified that meets genome-wide levels of significance' (Li et al., 2014: 116). Similarly, they note that studies of rare copy number variants are beginning to show patterned results, but that this line of work is in the early stages (Li, 2014). More precisely, Klein and col- leagues note that 'risk variants' – that is those gene variants associated with diagnosis

TABLE 6.1 'Hot genes' associated with ADHD

Gene (or variant)	Gene function and relationship to ADHD
SLC6A3 (also known as DAT1)	Solute carrier family 6, member 3 – a dopamine and serotonin transporter This is a neurotransmitter involved in encoding and transporting dopamine and serotonin. More than 60 studies have investigated the association of this gene to ADHD
SLC6A4	Solute carrier family 6, member 4 – a serotonin receptor This gene 'codes' a solute carrier protein. According to Klein et al. (2017) the protein coded by this gene is responsible for serotonin re-uptake and is the key mechanism that regulates the activity of serotonin in the brain. The specific function is to take serotonin from the synaptic cleft into the presynaptic neuron. A specific variation or 'functional polymorphism' of the gene in its 'promoter region' (known as 5HTTLPR) has been of interest to researchers. At this location there is a 44-bp insertion or deletion which create either and long (L) or short (S) allele respectively. The long allele has been associated with faster serotonin re-uptake which in turn means less serotonin active in the brain. A small number of resting MRI studies (sMRI) have sought to investigate gene × environment interaction in relation to the 5HTTLPR polymorphism in ADHD, with one study showing an interaction between stress, the 5HTTLPR S-allele, and increased severity of ADHD. Across studies, results for the relationship between this gene and ADHD remain equivocal.
SLC6A2	Solute carrier family 6, member 2 –a serotonin receptor This gene 'codes' a protein that is responsible for norepinephrine re-uptake, moving serotonin from the synaptic cleft to the presynaptic neuron. A number of studies suggest an association between the gene and ADHD but different gene variants (SNPs) are suggested across studies (Klein et al., 2017).
DRD4 (DRD1, DRD2, DRD3 and DRD5 have also been investigated but not associated)	Dopamine receptor D4 This gene is (codes) a protein receptor. A particular variation or 'polymorphism' of the gene – 48 bp VNTR in exon 3, where 2-, 4-, and 7-repeat alleles are found – has been targeted in association with ADHD. Particular attention has been paid to the 7R-allele which has also been associated with a broader set of behaviours that have been classified as 'externalising' (Klein et al.). Different variants have been associated with different continental ancestry (discussed in Chapter 1) with the 7R-allele associated with 'caucasian' continental ancestry. DRD4-7R has been identified as affecting receptor binding and producing a blunted dopamine response. Across the more than 60 studies that have investigated the association of DRD4 variants to ADHD, findings have been equivocal, with contradictory findings and a range of associations (not mechanistic) indicated.

The DRD4 gene has been shown to be expressed extensively in areas of brain considered to be affected in ADHD e.g. the orbitofrontal cortex and anterior cingulate in the frontal lobe. Association between the 7R variant and brain activity has shown variations in alpha and beta waves, and reduced activity has been related to lessened orientation of attention and preparation of responses in those with the 7R-allele. Likewise, longer DRD4 variants (including the 7R-allele) have been associated with lower levels of executive functioning. DRD4 variants have been explored for G x E interaction, and associations between response to stimulant treatment, quality of peer relationships and persistence of ADHD into adulthood have been suggested.

While many studies have focussed on the 7R-allele, findings remain inconclusive and the available evidence does not offer pathways from gene variant to identification of ADHD traits, diagnosis and/or adult outcomes.

At present it is not possible to say confidently that a clear correlation exists, or to identify a mechanism through which this variant is involved in or causative of ADHD. Nevertheless, genetic research in the field continues to explore the possibility that DRD4 variants affect brain structure/activity and so are involved in ADHD trajectories.

HTR1B (HTR2A and HTR2C have also been investigated)	5-Hydroxytryptamine (serotonin) receptor 1B, protein-coupled Klein: 135 HTR1B is a G protein-coupled receptor that inhibits cyclic adenosine monophosphate (cAMP) formation – a second messenger important in many intercellular signalling pathways. HTR1B is highly expressed in a brain region associated with the sleep/wake cycle (the dorsal raphe nucleus). It is also expressed in the striatum and dorsolateral prefrontal cortex (PFC). HTR1B has been studied in families with ADHD diagnoses and a particular variant – rs6296 G-allele – has been found to be more common in parents and children with ADHD diagnoses. This variant has been the subject of fMRI studies of response inhibition in which children are to respond to a stop signal, however, it was associated with both increased and decreased activation during both successful and failed stop trials.
ADRA2A (ADRA2C has also been investigated)	Andrenoceptor Alpha 2A – an andrenergic receptor The most prevalent noradrenergic receptor in the prefrontal cortex (PFC). Two variants have been associated with ADHD – rs1800544 SNP G-allele and rs553668 SNP T-allele. These variants have not been confirmed as risks for ADHD in meta-analyses. (Klein et al., 2017)

(Continued)

TABLE 6.1 (Continued)

Gene (or variant)	Gene function and relationship to ADHD
COMT	Catechol-O-methyltransferase – a catalyser of neurotransmitters
	This gene codes for the transfer of a methyl group from S-adenosylmethionine to catecholamines (these include dopamine, epinephrine and norepinephrine) and hence the metabolism of these.
	The gene is highly expressed in the frontal lobe and has a major role in the degradation of these neurotransmitters as well as the metabolism of catechol drugs. Studies of the association between COMT and ADHD have examined a particular variant (SNP) in exon 4 rs4860 (known as *Val158Met*) in which the amino acid valine is replaced with the amino acid methionine. This replacement leads to a 2-to-4 times decrease in activity and hence slower clearance of the neurotransmitters that COMT catalyses, notably dopamine. The role of the COMT Val158Met variant in ADHD continues to be researched and results remain equivocal for ADHD and for wider psychiatric diagnoses (e.g. associated with 'conduct disorder' (Thapar et al., 2013)).
	This variant has also been associated with brain structure, with the methionine-allele associated with diminished white matter structure and weakened white matter connexions. This has led to the hypothesis that higher dopamine availability may inhibit myelination. White matter connectivity has been invested in children with ADHD and damage to the myelin sheath of neurons (demyelination) affecting connectivity associated with functions identified as impaired in ADHD have been indicated in children with the Valine-allele (Klein et al., 2017: 134).
MAOA (MAOB has also been investigated)	Monoamine oxidase A – a catalyser of neurotransmitters.
	This gene codes for an enzyme which catalyses the 'oxidative deamination of amines, such as dopamine, norepinephrine, and serotonin' (Klein et al., 2017: 135).
	The 2 and 3 repeat alleles are low activity (MAOA-L) and so transcribe less well than the longer 'high activity' alleles (MAOA-H). MAOA-L have been associated with impulsivity and aggression. Investigation has not identified association with ADHD.
TPH1	Tryptophan hydroxylase 1
	This gene codes an enzyme that 'catalyses the reaction of tryptophan to 5-hydroxytryptophan, which is subsequently decarboxylated to form the neurotransmitter serotonin.
	The TPH2 gene codes for a rate-limiting enzyme in the production of serotonin in serotonergic neurons in the midbrain raphe nuclei; while TPH1 seems to be involved in synthesizing serotonin in peripheral tissues' (Klein et al., 2017: 137)

TPH2	Tryptophan hydroxylase 2
	Investigated in variant and animal model studies in relation to 'aggression' 'antisocial behaviour' also in GXE studies regarding aggression 'Risk alleles' of SNPs associated with ADHD on go/no go tasks – indicating an effect on ADHD-relevant prefrontal brain function (Klein et al., 2017: 137)
BDNF	Brain-derived neurotrophic factor
	This gene codes a protein involved in neuronal nerve growth, and so is involved in neuro development and plasticity.
SNAP25	Synaptosomal-associated protein 25
	This is a presynaptic plasma membrane protein that is involved in the regulation of neurotransmitter release. It has been associated with ADHD and targeted in at least 10 studies.
LPHN3 or ADGRL3	Latrophilin 3, official name Adhesion GProtein-Coupled Receptor L3 (ADGRL3).
	This gene codes for particular G-protein–coupled receptors (GPCRs). Subtype 3 is expressed in brain regions that have been associated with ADHD (the caudate nucleus, cerebellum, amygdala and cerebral cortex). The gene has been identified as being involved in gene expression regulation of monoamine signalling genes.
	It has been associated with hyperactivity in zebra fish and fruit flies.
	This gene has been suggested as having ADHD prevention and treatment potential.

Sources: Li et al. (2014) and Klein et al. (2017). See also Franke et al., 2012.

of ADHD – are often found in 'non-protein coding sequences' which, given the key role of proteins in cell functioning, means that 'the molecular consequences are difficult to evaluate' (Klein et al., 2017: 140).

Cortese et al. (2011) highlights the inconsistency of findings across studies in relation to particular genes/variants, and the very small odds ratios attributed to each in relation to ADHD. Likewise, Franke et al. (2012) notes that 'the genetic factors underlying ADHD (as well as other psychiatric disorders) are of even smaller effect size than anticipated, or are not well covered by current study designs' (Franke et al., 2012: 974). And Klein states that 'our understanding of the mechanisms underlying the action of genetic risk factors for ADHD is still limited'. (Klein et al., 2017: 138). What the field has to offer at present, then, is 'genetic susceptibility factors of ADHD' (Li et al., 2014: 119).

Accordingly, Cortese concludes that research into the genetics of ADHD should adopt a 'multifactorial polygenic model in which a plethora of genes each confer a small but significant risk to the disorder (sic)' and suggests that a 'multilevel approach has the potential to bring substantial convergence in findings' (Cortese et al., 2011: 514). We return to thinking about multilevel and multifactorial approaches in the last part of the chapter.

Brain imaging: volume, structure, function and networks

Neuroscience uses a range of measures to investigate ADHD, from DSM diagnosis, to child behaviour check lists, to brain imaging. This brain imagine work includes investigation of brain volume, brain structure, brain function and brain networks.

Volume

The international ENIGMA working group brings together brain imaging data from a series of studies across the world to create the biggest dataset of ADHD brain images so for interrogated. A mega-review by this group published recently in *The Lancet* identifies reduced volumes in a number of brain regions in children diagnosed as having ADHD (Hoogman et al., 2017). The researchers claim that these results demonstrate that ADHD is a 'brain disorder' of 'brain maturation delay' (Hoogman et al., 2017: 9), evidenced specifically by a pattern of higher age when brain volume peaks and when it begins to decrease among children diagnosed as having ADHD (Hoogman et al., 2017: 16). These volume reductions are not related to the medication status of children and, in line with the maturation delay analysis, are not seen in adults with the diagnosis. Yet while these differential volume-to-age findings are suggestive of ADHD as an effect of later brain maturation, in the mega-analysis brain volume did not correlate significantly with the severity of ADHD, suggesting that brain volume in itself may have limited or no relationship to the extent of ADHD. Hoogman et al. (2017) report a general smaller volume of females' brains irrespective of ADHD diagnosis. This volume difference is identified as '[c]onsistent with literature documenting smaller brains in females' and so is not treated as relevant in the analysis of ADHD. This leaves the question of why volume differences are considered relevant in relation to one factor (ADHD) but not another (sex).

Structure-connectivity

There is also emergent ADHD work that explores the structure of the brain's white matter, and the influence this has on connectivity. This research measures the way that water molecules move through the brain, treating this as an indicator of neuronal pathways and showing some evidence of different or 'disturbed' pathways in children diagnosed with ADHD (Klein et al., 2017: 117).

Region-function

While the ENIGMA project identifies brain volume differences in children with ADHD, it emphasizes region-function associations. These are correlations, not mechanisms, and the extent to which it is known what is happening within them is limited. In Chapters 2 and 4 we identified the current neuroscience of region-function relationships in the brain. While imaging dramatically enhances our capacity to see inside the active brain, region-function assertions continue the tradition of phrenology or 'blobology' (Hruby and Goswami, 2011).

Positron emission tomography (PET) and single photon emission computed tomography (SPECT) are recent brain imaging approaches that are able to image within brain regions or receptor systems and identify metabolic activity, blood flow, receptor binding, and neurotransmitter turnover. PET studies of ADHD have focused on the striatum region and the activity of the DAT gene which codes for the transport of dopamine. The striatum is part of the subcortical basal ganglia in the forebrain, has substantial glutamate and dopamine activity and is understood to have a key function in the motor and reward systems. In one study, the density of the DAT gene in the striatum was 14% higher in those diagnosed with ADHD than in a control group (Fusar-Poli et al., 2012 cited by Klein et al., 2017). This DAT density among people diagnosed as having ADHD was related to whether they had been prescribed psychostimulant drugs (e.g. Ritalin), with those with a history of this medication having higher DAT density than those without, a finding that makes it difficult to untangle whether DAT density is related to ADHD itself or to the medication prescribed to manage identified behaviours.

Region-function ADHD research reported by Schuch et al. (2015) examines what they call functioning 'abnormalities', especially 'hot' and 'cold' executive function associated with the prefrontal cortex of the brain, and suggests a key role for 'deficit emotional self-regulation' (Schuch et al., 2015). Here, 'cold' executive function includes attention, working memory and planning while 'hot' executive function includes tasks than need 'motivation and affect' (Schuch et al., 2015: 2). In this model ADHD is tied up with these 'hot' executive functions, associated with the orbitofrontal and ventromedial cortices specifically, and is suggested to result from 'deficit emotional self-regulation' (DESR) (Schuch et al., 2015: 2).

> DESR involves deficient self-regulation of the physiological excitation caused by strong emotions, difficulties inhibiting inadequate behaviors in response to positive or negative emotions, problems reorienting attention after a strong emotion, and dis-organization of coordinated behavior in response to emotional activation.
>
> *(Schuch et al., 2015: 2)*

About half of children diagnosed as having ADHD (according to DSM criteria) are also identified as having DESR. Schuch et al. (2015) suggests that it is this subgroup of children diagnosed with ADHD for whom outcomes might be most problematic.

This hot/cold executive function model is difficult to reconcile with sociological account, imagining as it does a relatively rational and self-knowing person (albeit one that is 'failing' in this regard) and sitting uncomfortably with understandings of a social subject and a social field through which affect flows constantly. This seems to represent a strange moment where ADHD becomes the incapacity to self-regulate a physiological response – as if biochemistry is under the control of the will. Is it, and if so to what extent? Can we 'do normal' and breath or 'mindful' our way out of it?

Consideration of the role of endophenotypes has contributed further lines of ADHD research. For instance, fronto-subcortical-cerebellar pathways are understood to 'control attention, response to reward, salience thresholds, inhibitory control, and motor behaviour' and so dysregulation of these, both in terms of structure and function and as identified through fMRI, have been suggested as potential ADHD endophenotypes (Klein et al., 2017).

FMRI studies in which participants are set specific tasks relating to working memory, self-control, and attention have focused on these region-functions. These studies have shown 'underactivation' of the fronto-striatal network, fronto-parietal network which 'mediates goal-directed executive processes', and ventral attention network which 'facilitates reorientation of attention towards salient and behaviourally relevant external stimuli' amongst participants with ADHD diagnoses in comparison with control groups. (Cortese et al., 2012 cited by Klein et al., 2017). In addition, Functional near-infrared spectroscopy (fNIRS) shows reduced 'oxygen metabolism within the frontal lobe' of subjects with ADHD diagnoses. (Klein et al., 2017).

That genes associated with ADHD appear to be expressed together in particular functional networks or pathways in the brain is suggestive of biological processes involved in ADHD (Klein et al., 2017). While this is not a mechanism, it does begin to suggest potential biological mechanisms that may be involved.

TABLE 6.2 The brain and ADHD

Brain region	Feature / Function
Amygdala	Smaller volume in children
Accumbens	Smaller volume in children
Hippocampus	Smaller volume in children
Caudate	Smaller volume in children
Putamen	Smaller volume in children
Prefrontal cortex	Executive function
Orbitofrontal and ventromedial cortices	Hot executive function and emotional dysregulation
White matter	Disturbed neuronal pathways
Striatum	Dopamine glutamate
Fronto-subcortical-cerebellar pathways	Attention, response to reward, salience thresholds, inhibitory control, and motor behaviour 'dysregulation'
Ventral attention network	Facilitates reorientation of attention towards salient and behaviourally relevant external stimuli
	Underactivation in ADHD diagnosed
Fronto-parietal network	Mediates goal-directed executive processes
	Underactivation in ADHD diagnosed
Fronto-basal ganglia networks – inferior frontal cortex	Inhibition
Fronto-basal ganglia networks – supplementary motor areas	Inhibition
Fronto-basal ganglia networks – anterior cingulate cortex (ACC)	Inhibition
Dorsolateral prefrontal cortex (PFC)	Attention
Parietal area	Attention
Cerebellar area	Attention
Ventral striatum	Reduced activation during anticipation and receipt phase of reward
Frontal lobe	Reduced oxygen metabolism

(*Sources*: Cortese et al., 2012; Klein et al., 2017; Schuch et al., 2015).

The interaction of genes and environment: G × E

The importance of the interaction between genes and environment, or G × E, is widely recognized in the biological science literature on ADHD (Cortese et al., 2011, Dillon and Craven, 2014; Klein et al., 2017). Yet understandings of significant interactions, and the mechanisms underlying these, is only now emerging. We discussed the field of epigenetics in Chapter 2. In relation to ADHD, a whole slew of environmental factors have been cited as not just themselves influencing ADHD, but as provoking epigenetic changes in gene regulation and expression which are involved in the manifestation of traits associated with ADHD. Indeed, epigenetic influences may be involved in the function of genes such as those 'hot genes' we discussed earlier. Schuch et al. (2015) identifies:

- psychosocial adversities
- maternal mental disorders
- violence
- stress
- smoking and alcohol exposure
- family dysfunction
- lack of social support for mothers
- adverse life events, and disagreements in the course of pregnancy
- violence in intrauterine life and childhood, including domestic violence
- exposure of pregnant women to stress in the third trimester
- premature birth
- social adversities, expressed as a low maternal educational level, birth size.

Smoking and alcohol exposure, for instance, have been shown to cause changes to 'cell dynamics' that have knock-on effects on the activation of receptors, thereby modulating the plasticity of cell function. A three-way relationship between specific gene variants, exposure to smoking and ADHD have also been shown (Schuch et al., 2015: 3). Likewise, an interaction of a particular protein (5HTTLPR – a serotonin transporter which is a long and short allele polymorphism on the protein coding gene SLC6A4) and stress has been associated with the severity of ADHD and brain substrates that mediate this interaction have been shown (Klein et al., 2017 citing van der Meer et al., 2014).

This highlights the complexity of the regulation of the G × E interaction and mean that G × E researchers must identify and understand:

> [P]athways from genes to phenotypes in complex disorders, such as ADHD, which involves different biological and non-biological factors acting synergistically during an individual's developmental trajectory.
>
> *(Klein et al., 2017: 138)*

Many of these influences that are defined as environmental go to what is known in the psychology, genetics, neuroscience and social care and welfare literature as 'early childhood adversity'. Thapar et al. caution against mapping early adversity onto ADHD especially as causal – but do identify (general) epigenetics as important.

The promise of understanding (the biology of) ADHD

Dillon and Craven, 2014 argue that understanding the aetiology of ADHD is important as it has potential treatment implications, but at that same time a genetic model has the potential to limit consideration of psychosocial interventions. This signals two tensions, first the fundamental tension over whether or not we recognize

ADHD at all, and second the tension over how ADHD might be responded to and, potentially, intervened into.

Phamaceuticals

Critical sociological accounts of the psychopathologization of the set of behaviours identified as ADHD have been concerned with the way that this lends further force to an already massive trend in the use of psychostimulant medication for the treatment of children diagnosed with ADHD (Harwood and Allan, 2014). A persistent presence in Harwood and Allan's analysis is methylphenidate (Ritalin) and related psychostimulant drugs prescribed from children's early years and insisting themselves upon the child/young person as well as their caregivers who must be 'compliant' with their prescribed medication. Harwood and Allan's analysis of the persistent place of these pharmaceuticals in the lives and bodies of children and young people – disproportionately poor and from minoritized race and ethnic communities – is arresting in the face of the unknown long-term effects of prolonged exposure to these drugs during childhood and adolescence.

Genetic scientists argue, however, that recognizing and researching genetic influences on ADHD does not in itself suggest or promote a pharmaceutical response (Cortese et al., 2011; Dillon and Craven, 2014). Indeed, Cortese argues the potential for the reverse to flow from genetic research:

> Gaining insight into the neurobiological correlates of ADHD may help us understand how non-pharmacological treatments work, as well as in which patients (and why) they do not work.
>
> *(Cortese et al., 2011: 515)*

Furthermore, research in the genetics of ADHD has begun to identify gene involvement (eg DRD4, SLC6A3) in response to psychostimulant medication (methylphenidate) (Li et al., 2014: 19).

Stigma

Neuroscientists involved in imaging research into ADHD suggest that the brain imaging findings of the ENIGMA Working Group promise a route to interrupting the stigma associated with ADHD by identifying an organic basis and so refuting perceptions or suggestions that ADHD is the result of poor nurture or simply bad behaviour:

> ADHD is a disorder of the brain. This is a clear message for clinicians to convey to parents and patients, which can help to reduce the stigma that ADHD is just a label for difficult kids, and caused by incompetent parenting
>
> *(Hoogman et al., 2017: 18)*

While for the authors these findings promise to redress deficits and discriminatory accounts of children with ADHD and their families, there seems no reason to assume that identifying ADHD as a brain disorder will deflect criticism of parents and their childrearing practices. The increasing attention to the possibility of multiple influences on ADHD and in particular biology-environment interactions mean that it does not follow that particular patterns of brain maturation rule out or are independent of social influences such as modes of parenting. While parenting is not evident as a potential factor for analysis in the recent genetic and brain research that we examine here, the work on rat lick-groom that explores through animal models the potential epigenetic influence of parenting (that we explored in Chapter 3) does identify the impact of care relations on the brain's 'stress axis' and contributes to the targeting of candidate genes that and are part of that wider array of 'hot genes' for ADHD.

Complexity

In the current genetic science there is growing consensus over the complexity of ADHD: 'multidimensional mechanisms influence the behavioural phenotype'. (Schuch et al., 2015: 1). Klein and colleagues offer substantial detail to this model of biological complexity:

> imaging genetics analyses of the human brain provide information on the effect of ADHD risk genes/variants on brain structure, activity, and connectivity, but other levels of investigation are needed to provide a more complete picture [. . .] We also need information about the molecular networks, in which an ADHD gene acts, and the cellular processes that are affected by it.
> *(Klein et al., 2017: 141)*

Here we see combined brain imaging at different scales and concerned with different structure, regions and neurogenetics to understand more globally the ADHD influence of:

- foetal development
- chromatin structure
- neurite outgrowth
- steroidogenesis
- synaptic function
- neuron-glial signalling (Klein et al., 2017).

In particular, within a disease model, seeking 'pathways from gene to disease' Klein et al., 2017: 141) suggest systematic integration of the range of data from animal models, genetic studies, brain imaging. Bringing together data about a whole range of potential genetic influences – all the 'hot genes' – to integrate knowledge about clusters of genetic functions, the interaction of proteins, patterns of gene co-expression together with animal models that allow genes to be manipulated in order to understand causal relationships between genes, gene variants and processes at molecular and cellular levels. Specifically, research on the DAT1 gene variant induced in animals allows researchers to:

> [E]valuate the contribution of dopamine-related processes to brain patho-physiology, to analyse the neuronal circuits and molecular mechanisms involved in the action of ADHD medication, and to test novel treatments for ADHD.
>
> *(Klein et al., 2017: 141)*

Similarly, research on 'spontaneous hypertensive rats' has shown that in rats with ADHD-like behaviours there is different expression of proteins in the striatum region of the brain and PFC GABAergic system that are involved in energy metabolism, neurotransmitter function, neural development, and myelination (Klein et al., 2017). Finally, the reprogramming of human cells in vitro (cells studied outside the body in the laboratory) is now allowing researchers to generate neural stem cells or neurons. This technique has been used in the study of schizophrenia and is thought to have potential for the study of ADHD.

Yet across these biological accounts, multi-dimensional mechanisms tend to remain within the biological, as do their effects – they are presented as resulting in a phenotype, rather than, for instance, a difficult encounter between a child and the requirements of a particular schooling regime, as might be identified in the critical education literature. Nevertheless, the influence of environment is recognized:

> ADHD seems to result from a combination of genetic and environmental factors that alter the developing brain, resulting in structural and functional abnormalities.
>
> *(Schuch et al., 2015: 2)*

This predominance of associations in the science research begins to unsettle the hard distinction between science and the social – bioscience rarely offers a one to one causal relationship, and the interpretive work of sociology remains necessary to explain the nature of associations, in particular those that have dimensions in the social environment. Further the (imagined?) desire for mechanism, often presented as a counter to sociology, may not be so far from a sociology concerned with processes and practices, relationships and affects and **how they make things happen.**

Mapping and understanding complex influences

At various points in the book we have talked about the difference between associations and mechanisms in science and influences, processes and forces in sociology. We have been at pains to do more than note the difference between these, and the difficulty of integrating research with these different concerns. Rather we have wanted to specify these differences and begin to offer precise accounts of how they intersect or, indeed, interact, and how we can research across them. As we have done this we have talked 'phenomena' as 'assemblage' and about 'multifactorial complex causality' – something that is caused by the complex interplay of a number of factors, factors that may well span the domains of particular disciplines and that might reach across scales from the molecular to the macro.

This need to map and understand the influence of factors from across domains and across scales is recognized in the scientific literature concerned with ADHD. Figure 6.1 is one attempt at this mapping from within the field of human genetics. Versions of this schematic can be found in this major review of genetic and brain research into ADHD by Klein et al. (2017) but is adapted from a piece examining GWAS approaches to ADHD by other researchers from their institute (Franke et al., 2009).

Klein and colleagues explain the figure as follows. Polygenecity – the idea that multiple genes contribute to a function or process or 'causing gene symptoms' (Klein et al., 2017: 140) – is represented as gene A to I in the figure, and a smaller number of these genes are said to be involved in the endophenotype (we discuss this earlier in this chapter) and so need to be studied at a range of 'biological levels', These levels, as shown in the figure, are biochemical processes and cell function (studies through assays in cells or animal models – e.g neuron morphology, synaptic functioning); brain morphology (studied through imaging methods); and brain unit function (studies through fMRI or neuropsychological tests). Klein et al. suggest that 'aberrations' at brain unit function level 'can result in altered behaviour and disease related behavioural traits that subsequently lead to disease symptoms' (Klein et al., 2017: 140). Environmental influences are suggested as having the potential to impact at all levels but need of further research. Finally, bioinformatics/network analysis are suggested to integrate data and 'identify molecular networks or cellular processes ADHD-related genes are enriched' (Klein et al., 2017: 140).

The schematic usefully sets out a series of influences on ADHD at a range of levels and attempts to map pathways from the gene to 'trait' or 'symptom'. Furthermore, it acknowledges that 'environmental influences' might act across these levels. As a way of thinking of the movement from gene to 'trait', 'symptom' or what we might call with a less diagnostic orientation 'way of being in the world', the scheme alerts us to both multiple levels of biological function and multiple orders of influence i.e. the biological and the environmental. Furthermore, as these orders of influence interact across these levels (we have generally used the term 'scales' elsewhere), we begin to have a sense of the three-dimensionality of these processes. Yet at the same time as noting the usefulness of the schematic, not just in relation to ADHD but generally, for thinking from gene to way of being, it also contains important gaps that we wish to elaborate.

However, research in molecular biology demonstrates that the movement from gene to biochemical process is an entire field of study in itself which comprises multiple layers or levels. First of these is the movement from gene to gene expression; next the regulation of gene expression which, itself controlled by gene expression,

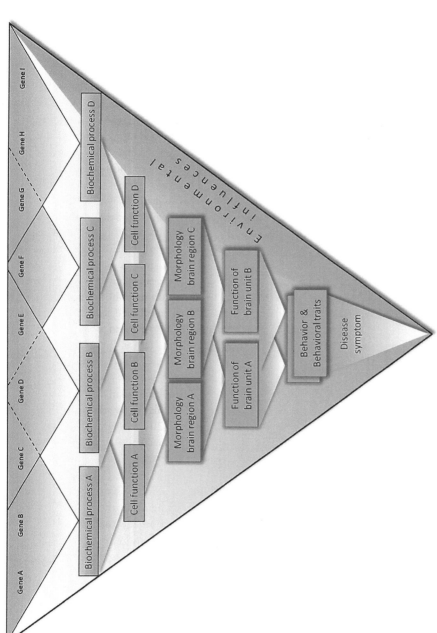

'This schematic representation of the endophenotype concept shows the pathway from gene to disease at different levels of complexity in psychiatric genetics'. (Klein et al., 2017: 140 adapted from Franke).

FIGURE 6.1 A biological model of complexity

Source: Klein et al. (2017).

is an ongoing cycling of interaction and influence; next is the assembly of protein from amino acids; next the movement from protein expression to protein; and finally the protein involvement in the biochemical process.

Established biosocial approaches

There is a growing body of research and editorial that asserts the biosocial nature of ADHD and seeks to demonstrate this empirically. This assertion can be found in the genetics and neuroscience literature as well as in the social science and education literature. Indeed, a reading of current ADHD research might lead us to think that the orthodoxy is for biosocial ADHD. Critical sociology, inclusive education and disability studies (where Deborah's previous work has been located) are disciplines where the strongest resistance to biological readings, and so biosocial readings, of ADHD remain.

It is possible at this juncture, then, to assert that ADHD is recognized as complex and that multiple factors – genetic, social and environmental – are involved in its emergence (Klein et al., 2017; Li et al., 2014; Schuch et al., 2015). For instance, education psychologists Dillon and Craven say that:

> [C]ontemporary life sciences tell us that we do not have gene-directed processes but rather gene-dependent processes. Therefore, the question of interest is not if genes are implicated in ADHD but rather to what degree are they implicated.
>
> *(Dillon and Craven, 2014: 24)*

Cooper (2008), writing in the *Journal of Philosophy of Education* and looking across research into biological and familial influences on ADHD argues for a biopsychosocial approach:

> ADHD is a biopsychosocial phenomenon – that is, a behavioural manifestation with its origins in a biologically based predisposition. The biological predisposition and the behavioural outcomes, however, are mediated by social, environmental and other experiential factors.
>
> *(Cooper, 2008: 461)*

With this orientation Cooper sets aside thorough going critical analyses of ADHD such as those found in the inclusive education literature, in order to assert the interplay of **social construction**, in particular through 'patterns of institutional control and pedagogical practices' (Cooper, 2008: 461) and **biological predisposition**:

> Certain individuals, by virtue of their biological inheritance and social circumstances, are more prone than others to being constructed as being 'disordered' in this way.
>
> *(Cooper, 2008: 461)*

This is useful in that it refutes the idea that biological influences are equivalent to determinism, or monism, and pre-figures epigenetic analysis without appearing to know the field (which was only in the very early days in 2008 when the paper was published).

> In other words, children who are biologically predisposed to develop ADHD are disadvantaged by culturally based assumptions about what appropriate behaviour in schools and classrooms looks like. This is not the fault of the clinicians who drafted the criteria; on the contrary, the ubiquity and persistence of ADHD and its diagnostic forerunners and equivalents reflect, unintentionally but accurately, one of the most persistent criticisms of Western mass education, namely that it stresses rigid authoritarian values and is relatively unresponsive to individual differences and needs.
>
> *(Cooper, 2008: 466)*

This, then, is a call to apprehend ADHD as a 'cognitive style' (Cooper, 2008: 467) that requires pedagogical and organizational approaches that are not commonly found in the rigidly organized and didactic classrooms of contemporary education systems. Nevertheless, Cooper does not seem to perceive any tension or problems of compatibility between the accounts here being put together. The concept transformation that such transdisciplinary working ought to provoke is unrecognized by Cooper, as is the degrounding that this entails.

Assemblage – biosocial ADHD

The assertion of ADHD as biosocial is not a straightforward one. While at first sight it might seem reasonable to say that social and biological processes are both in play and in some cases are interacting, when we begin to work through the details of such a claim we find fundamental contradictions between underpinning thinking, abiding in-discipline or in-domain approaches to what is 'really' important, as well as a continued reluctance amongst critical to acknowledge bio or even existence of ADHD as a 'real' disorder at all. Key points of tension include:

- the respective extent of social and biological influence
- the nature of these social and biological influences
- the relative importance of any interplay across social and biological influences
- whether (any particular) behavioural, social or biological influences should be foregrounded
- whether any particular strands of research or methods are most informative
- whether there are influences that are so small or so little understood as to be unhelpful.

These tensions leave a critical biosocial position with a pressing question: if we can move past the psychological language of deficits or the neuroscience and biological languages of psychopathology and pathophysiology to a language of multiplicities of ways of being human – then can we then concede the 'ADHD' 'difference' is an actual fact?

We suggest a move to think about ADHD, indeed about SEN, as phenomena, as the effect of an assemblage of productive forces. Subjectivation is one of these productive forces, as is the governmental effects of bio-politics, but physiology, genetics and the environment-body interface are also part of this assemblage. ADHD assemblage, then, might map geneotype, phenotype, endophenotype, behavioural trait, patterned response, institutional forms, expert knowledges, subjectivation, recognition, identification, affective flows, biochemical reactions and processes. Such an approach needs to be able to tolerate and work with the disarticulation between gene studies (whether candidate, endophenotype or GWAS), molecular functions, G × E and analyses of social institutions, social processes, everyday life, relationships, subjectivities and feelings.

Duschinsky and colleagues make a similar move in relation to work on attachment:

> Our approach is aligned with sociological scholarship which attempts to move beyond social constructionism by considering processes and forces conventionally articulated as 'biological' and 'social' to be mutually constitutive rather than ontologically distinct.
>
> *(Duschinsky et al., 2015: 174)*

In articulating attachment as assemblage, Duschinsky and colleagues emphasize 'the ways in which child–parent relationships plug into, affect and are affected by other processes at different levels', foregrounding 'biological, social and political assemblages' and the operation of these 'below and beyond the level of the human subject' (Duschinsky et al., 2015: 175). Once again, the likely 'rough and tumble' of destabilized disciplines is evident.

Elizabeth Wilson presses for the suspension of a sceptic versus enthusiast division. She suggests that this will:

> [B]ring to light a systemic traffic in disquiet that cannot be fully grasped by either neuroscientific or critical texts, but can be glimpsed at these moments of disjuncture where neurological data and critical inquiry meet and cut across (cleave) each other.
>
> *(Wilson, 2015: 176)*

As is evident from this exploration, biological research into ADHD covers a broad range of concerns and approaches, stretching from brain volume to analysis of particular variants. Across this variation, a commonality is that findings remain associational and complexity and the influence of multiple factors, are increasingly recognized. The bioscience work that has a G × E orientation and looks to gene-environment or body-environment interaction may be particularly helpful for thinking about how ADHD is produced.

In sociological accounts this recognition of complexity and multiple influences is also evident within critical interpretive accounts that demonstrate processes through which ADHD is socially, institutionally and discursively constituted. While the terms of these sociological and biological analyses are not immediately compatible, their assertions of the multiplicity of influences is, and there is real potential for an investigation of the relationship between these social processes and bodily mechanisms to generate a step change in understanding. Sociological analyses will rightly continue to critically deconstruct the productive force of diagnosis of ADHD and the practices flowing from these as processes of psychopathologization. Indeed, research with this orientation might interpret the genetic research into ADHD we have set out here as exemplifying a movement from psychopathology to *pathophysiology* at the level of the genome.

Yet we see this biosocial orientation as bringing the potential to generate a movement from things and names (the child with ADHD) to things and functions (what a molecule, a pedagogic relationship or a diagnosis makes happen). We return to the question *what can a body do here?*, informed by the expectation that what a body can do will be made possible and constrained by the infolding of genetic inheritance; gene regulation, including through environmental influence; bio-politics that push for diagnosis, intervention and, ultimately, separation; flows of money, to pharmaceutical companies and to schools and families in receipt of resources predicated on formal ADHD diagnoses; and subjectivating processes of recognition and identification and, perhaps, abjection. In this analysis, the transformation of the concept of ADHD can be apprehended to also 'a change of form' as the biosocial assemblage ADHD begins a sort of ongoing metamorphosis. (Malabou, 2009: 63).

7

BIOSOCIAL LEARNING

Learning as phenomena

Thinking biosocially about education, and in particular education in school and other institutional settings, leads us to what seems to be a fundamental but under-asked question: *what happens when we learn?*

Joining together biological and social research in order to avoid nature versus deadlocks and better understand the entanglement of institutions, social forms and practices, relationships and bodies leads us to think differently about learning. It suggests that shared meanings, gene expression, electrochemical signals, the every-day of the classroom, and a sense of self are actually all part of one phenomenon that is learning. Reconceptualizing learning as a complex biosocial phenomenon produced through multiple influences and processes that are trans-scalar, contextualized and moving suggests an expansive array of productive forces, retaining sociological insights on productive power, discourse and subjectivation, performativity, recognition and identification and adding to these further influences, some that are bodily and others that are non-human. This approach offers the possibility of including in analyses of learning new sets of evidence from biosciences at the same time as it remains engaged with the range of evidence from critical education research and maintains in analysis the complex intra-actions of multiple productive forces.

What happens when we learn?

A move to a focus on learning as phenomena is not straightforward. In the multi-disciplinary field of education approaches to learning reflect the concerns and research traditions of particular fields – such as sociology, curriculum and pedagogy, developmental psychology – proceeding with distinct problems, conceptual tools and units of analysis. Indeed, through this chapter we show that the field of education is able to offer only a partial and fragmented understanding of what constitutes learning, what learning is influenced by, and what the mechanisms of learning might be.

Learning as testing

There is a global policy tendency to foreground performance in standardized tests, from the global PISA administered by the OECD to the batteries of tests utilized by individual education systems and institutions. These tests allow comparisons to be made between students and populations and over time. Test performance is not claimed to be the sum total of or equivalent to learning, but the relationship between learning and test performance is blurred. Test developers offer increasingly sophisticated test instruments said to measure an array of cognitive skills; be predictive of future performance; and enable in-test adjustment in response to the student's performance in real time (Gillborn, 2010, 2016; Thompson, 2016). As standardized test performance functions as a performance indicator and accountability mechanism, in practice such tests can become the focus of learning, especially where students struggle to reach targets in these tests (Booher Jennings, Darling Hammond). In the media and in policy – and increasingly in school too – the emphasis is often on students' performance in tests, taken at set points in their education. This can easily leave us thinking that learning and how students do in tests is the same thing. Standardized tests make inequalities visible and offer accountability, but they also impose demands that impact how institutions operate, how teachers and learners behave and see themselves, the opportunities available to differently recognized students, and, as we saw in the preceding chapter, even feel (Youdell, 2011; Youdell et al., 2017). The 'high-stakes' (Apple, 2006) attached to test performance has been shown to transforms institutional and pedagogic practice, with 'educational triage' (Gillborn and Youdell, 2000; Youdell, 2004) deployed to inform organizational practices and target resources in ways believed to maximize performance at the target levels. As triage decisions are made, students are allocated to teaching groups and resources distributed in ways that support the learning of some but impede the learning of others. These perverse consequences of the use of performance indicators as accountability measures impact particular minoritized and poor students disproportionately (Booher-Jennings, 2005; Bradbury, 2013; Gillborn and Youdell, 2000). Test performance is only what a student does in that test, on the day of that test. It might say something about what they have learnt, the limits of what they know and can do, but it might not. Test performance can only speak to what the test itself allows for as knowledge or skills. And it is not the learning itself.

Learning styles

Outside the debate over testing, a dominant approach to learning itself in education foregrounds different learning styles, the ways that these 'styles' influence students' learning and, therefore, how teachers' practices should respond. There are many different models of learning styles, but predominant across these are distinctions between 'visual', 'auditory' and 'kinesthetic' learning. Learning styles are often closely associated with 'cognitive styles' found in the developmental psychology literature, and, models of differential types of 'intelligence' or 'multiple intelligences' (Gardener, 1993, 2006). The principles underlying learning styles models are that individuals have a learning style or preference that will be expressed; that individuals show differences in ability to learn about different types of things and through different sorts of approaches; and that teaching should be matched to the learning style of individuals.

There have been numerous critical reviews of the notion of learning styles. Indeed, education neuroscientist Paul Howard-Jones recently noted that '[p]erhaps the most popular and influential [neuro]myth is that a student learns most effectively when they are taught in their preferred learning style' (2014: 817). Critical analysis of learning styles highlights the way that these models assert for each individual a singular learning style, rather than gradations of each, and note how this harks back to prior notions of personality 'types'. This manifests the underpinning assumption that learning styles are 'states' (i.e. the fixed properties of the person) rather than processes that are mobile, changing over contexts and in relation to learning opportunities. The consensus in the education research community then is that learning styles are without evidence and in fact can do harm by restricting both learner and teacher conceptions of individuals' capacities and over-emphasizing efforts to 'match' teaching to an ascribed style which in turn acts to foreclose other opportunities or engagement with and take up of more effective pedagogic approaches (Coffield et al., 2004; Pashler et al., 2008; Howard-Jones, 2014; Newton, 2015).

Despite the absence of positive research evidence supporting learning styles, and the evidence against in terms of over-simplification and restriction, learning styles are embedded in the popular imagination and circulate as curriculum, teaching and parenting resources. For instance the *time4learning* website confidently states: 'There are currently seven "Learning Styles"' and goes on to list these as follows:

- Visual (spatial): You prefer using pictures, images and spatial understanding.
- Aural (auditory-musical): You prefer using sound and music.
- Verbal (linguistic): You prefer using words, both in speech and writing.
- Physical (kinesthetic): You prefer using your body, hands and sense of touch.
- Logical (mathematical): You prefer using logic, reasoning and systems.
- Social (interpersonal): You prefer to learn in groups or with other people.
- Solitary (intrapersonal): You prefer to work alone and use self-study.

(*Time4Learning*, www.time4learning.com/learning-styles.shtml)

Similarly, schematics representing learning styles and the 'multiple intelligences' that many of these reiterate abound on the internet (see Figure 7.1), constituting these styles and further sedimenting their divides and the certainty about their bounded

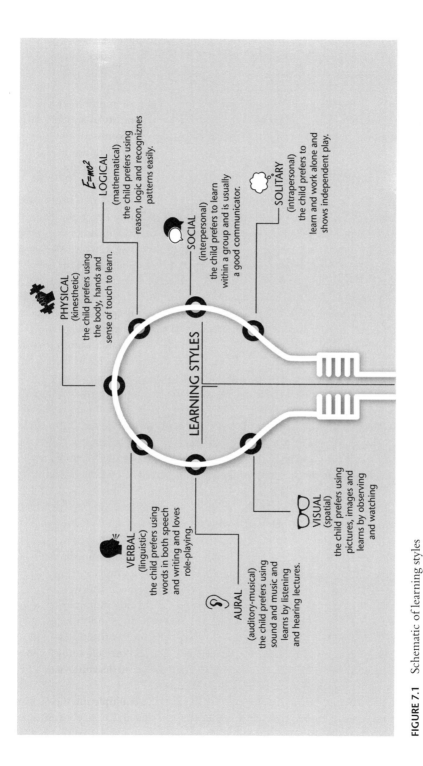

FIGURE 7.1 Schematic of learning styles

PHYSICAL
(kinesthetic)
the child prefers using
the body, hands and
sense of touch to learn.

LOGICAL
(mathematical)
the child prefers using
reason, logic and recogniznes
patterns easily.

SOCIAL
(interpersonal)
the child prefers to learn
within a group and is usually
a good communicator.

SOLITARY
(intrapersonal)
the child prefers to
learn and work alone and
shows independent play.

LEARNING STYLES

VERBAL
(linguistic)
the child prefers using
words in both speech
and writing and loves
role-playing.

AURAL
(auditory-musical)
the child prefers using
sound and music and
learns by listening
and hearing lectures.

VISUAL
(spatial)
the child prefers using
pictures, images and
learns by observing
and watching

$E=mc^2$

nature and also constituting learners in these terms. Learning styles are big business (Pashler et al., 2008; Howard-Jones, 2014). For instance, the *time4learning* website offers a mix of free and paid for content, including learning styles-informed curricular and pedagogic content at a subscription cost of $30 a month per student. Despite the lack of underpinning research evidence and potential limiting effects of these models and the approaches that flow from them, learning styles remain embedded as educational truths in many schools and classrooms.

Curriculum, pedagogy and assessment

In much curriculum, pedagogy and assessment research the focus is on what is learnt, through what processes, and with what outcomes (James et al., 2006; Pollard et al., 2005). Learning here is figured as dynamic and open to intervention by approaches developed through education scholarship that aims to maximize learning. Learning how to learn (James et al., 2006; the embedding of formative assessment (Wiliam, 2011); and assessment for learning (Swaffield, 2008) each seek to develop students' capacities to learn in the classroom by orientating teachers to a learning-assessment-reflection cycle, supporting students' structured reflection on how they learn, systematically communicating to students what they have learnt and what they need to learn next, and what they need to do to improve. This emphasis on explicit reflection is also seen in educational accounts of how teachers and their practices can support learning (Wiliam, 2011), with practicing as a 'reflective teacher' (Pollard et al., 2005) an integral part of professional education and development and an important aspect of 'effective pedagogy' (James and Pollard, 2012). Reflective approaches have traction in education policy and practice but include tensions. Realizing the ideal of the 'reflective teacher' is not easy; indeed, the possibility of enacting the 'good teacher' (Moore, 2009) has been questioned. Reflection suggests a teacher and a learner who can reflect and act without constraints of context or self-knowledge (Youdell, 2006b, 2011; Moore, 2009), and, adopted and enacted in competitive markets, such processes are commandeered in the pursuit of outcomes where this incitement to reflection and ever-improved practice comes to act on and define the "terrors of the teachers' soul" (Ball, 2003).

Critical approaches

In critical education research, ideas about learning as gaining skills and knowledge have been replaced by ideas that try to account for all sorts of social influences on learning, including the influence of inequalities as these structure institutions and also as they are made and remade through the practices and encounters of everyday life. The revolutionary educator Paolo Freire criticized education based on 'banking' important information in the minds of learners. He saw learning as tied up with the social, economic and political situation that learners are in. This led him to think of learning as 'conscientization' – the learner coming to see and understand their situation and generate strategies for engaging with and transforming it (Freire,

1970). Freire's revolutionary project has slipped from most education theories of learning, but the idea that central to learning is criticality and a struggle for justice remains foundational to critical, anti-racist and politically orientated approaches to pedagogy (Youdell, 2006a, 2011).

We can see these commitments reflected in productive pedagogy, an approach developed through a major action research collaboration between education schol-ars and the Queensland Government. Productive pedagogy is unique in the way it was generated but more importantly in the way that it brings together both peda-gogic and social justice concerns, recognizing that learning requires pedagogies that offer intellectual quality, connectedness to learners' worlds, a supportive classroom environment, and a valuing of and working with difference (Gore et al., 2004; Lin-gard et al., 2001; Mills et al., 2009). Here the gap between concerns for social justice and inclusion in education on the one hand and concerns for effective pedagogies is bridged, situating learning in the nexus of the art of teaching and the politics of schools, classrooms and everyday lives.

Critically orientated education research also emphasizes the influence on learn-ing of teacher-student relationships (Bibby, 2011, 2017). Psychoanalytic research introduces psychic processes into this dynamic social field, understanding learning as involving the loss of what is known and its replacement with something new, and showing how the loss intrinsic to learning can make learning unsettling and open up the risk of learning being blocked (Bibby, 2011). Bibby (2011) foregrounds teachers engagement in the psychic dimensions of learning, in particular the rup-tures experienced by learners and the need for the learner's discomfort at the new to be recognized and for the learner to be 'held in mind' (after Winnicott, 2017) if they are to be able to learn. Teaching and learning is a relational, not simply a rational process. These orientations to learning insist it is not the acquisition of external knowledge, rather, it is a complex social and psychic process that produces people and communities as well as the thing learnt.

Relationality is also foregrounded in contemporary theories of learning that model learning as fundamentally social (Engerstrom, 2009; Wenger, 2009). These theories suggest a complex interplay of social, personal and educational factors in which community is key and which together in interaction influence learning. Research that uses activity theory to understand learning suggests that it is a process of mediation in which social rules, community structures and available artefacts or tools mediate between the person who learns and the meaning that can be made of a learning object (see Figure 7.2).

Research that examines communities of practice extends this understanding of socially situated learning, showing dynamic, productive relationships between the thing learnt, the person who learns and the community in which this learning is embedded. Here learning results from processes of doing, belonging, experience and becoming, all of which construct and are held within 'communities of practice' with shared meanings, practices and identities (see Figure 7.3).

Long-term literacy research by Deb Hayes and colleagues shifts attention from the learner to the teacher and her/his 'body of work'. This work shows that when

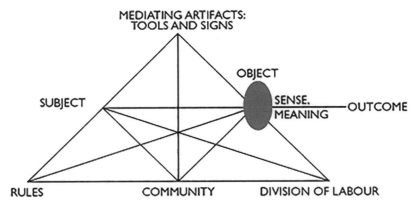

FIGURE 7.2 Engerstrom's activity theory of learning

Source: Illeris, 2009.

FIGURE 7.3 Wenger's learning and 'communities of practice'

Source: Illeris, 2009.

teachers in the most disadvantaged schools use 'common pedagogical approaches', namely the evidence-based interventions with built in evaluation and assessment of the sort favoured by government education departments, children's performance is not improved. This is because these approaches promote scripted lessons, a focus on skills that can be tested, a narrow curriculum and a normative model of learning as staged and developmental. In contrast, Hayes and colleagues suggest that children learn when teachers use 'uncommon pedagogies' that situate curriculum and testing requirements within a 'rich repertoire of teaching practice' that brings together the knowledge and experience of students, connexions to families and communities, open-ended tasks, complex thinking, engagement with issues that are significant to the children in the classroom, and the drawing on and building of strong relationships. This 'body of work' approach, they argue, is able to foreground and respond to the complexity of teaching and learning and thus support children's learning. (Hayes, 2018). Yet once again it does not tell us what happens when we learn.

In critical policy and sociology research the focus tends to be on the structures, systems and everyday practices that form the contexts in which learning takes place (Youdell, 2011; Ball, 2013). This research explores the influence of institutional and social structures, processes and practices on learning (Gillborn and Youdell, 2000; Youdell, 2006a, 2011). Teachers' judgements about students' learning, often couched in terms of 'ability' and 'performance', augment formal performance measures with knowledge about what students can do and 'who' they are. Yet the knowledge about students that circulates in schools is informed by dominant thinking about ability and learning and this feeds into teachers' explicitly and implicitly held values and perspectives. Engrained and overlapping discourses about race, religion, gender, social class, and intelligence inform and constrain teachers' sense of the possible (Bradbury, 2013; Gillborn, 2008; Youdell, 2006b, 2011).

Deborah's sociological work on how students come to be seen by teachers and by themselves as 'ideal' or 'impossible' learners has paid close attention to the nuances of everyday life in classrooms, looking especially at processes of subjectivation and how meanings stick to particular sorts of people and activities. How children behave, how they speak, what they value, how they play, the skills they can show all come together to inform not just teachers' beliefs about students, but also the sort of recognition that the teacher offers the student. Processes of recognition are social and psychic, informed by 'facts', discourses and gut feeling. They are not simply responses to external facts, but are constitutive – performatively producing the person, or subject, that they recognize (Butler, 1997; Youdell, 2011). In turn, recognition, and the absence or refusal of recognition, becomes enfolded into the student's own identification These nuanced processes are ongoing, open to contradiction and change but also readily sedimented. They also have implications for student-teacher relationships; these may well become blocked when a child is not recognized by her teacher in ways that sustain her identification. As multiple factors from socio-economic status and prior attainment to linguistic forms and cultural capital coalesce in particular settings, they constrain 'who' it is possible for a student to be, they constitute 'ideal' and 'impossible' learners (Youdell, 2006a). This tells us a lot about how students are included (or not) in classrooms, and why some students are thought of and think of themselves as good learners while for others this recognition and identification is foreclosed.

Across education scholarship, the common-sense understanding that to learn is to gain skills and knowledge has been supplanted by recognition of the complex, dynamic and social processes of learning. This recognition of the dynamic and situated nature of learning, and the multiple and sometimes unintended effects of policy initiatives shows how learning is inseparable from institutional and social processes and practices. These critical understandings of learning make sense, yet all of this education research remains a step removed from learning; it still does not quite tell us what happens when we learn and any physiological mechanisms and effects of learning remain well out of reach.

Biosciences and learning

A turn to bioscience does not simply resolve the difficulty of accessing what 'happens' when we learn. Research in molecular biology and neuroscience has new thinking to offer to our understanding of learning, with emerging knowledge about the influence of the environment on the regulation of genes and on brain function, combined with the mutability of these effects, suggesting the potential for collaborative transdisciplinary work investigating *biosocial* influences and mechanisms in education.

Epigenetics and learning

Engaging epigenetic research on the way environmental influences effect the way genes are expressed, and therefore how the cells of the body function, has led us to some unexpected work on learning. In epigenetics the nature of the question and its answer is quite different. We find learning taken to be the making of memory, and memory taken as the biochemical changes in the brain that occur when something is learnt. As we cannot take tissue samples from human brains while they learn, epigeneticists set up experiments in which model animals (rats, mice or flies) learn and then the animal is killed so that its brain tissue can be examined. When rats learn fear of/in a new environment by being given an electric shock through the floor, and then are subsequently re-exposed to the environment, either with or without foot shock, the learning shows up in their brain tissue. The rats are then killed at fixed points after exposure and, as represented in Figure 7.4, on examination their brains show histones (that DNA is stored around) in certain parts of the brain are differently methylated, impacting the expression and regulation of the genes proximate to these sites (Molfese, 2011). These findings suggest that the making of memory – if we accept this as the fine grain empirical instance of learning – includes epigenetic changes the brain.

To an educator this is likely to seem strange, perhaps somewhat discomforting, and a long way from the various conceptions of learning that circulate in education knowledge and practice. Yet it begins to demonstrate the sorts of questions that epigenetic research into learning using model animals is likely to ask, and the sorts of findings this work can offer. The space between demonstrating histone methylation as a result of trauma-induced learning and children learning in classrooms is, we hope, quite extensive. Nevertheless, when we reflect back on the place of feeling in learning that we explored in Chapter 5, the importance of understanding that stress

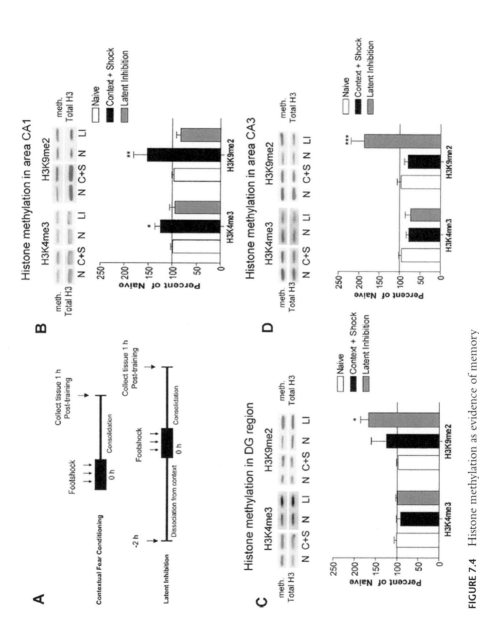

FIGURE 7.4 Histone methylation as evidence of memory

Source: Molfese, 2011.

blocks learning – potentially including at the level of the histones around which our DNA is coiled – is underscored.

Neuroscience of learning

In educational neuroscience Usha Goswami and colleagues have contributed significantly to developing debate over the conceptual and methodological needs and directions for educational neuroscience, and have been forthright about what educational neuroscience knows and does not know to date and what it might be able to tell us in the future. As we move to consider the contribution of education neuroscience to understanding learning, it is important to remember the massive variability and plasticity of human brains (Hruby and Goswami, 2011); that brain anatomy, biochemistry and function relationships remain largely associational (Bhide et al., 2013); and that 'activation' of brain regions and networks under test conditions is indicative of the familiarity or difficulty of the test task, not of a 'baseline' of activity necessary for the task to be performed (Hruby and Goswami, 2011). Indeed, Hruby and Goswami suggest that neuroscience is unlikely to provided precise identification of brain subprocesses that would override professional teacher assessments.

Education neuroscientists alert the wider education audience to the 'neuromyths' that circulate in education, and are particularly sceptical about much work in education that claims to draw on knowledge of the brain. Just as critical education sociologists highlight the fragile foundations and dangerously wide reach of 'brain-based' education (Baker, 2018), neuroscientists say that 'the one small way that neuroscience relates to most "brain-based education" is that students and other learners have brains' (Fischer et al., 2010: 70). Despite this careful stance amongst the experts, the idea that education can be 'brain-based' persists and there is much professional development material targeting professional educators that moves from this foundation. One high profile example of this is the 2016 report, *Lighting Up Young Brains*, by the children's charity Save the Children, but there are many examples of free and at-cost 'brain-based' approaches.

Moving from the popularized idea of 'brain-based' approaches to neuroscience research itself, we can find ourselves somewhat abstracted from applied questions about learning in schools. For instance, leading-edge research in neuroscience uses fMRI scanning, often combined with other imaging approaches, to identify learning inside the brain as it happens. But 'learning' in such experimental laboratory-based work is often not the sort of learning that we might look for in classrooms. One key area of neuroscience research concerned with learning investigates 'working memory' and demonstrates patterned brain activation in particular regions of the brain in response to different sorts of stimuli. Figure 7.5 shows differential patterns of brain activation in response to different types of stimulation, in this case colour and shape.

The capacity to explore patterns of brain activity in real-life settings that the development of portable EEG devices offers has begun to see research into brain

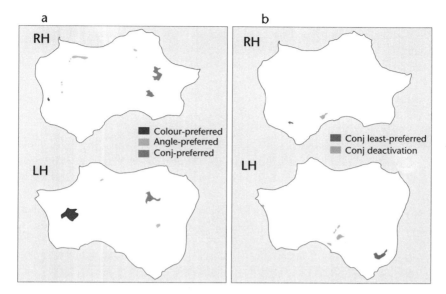

FIGURE 7.5 Brain activation and working memory

Source: Jackson, 2011.

activity inside classroom settings. Here students wear caps with electrical pick-ups that monitor activity and in particular connectivity across brain regions and feed this data wirelessly to a local laptop. One recent study used portable EEG with a class of high school students to explore brain activity in the context of a variety of individual and group activities inside the classroom. This research found that students' brain activity became 'synchronised' when they were engaged actively in learning activities, in particular when these involved face to face encounters between learners. It also found that the extent to which students' brain activity showed synchrony was related to observed engagement, in particular shared attention, in the classroom (Dikker et al., 2018). This is emergent research but begins to suggest how portable EEG might usefully be deployed to help us to better understand learning. For instance, researchers at Stockholm University are using EEG to help to understand the effects of different approaches to literacy learning (Lenz Taguchi, 2018).

Educational neuroscience has also begun to explore the potential for transcranial direct current stimulation (TDCS) and transcranial random noise stimulation (TRNS) of targeted brain regions to enhance learning, in particular mathematics skills as well as general attention and cognition. This work has shown effects in university students that has been sustained for 6 months after the intervention (Cohen Kadosh et al., 2010). Positive results have also been found in clinical trials with patients experiencing depression and with patients who have movement and language impairments following a stroke. Outside the research domain, gamers are using transcranial stim devices to improve gaming performance and this has led to concerns being expressed over the easy availability of kits marketed at gamers, rather than as licensed medical devices, for self-use at home(Hogenboom, 2014).

Engaging with work of this sort shows how it is by no means straightforward to move from neuroscience research concerned with learning through to classroom learning. Fischer and Goswami argue that educational neuroscience research must attend to the 'neural, genetic, cognitive and emotional components of learning' (Fischer et al., 2010: 70).

This is an approach which, even within the confines of a discipline, emphasizes the complexity and multifaceted nature of learning. As they pursue an educational neuroscience of learning they stress a series of core principles and concerns: that a distinction must be maintained between mental activity and brain activity underscoring, as we did in Chapter 4, that the former cannot simply be read off the latter; that if educational differences have biological and neural elements, then the mechanisms of these must be understood; and that, if such difference and mechanisms are identified, these differences must be understood as reflecting a range, rather than constituting distinct profiles. These are important provisos as they emphasize the importance of understanding the mechanisms that generate difference, rather than relying on correlational measures) at the same time as we avoid developing profiles or typologies of learners. This is an orientation that we think articulates well with the sort of biosocial approach that we are advocating.

Learning to read

In Chapter 3 we discussed education neuroscience research into reading in order to explore the possibility that 'optimizing humans' through reading interventions might be the 'right' thing to do. Here we return to this field of work as an example of research that is seeking to understand the *how* of learning.

Reading is understood as the process of 'recoding print to sound', i.e. matching written letters, graphemes and words to the sounds and meanings in language. According to Goswami (2014) this is 'one of the most complex cognitive feats that the brain achieves' and that involves visual, spatial, auditory and attentional processing and literally changes the brain (Goswami, 2014: 3100). There is not a consensus, however, on the way in which the brain achieves reading.

Neuroscience reading research with a region-function emphasis has been interested in the left occipitotemporal cortex which is involved in object recognition, including printed words, and so also known as the *Visual Word form Area* or VWFA. EEG research measuring activity in the VWFA during word recognition tasks shows slower response times to words and nonsense words in children identified as being at 'family risk' of dyslexia i.e. other family members already have a diagnosis of dyslexia. When congruous and incongruous sounds and letters are shown together, EEG shows activation of the VWFA and nearby brain areas, as well as speech recognition areas. Again, children identified as being at family risk of dyslexia have distinct brain activation patterns, which include the absence of changed activity in response to sound-letter incongruence (Hruby and Goswami, 2011). For neuroscientists, this research into the VWFA provides new insight into brain activation associated with word/letter/sound recognition, and the distinct patterns of activation amongst potentially dyslexic or struggling readers, that may be able to inform interventions to support the reading of these children. Furthermore, EEG research is considered particularly useful because the fine temporal grain size of EEG measurement captures the time course of brain activation patterns with precision and in a way that could not be captured through observation alone.

In her 2015 *Nature* review paper Goswami examines a series of theories of reading, setting out their premises and the research they are based on and reviewing some of the limitations of these. One area of focus is *Magnocellular theory* which, like VWFA discussed earlier, suggests a core role for the visual system in reading. Deficits in visual field, including motion and spatial information are thought to result in reading difficulties such as dyslexia. However, Goswami's interrogation of the evidence presented suggests that differential results are due to the reduced reading experience that flows from reading difficulty and not from dyslexia itself. Likewise, limited visual attention span is argued to be an artefact of reduced reading experience rather than a result of dyslexia. These are important distinctions because, in flipping the direction of the relationship between dyslexia and the visual, they begin to question the dominant assumption of the central position of the visual in reading.

Reading as hearing (not seeing) – a mechanism for reading difficulties?

The accepted education neuroscience account of reading, and reading difficulty, drawing on structural and functional imaging, shows a 'reading network' (Turkeltaub et al., 2003) comprised of:

> extensive activation in brain areas related to audition, vision, language, spatial and cross-modal processing (e.g. posterior superiortemporal cortex, occipito-temporal cortex, temporal and parietalareas, inferior frontal gyrus).
>
> *(cited in Goswami, 2014: 3100)*

Studies show that this activation is initially 'bilateral' – occurring on both sides of the brain – but that as reading skills develop this becomes 'left-lateralized, and more focused on the occipitotemporal and posterior superior temporal cortices' (Goswami, 2014: 3100). In this model, reading is multi-sensory but the visual is at its core.

Yet Goswami builds a novel alternative account of reading, and reading difficulty, in which sound, as processed through the auditory cortex, is at the centre. Furthermore, Goswami suggests that this offers not just correlational evidence but that research is beginning to show a *mechanism* for the role of sound in reading.

Goswami explores impaired auditory processing as a potential cause of dyslexia. This is a novel line of investigation and, importantly, one which may move the field on from correlations between brain regions and reading to actually identifying neural mechanism of reading and reading difficulty. Research focusing on auditory processing has explored rhythmic processing; exploring rapid auditory processing and sensitivity to intensity and pitch of 'rise times' (the amplitude modulation) in onset-rime and phoneme. Findings suggest that rise time sensitivity and rhythmic processing are affected in children with dyslexia, and persist over the primary school years. Particularly noteworthy is the finding that pre-reading children's awareness of music rhythm is a better predictor of reading than letter and phoneme sound awareness (Goswami, 2015).

Goswami also considers theories of language and reading that suggest 'representations for words are stored in continuous time as high-dimensional spectrotemporal auditory patterns' (Goswami, 2015: 45). This suggests that awareness of word sounds 'is an emergent property of acoustic structure' and that for pre-readers speech rhythm is prioritized by the brain as it makes sense of language. Goswami suggests that:

> [R]ise times function as auditory 'edges', resetting ongoing neuronal oscillations so that oscillatory peaks are aligned with amplitude modulation peaks. Atypical oscillatory alignment would thus affect the perceptual organization of amplitude modulations, meaning that stressed syllables, syllables and the onset-rime division would be poorly encoded.
>
> *(Goswami, 2015: 51)*

Goswami examines specifically a Norwegian longitudinal study from pre-reading children age 6, through to age 11 using fMRI to measure cortical thickness at three points in the study. Using family history to identify children at risk of dyslexia, the longitudinal study traced an at-risk and control cohort over the 5-year period. Importantly, this research found no structural brain differences between the at-risk and control cohort pre-reading. At this pre-reading stage differences in cortical thickness were evident 'suggesting that sensory processing and executive control might already differ pre-reading' (Goswami, 2014: 3100). A difference in thickness of the primary auditory cortex persisted over the course of the 5-year study. Goswami argues that the structural differences demonstrated by this research provide evidence that '[a]uditory impairments are primary in the etiology of developmental dyslexia' (Goswami, 2014: 3101) but that this research is not able to address the question of the mechanism(s) involved (see Figure 7.6).

Goswami suggests that speech comes to be understood when the auditory cortex – the part of the brain that is believed to be centrally involved in processing sound – comes to recognize the timings and rhythms of the sounds that make up speech. Neuroscientists refer to such processes of repeated exposure that lead to familiarization and embedded patterned activation responses as 'entrainment'.

Goswami's research suggests that it is the particular nature of these timings and rhythms, and responses to these in the auditory cortex, that establish the mechanisms for reading and, indeed, for reading difficulty.

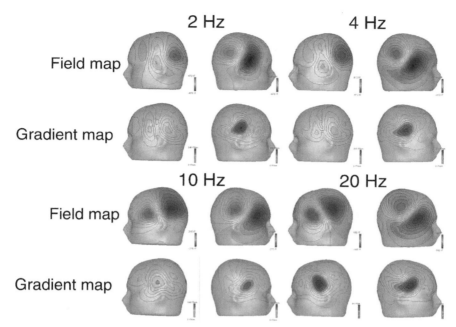

Schematic depiction of the MEG field and gradient maps of neural activity in response to amplitude modulations delivered at different temporal rates (2, 4, 10 and 20 Hz). Source localization of these field maps suggested different sources in auditory cortex for the slower (2 Hz, 4 Hz) and faster (10 Hz, 20 Hz) rates. Dyslexic participants showed significantly reduced phase locking compared to control participants in auditory cortex in the right hemisphere for 2 Hz amplitude modulation stimulation. (Hamalainen et al., 2012 in Goswami, 2014).

FIGURE 7.6 Auditory cortex and learning to read

In order to understand Goswami's account of the auditory cortex's role in reading, it is necessary to understand the fundamentals of how the brain processes stimuli. Incoming stimulation, in this case particular sorts of sounds, provokes rhythmic electrical oscillatory activity or 'brain waves'. These electrical oscillations vary in terms of frequency, phase and amplitude and these variations are thought to be fundamental to the coding of information in the brain. Amplitude measures the strength of the wave, that is the distance of the peak of the wave from its neutral state, while the frequency of oscillatory activity measures the waves per second in hertz (Hz), with waves sub-categorized according to this: delta waves have a frequency of 0.5–4 Hz; theta waves have a frequency of 4–8 Hz; alpha waves 8–12 Hz: beta waves 12–38 Hz; and gamma waves 40 to 100 Hz.

Modulation of amplitude is the variation in the wave form. This modulation can be provoked by the phasing of waves across neurons and also by neurotransmitters. Brain waves, then, are inherently temporal – the wave happens over time and amplitude and modulation determine over *how much* time (Scott et al., 2010). Speech, then, is understood by the auditory cortex becoming entrained to the timings and rhythms of the 'amplitude modulation patterns' in speech.

> In multi-time resolution models of speech processing, endogenous oscillatory activity in the auditory cortex becomes rhythmically-entrained to amplitude modulation patterns in the speech signal at different temporal rates, thereby encoding speech information at multiple timescales
>
> *(Giraud and Poeppel, 2012 cited by Goswami, 2015)*

Goswami draws attention in particular to differences in delta wave band across readers, with dyslexic children and adults appearing to have impaired entrainment to delta waves. Goswami and colleagues use a stream of speech sounds, in particular phonemes that make up the onset of a word such as 'ba', to study with EEG the differential oscillatory activity (brain wave amplitude and modulation) in the auditory cortex.

Delta waves, with slow amplitude modulations, are related to the ways in which syllables are stressed in speech, with the 'rise time' from the beginning of the wave to its peak larger when the syllable is stressed. Furthermore, these rise times 'appear to reset ongoing neuronal oscillations to achieve phase alignment' (Goswami, 2015: 3102). This phase alignment is atypical in children diagnosed with dyslexia, for whom the auditory cortex appears to be entrained to 'less informative points of the speech signal' (Power et al., 2013 cited in Goswami, 2014). Goswami suggests that when the brain is not entrained to discriminate the rise time of the delta wave, then problems arise in syllable and syllable stress (prosodic) level language, which in turn impacts on readers' awareness of phonemes (Goswami, 2014). It is noteworthy that these findings are consistent across a range of transparent, non-transparent and ideographic languages (Goswami, 2011 cited in Goswami, 2014).

> The strong prediction from the delta entrainment acoustic hypothesis outlined here would be that differences in prosodic [syllable stress] and syllabic awareness would be most marked in *pre-reading* at-risk samples.
>
> *(Goswami, 2014: 3102, my emphasis)*

This is early research and further work is required; according to Goswami this needs to include auditory, visual and executive function in order to generate sophisticated insight into the mechanisms of reading and causality of reading difficulties.

This education neuroscience research into reading is important because it begins to demonstrate not just associations between brain regions, patterns of brain activity, networks and cognitive functions, but goes beyond that to begin to identify specific mechanisms involved. This offers a way into thinking about neural mechanisms of learning more widely, as well as mechanisms that might inhibit learning. In addition, a biosocial approach to learning to read might provoke us to think beyond these delta waves to consider further influences of different types and at different grain sizes. Factoring potential influences such as stress and pleasure, the social dynamics which provoke and protect against these, the nuances of pedagogies and pedagogic relationships, and their impact on neurotransmission along with nutritional influences on neuronal membranes and neurotransmission into analyses of reading would begin to generate a rich multifactorial biosocial account of interacting influences and mechanism.

Nutrition and learning

In previous chapters we have explored research into the importance of Omega-3 for the functioning of cells. While much of the focus of Omega-3 research has been on immune function and inflammatory mediation, researchers have also attempted to identify the educational significance of Omega-3 levels and Omega-6:Omega-3 ratios. There is emerging research in molecular biology that may relate directly to the capacity to learn through its focusing on Omega-3 in the brain. Work from the Cohen-Cory lab sets out research on DHA, an Omega-3, and its role in the development of neurons (Igarashi et al., 2015). Working with adult female frogs and their tadpole offspring, this research shows the impact of reduced DHA on the trans-generational transmission of less-developed neurons as well as its reversibility.

This study fed female frogs differential DHA-content diets and examined neuronal development in tadpoles over 60 days. The study showed that offspring of frogs fed a DHA-deficient diet themselves had a 57% reduction in DHA in the brain by week 60 and developed neurons that were 'morphologically simpler' (p6079) than offspring of frogs with non-DHA-deficient diets (see Figure 3.1 in Chapter 3). It also showed that the offspring of DHA-deficient frogs had a 40% reduction in key proteins involved in DNA transcriptions (BDNF mRNA) – meaning that the myelin sheath that provides connectivity between neurons is compromised. These effects were reversed when the offspring were fed Omega-3 enriched diets. This study shows that DHA 'is an essential component of the nervous system, and maternal n-3 [Omega-3] polyunsaturated fatty acids (PUFAs) are an important source for brain development' (p. 6079). However, the study is not able to say what the effect of these differences might be, if they are associated with tadpole survival/thriving, if there is any particular phenotype in the adult frog, and it is certainly not able to identify any cognitive implication.

Moving from frog brains to human brains can only be done with great caution, and we are not able to say straightforwardly that we would expect to find similar differences in humans with DHA-reduced diets and we are certainly not able to say that a cognitive impact could be expected in humans. Furthermore, in contrast with the Igarashi paper, recent research by Bou and colleagues (Bou et al., 2017) on the effects of Omega-3 deficiency in salmon finds differential Omega-6:Omega-3 ratios across specific tissue types in single subjects. This suggests that in salmon there is a cellular mechanism that maintains a 1:1 Omega-6:Omega-3 ratio in brain tissue irrespective of overall dietary levels, with very different ratios in other tissues e.g. muscle, plasma and gut. Such a mechanism would appear to protect the brain from the effects of Omega-3 shortage, at the same time as severe Omega-3 deficiency-related damage occurs in other tissue. Once again, we are forced to make the move from animal models – here frogs and fish – to humans, in order to consider the potential implications of this research for understanding influences on children's learning. And once again we are faced with findings that are in tension, with Igarashi's findings appearing supportive of an Omega-3-brain health mechanism, and dietary finding from Bou potentially undermining such evidence for supplementation/dietary intervention for human children on grounds of cognitive development, and perhaps beginning to shed light on the limited findings of education-based Omega-3 research to date.

Sleep and learning

It is widely understood that children need adequate amounts and quality of sleep to thrive, with sleep understood to have an important role in memory formation and, therefore, learning (Hill et al., 2007). Sleep duration and quality is predictive of white matter differences and waking functional connectivity (Khalsa et al., 2017, 2016) and of children's educational attainment (Gruber et al., 2010; Kelley et al., 2015), and early sleep problems in childhood are associated with later difficulties, such as substance abuse (Wong et al., 2004). However, to date this work is largely associational and we do not yet have any mechanisms to show how sleep functions to enhance learning. Recent research has established intracellular molecular mechanisms that guide cycles of sleeping and waking and epigenetic influences on 'clock genes' whose variation suggests 'chronotypes' (Foster and Kreitzman, 2014). This has underpinned research into the potential learning benefits of varying the timing of the school day for adolescents and developing sleep education Education Endowment Fund, 2016). This research is still underway and we are some way away from system-wide changes to school start times, for instance.

Health and learning

Consideration of factors such as nutrition and sleep suggest a wider engagement with children's health and learning. Poor educational achievement is known to be strongly associated with poor health outcomes across the life course. However, it is often the case that background characteristics, and in particular relative deprivation or poverty, are foregrounded as key influences on both health and education outcomes. For instance a major enquiry by the UK Parliament with a focus on health over the life course, *Fair Society, Healthy Lives* (Marmot, 2010), identified factors pertaining to background, parents, peers and the child as influences on education, but did not consider child health as itself a potential influence. Similarly, the World Health Organization report *Health 2020* (WHO, 2013), argues for the importance of synergy between health and education sectors in pursuit of greater equity in health and well-being. However, it frames education as a determinant of health outcomes, and does not explore how children's health might influence their capacity to learn.

Reading across state-of-the-art evidence from education, sociology, molecular biology, analytic chemistry and neuroscience suggests that education does not just influence health outcomes by opening (and closing) life opportunities. It also suggests that children's capacity to learn is likely to be influenced by their health and well-being. It is too simple to say that health or well-being as generalized states influence learning in a linear way. Rather, particular aspects of health and well-being – from children's relationships with carers, teachers and peers and their sense of self, to the food they eat, the way they play and exercise and the way they sleep – influence each other as well as a child's capacity to learn. This suggests that we should think of children's health, well-being and learning as a complex set of inter-related biosocial phenomena influenced by multiple interacting biological, social and economic factors that span fields of daily life, scales of granularity and domains of knowledge and whose mechanisms of influence are yet to be understood.

Impeding learning

The idea of 'ability' which circulates in schools and education policy as well as in popular and media accounts is a key impediment to learning. Ability is one term in a wider lexicon – intelligence, IQ, potential, aptitude, capacity, capability, talent, gift – all of which rest on the same underlying assumptions. Whether understood as innate 'ability' or 'intelligence', a point of 'development', or reframed as 'prior attainment', the idea that the intellectual ability is innate to the person and is unevenly distributed across the population remains profoundly influential. As does the idea that some people have particular aptitudes, special skills or 'gifts' and 'talents' in specific domains. Following from these ideas is the implication that some people will all but inevitably do better in school than others.

In this book we have foregrounded current research in biological sciences that emphasizes mutability and social-biological interaction. 'Intelligence' is one area of neuroscience research that tends away from this mutability and interactivity. Most notably, the work of Robert Plomin's laboratory which uses genome-wide association studies – a technique that analyses a section of genome from a relatively large population predicated on the expectation that a trait is produced by many genes, each having small effect – to investigate a genetic basis for 'generalized intelligence' or 'g' (Ashbury and Plomin, 2014; Plomin and Deary, 2015). So far these studies have shown much less genetic variance than suggested by earlier twin studies, but the programme of research is ongoing, with expanded samples, and the authors anticipate being able to increasingly identify complex genetic causes for 'intelligence'.

Despite a large body of critical education research against ability, work such as Plomin's is highly influential and ability remains a staple of education policy and guidance and part of common sense. Indeed, it is a cornerstone of the idea that we live in a 'meritocracy' in which we each get what we deserve (ability plus effort equals merit), and it is used as a key organizational and explanatory device in many schools, structuring the everyday landscape and experience of schooling. Advocates of ability or 'IQ' have persisted in suggesting that its uneven distribution across race and class groups is an uncomfortable fact that society must accept and that education systems should respond to, or, in particular in the light of vigorous criticism from anti-racist scholars, they claim that it has a 'normal distribution' and leave race out of their commentary (Gillborn, 2016).

As a way of navigating this difficult and contentious terrain, many educators advocate focusing on prior-learning, pre-existing skills, preparedness, readiness – but each of these might, or might not, still rest on the idea of ability. This resonates with the now internationally widespread endorsement of 'differentiation' and 'personalization' of the curriculum and teaching (Prain et al., 2013; Williamson and Payton, 2009). Yet while there is a good deal of support for personalization in principle, its definition is slippery – note the movement across personalized curriculum and pedagogy to personalized learning – and models for implementation vague (Prain et al., 2013). There is also substantial criticism of 'personalization'. This spans concern over the central role of information technology that harvests data at the same time as it generates apparently personalized learning opportunities (Herold, 2017) through to concern that the notions of the learner and learning that underpin personalization remain infused with a notion of ability and act to reinscribe already existing educational advantages and disadvantages (Prain et al., 2013).

Education research shows the harm done by ability. It has long been used as the basis for sorting, selection, setting and streaming in schools (Gillborn and Youdell, 2000; Gillborn, 2008). Research by Sue Hallam and colleagues (2013) shows that using 'mixed ability' groupings is better for everyone. Nevertheless, policy continues to very actively promote setting by ability. Setting by ability not only sorts and separates, it makes hierarchies – when selection and setting based on ability are part of the fabric of an education system, some students come to be 'better' than others. Children in the bottom set know they are in the bottom set, and, as Rauch's research shows, children sat on the 'circles' table know what is implied by the fact that circles have many less sides than hexagons (Ball, 2013). Deborah's own research shows how, through mundane everyday practices ability makes differently valued learners. Day-in, day-out, schools and teachers recognize some students as good learners, and others as difficult, troubling, or troubled learners – modes of recognition that become bound up in students' sense of themselves – the child recognized as bright understands herself as bright and manifests her brightness in the classroom, while the child recognized as struggling understands himself as struggling and manifests his struggles in the classroom. Ability is used to predict and fix – many schools pay large sums to private education companies that predict students' subject-by-subject outcomes in terminal exams based on measures of their ability taken years in advance, explaining away inequalities by making them natural, unavoidable and down to the individual. Ability is also used to allocate resources, and when resources are limited and performance indicators drive not just a school's reputation but its continued autonomy and even its continued existence, ability is used to perform 'educational triage'. When Deborah and David Gillborn first observed schools performing what looked to us like educational triage in the late 1990s we were shocked – schools were not prioritizing the most disadvantaged or lowest attaining students as we had expected. Instead, these students were deemed 'hopeless' and the often more socially and economically advantaged students performing on the borderline of the performance indicator – the suitable cases for treatment – got the resources. These once shocking practices are now standard in schools.

Finally, but perhaps most profoundly, ability stops us from thinking differently about learning. It stops us from conceptualizing capacities for learning as potentially available to all children and across a whole range of moments. When ability is embedded in our thinking we anticipate hierarchically different outcomes for children who by extension become hierarchically arranged and we offer hierarchically different opportunities for learning to them, thereby compounding the problem. Furthermore, when ability is embedded in our thinking what we can do as an educator is curtailed, we can only teach within the constraints of ability, rather than being able to open up endless possibilities for learning to all children.

If we reject ability and think in different ways about learners and learning, if we understand learning as a biosocial phenomenon that is profoundly mutable – from the capacity for connectivity across myelin sheaths to the possibility of being recognized and identifying as a learner – then we might have a real chance of removing the current limits on children's capacities for learning.

What rats can teach teachers

Over the course of this book we have returned at various points to research on rat brains and behaviours and how they are changed by the sort of care they receive. This research, which looks at rat mothers' licking and grooming behaviour, shows that rats that get lots of licking and grooming are different from rats that do not. Rat offspring that experience 'low' licking and grooming show hormonal changes in the 'HPA axis' (hypothalamic, pituitary and adrenal activity) – also known as the 'stress axis' – that together mean that licking and grooming effects how rats' neuronal stress responses work and how the rats then respond to stressful situations. While these patterns can repeat over generations, importantly they can also be changed inside generations – when infant and adolescent rats are fostered to rats with different licking and grooming patterns, their brains change and so do their behaviours.

This capacity for change at the neuronal level is fundamentally important to our thinking about capacities for learning. The study of the effects of foot shock on rats that we discussed earlier in this chapter not only showed methylation resulting from the fear-exposure, it also showed *varying* methylation over the hours and days post-fear exposure (Molfese, 2011). And research with monozygotic (single egg) twins which compared DNA methylation in specific genes at age 5 and age 10 found that methylation varied *across* twins at age 5 and that methylation was not stable *within* individuals between the ages of 5 and 10 (Wong et al., 2010). That is, the brain undergoes significant changes to its structures, activities and functions over the life course and many of these changes occur in interaction with environmental factors.

Epigenetic changes take place at the scale of the cell and the molecules that make it, but scale up (in complex and often little understood ways) into 'phenotypes' (the characteristics of a creature) and behaviours. The genome itself does not determine how a creature will be and behave – the genome provides a resource that, in interaction with other influences, is embroiled in the action of molecules, cells and the creatures these make up. The potentialities of a body are vastly greater than the genome (Frost, 2016; Molfese, 2011; Rose and Abi-Rached, 2013; Tognini et al., 2015).

This plasticity of the brain's epigenetic responses to environment and experience offers a positive alternative to the now well-established policy emphasis on early intervention (Allen, 2011; Feinstein, 2003). Early intervention policy has been criticized for over-emphasizing the responsibility for children's educational attainment on mothers, especially when it insists that 'two is too late' for the educational effects of 'poor parenting' to be undone (Edwards et al., 2015; Gillies, 2008). What the rats suggest is that two is not too late, that mothers of toddlers can't possibly be held responsible for their children's entire educational futures, that different forms of care affect different children in different ways, and that, in terms of these brain effects anyway, we may not need to get our care from our mothers.

We have to take care translating from rats to humans. Children's worlds are complex. Their days are filled with numerous experiences and encounters that will provoke a whole range of biochemical, affective, intuitive, social and meant responses. These responses, the rats tell us, vary between children but also potentially vary in the same child over time. And in the movements and flows of the day, it might not always be so easy to know what might count as a stressor and what might count as careful, and to which child. Children's relationships are also complex. They form deep attachments to carers, family members, peers, teachers, including when people do not care for them well. Children's relationships with individuals shift and change, and children can have caring, supportive relationships with some people, and uncaring and unsupportive relationships with other people. And the impact of relationships can endure long after the relationship has ended.

It is not straightforwardly clear what might be the equivalent of rats' licking and grooming for a child. Certainly we would not want to suggest that it is a model of attachment carried directly from Bowlby or Ainsworth, or the dominant account of the 'good' parent that prevails in policy and seems to say there is just one correct way of parenting. But even if we were to say that the human equivalent of licking and grooming might be lots of physical affection, attentive dialogue, responsiveness to needs, validation of feelings and an orientation to discovery, the point the rats are making is that this does not all need to be done in infancy, and it is not all down to the mother. What the rats teach teachers is the fundamental importance of caring for children in classrooms. They remind teachers that if we get a report from another professional telling us 'what' and 'who' a child is, what their 'ability' is, and what they are 'able' to learn, teachers should engage with this information knowing that children and their capacities for learning can change and that these capacities can be opened up to change. Building strong relationships of care is a key to this change. The rats teach teachers that when a child is not doing something the teacher wants them to do, it might not be because the child is recalcitrant, disordered or disruptive – it might be because their stress axis or their social behaviour network needs some care. Finally, the rats teach teachers that stress and learning do not go together, that we should keep stressors – from social policing to high-stakes testing – away from children. According to the rats, everyone involved with children and young people should have care and support at the heart of their encounters.

Biosocial learning

What happens when we claim that all of these accounts of learning might be true at the same time? The transdisciplinary evidence that we examine here leads us to analyses of multiple intra-acting productive forces that might be influences on or mechanisms of learning – that might be understood as the phenomenon of learning. These forces might include institutions, social milieu, politics, policy, discourse, subjectivity, pedagogy, relationships, feelings, food, physical activity, sleep, objects, fauna, flora, and architectures, each of which may be productive at a range of scales of granularity – from the macro to the molecular. As we have stressed throughout this book, much is still unknown about the molecular mechanisms that drive the particular functioning of particular cells and new biosciences are themselves diverse and proceed with different orientations to learning.

This book makes the case that learning is a complex biosocial phenomenon impacted by multiple influences and achieved through multiple mechanisms. We represent this in Figure 7.7, although the representation is itself limited because it does not capture the interaction across influences and the multiple directions in which these interactions might flow. Learning is an interaction between a person and a thing; it is embedded in ways of being and understanding that are shared across communities; it is influenced by the social and cultural and economic conditions of lives; it involves changes to how genes are expressed in brain cells because it changes the histones that store DNA; it means that certain parts of the brain are provoked into electrochemical activity; and it relies on a person being recognized by others, and recognizing themselves, as someone who learns. And these might be interacting with each other – shared meanings, gene expression, electrochemical signals, the everyday of the classroom, and a sense of self are actually all part of one phenomenon that is learning.

This sort of thinking is just beginning to generate new thinking and new approaches in education research. For instance, current research by Hillevi Lenz Taguchi and her team at Stockholm University is seeking to develop 'neuro-sensitive' pedagogic practices that are embedded in a transdisciplinary approach to learning, bringing together insights from pedagogy, linguistics and education neuroscience to compare the effects on children's language and communication skills of social and emotional approaches to learning and computerized attention training techniques (Lenz Taguchi et al., n/d).

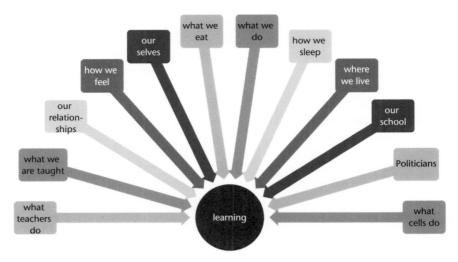

FIGURE 7.7   Biosocial influences on learning

Our consideration of the multiple social and biological influences on learning leads us to a number of initial suggestions for what we might do differently in education.

Fish oil supplementation: Omega-3 has been a recurrent interest in this book, having been shown to have a key role in cell membrane function and neurotransmission. While supplementation results in education are to date not definitive, the suggested importance of Omega-3 means it is essential to clarify Omega-3 effects and address both Omega-3 levels and Omega-6:Omega-3 ratios. Dietary interventions that regularly serve oily fish as part of school meals are already underway, for instance the twice-weekly serving of well-chosen fish), although minimizing the intake of excessive Omega-6 found in vegetable oils is more challenging. Omega-3 supplements, particularly of the sort that can be taken as a fruit drink that children enjoy, may well merit being the next school milk.

Caring relationships: As we have shown across this book, the quality of relationships have social, psychological and molecular impacts. Animal models suggest that caring relationships between adults and children have epigenetics effects, in particular on the brain's stress axis, which have down-stream effects on social behaviour and learning. Importantly, these effects can be positively impacted by intervention – no child should be regarded as too troubled or too difficult to learn, with the right support built on the foundation of a profoundly caring relationship between the teacher and learner it is never 'too late'. Underscoring this, psychosocial work shows the benefits of 'holding learners in mind' as they encounter the sometimes difficult feelings of learning. With a very different framework that foregrounds quantitative measures of effectiveness, John Hattie's (2009) influential review of research into effective teaching shows the central importance of relationships between the teacher and the learner. Caring relationships between teachers and learners are central to learning and should be regarded as at the core of professional pedagogic practice.

Destressing schools, jettisoning ability and promoting happiness: Across this book the negative effects of thinking in terms of ability and intelligence have been shown, as have the negative consequences of high-stress education systems and the classrooms that these provoke. The evidence we have explored suggests the sorts of schools and classrooms indicated by inclusive education and productive pedagogy: where curriculum and pedagogies offer intellectual quality, connectedness to learners' worlds and draw on and develop teachers' body of work; where children are involved in negotiating, leading and reflecting on their learning; where there is a supportive learning environment accessible and responsive to all students; where there is a valuing of and working with difference; and where notions of ability and associated setting practices have no place. And our exploration has also indicated the need to recognize and allow feelings to flow in classrooms and the potential that happiness and pleasure should pursued in and as a medium for learning.

Making good use of neuroscience: Education neuroscientists are strenuous in their advocacy for continued development of basic neuroscientific insight into brain mechanisms before a rush to implementation in classrooms. That said, some important connexions between mechanisms and interventions have already been found. For instance, there is amassing evidence that learning is accelerated for children with particular language and reading difficulties by computer-based language and reading games, e.g. *Graphogame rime*, that build on findings about brain activation and networks such as Goswami and colleague's auditory mechanism for reading difficulty. As biosocial education approaches develop, these will be important lines of work to develop.

Giving more resources to the poorest children: Over and again research in education has shown that well-resourced schools can support the most disadvantaged children best. Now neuroscience research shows that providing even modest financial uplift for the poorest families benefits children – development and outcomes are driven by access, opportunities and experiences, not social class itself. Rather than intervening into the parenting of families living in poverty and facing multiple challenges or endlessly reforming education systems, curriculum, pedagogies and assessment in attempts to address educational inequalities, redistributing wealth to eradicate the worst economic inequalities is the best way of achieving socially just education.

Difficulties, dangers and a biosocial education

Separating biological sciences and the findings they generate from policy, media and popular uses and misuses is tricky, as is ensuring that these findings are articulated with or nested in amassed knowledge about education. Substantial, compelling criticism of the 'new bio-rationalities' or 'molecular rationalities' has been offered that give pause to critical educationalists engaging with biological sciences

(Gulson and Webb, 2016, 2017; Williamson et al., 2017). Yet we want to maintain that the ways that politicians, lobbyists and other advocates call up particular findings or fragments of findings from biological sciences and use these to 'evidence' particular positions and changes in policy and practice *is not the science itself* (Youdell et al., 2017).

Concerns have been raised that despite good intentions, new biological knowledges, and biosocial approaches that take these up, will ultimately serve the interests of capital and already privileged groups, and further entrench disadvantage and exclusion along lines of race, ethnicity, region, religion class, gender, sexuality, disability etc. This is a particularly important concern in the context of the history of the creation of racial hierarchy as a core part of the colonial project and the historical invention and uses of scientific race in the justification and structuring of the colonial global order (Gillborn, 2008; Meloni, 2016). Critical Race Theory (CRT) offers important tools for understanding how White Supremacy is made and remade in changing circumstances (Delgardo and Stefancic, 2001; Gillborn, 2008). CRT insights into the business as usual of racism, the rule of racial standing, and the convergence of White Interest with the demands of minoritized groups as the driver for change, all warn that new biological sciences and biosocial approaches might be commandeered and deployed in the interest of White Supremacy. Indeed, as has been noted in relation to policy deployments of attachment theory and the epigenetics of attachment, scientific research is already being used in ways that reinscribe the fault and failure of poor and minoritized women (Edwards et al., 2015). And research in behaviour genetics is reinscribing the intellectual inferiority of Black and other racially minoritized groups (Gillborn, 2016).

But behavioural genetics is just one area of work in the new biological sciences, and it seems to ill-represent a broad discipline where plasticity and social-biological interaction are foregrounded. Furthermore, the figure of the scientist either actively aligned with oppressive political movements or defaulting to a naive position of 'scientific neutrality' unaware of their culpability, seems an insulting strawman that ignores the diversity of political positions across a massive professional body as well as the creative curiosity and ambition to do social good that drives much research in the biological sciences. Rose and Rose (2013) have suggested that scientists themselves should do more to counter policy and popular misuses of scientific findings. In the context of a university sector where funding begets funding and the demand to evidence 'impact' in the 'real world' is intensifying, it is not a case of asking scientists to make a simple 'ethical' choice – their careers are at stake when they call out policy excesses or the aggrandizement of their colleagues. Furthermore, while the scientific evidence is complex and partial, policy solutions seldom are, and so claims that science is being misused are likely to oversimplify the processes of knowledge selection, circulation and influence. It is not always easy to 'do the right thing'.

Developing a biosocial approach for education does not mean swapping education studies or sociology of education for biology – it is not a case of throwing away our recognition of the importance of the social and insights into social processes and replacing these with biology. Nor is it a case of finding a single line of research in a single field of biology and foregrounding this as the new explanation for educational successes and failures. It is not either, attachment, the brain's stress axis, or Omega-3 that needs to be addressed – it is all of these acting together and with further biological and social forces. This book is the beginning of an attempt to map these intra-acting social and biological forces and work through the implications of these for education. We are certainly biological organisms but biological life proceeds in complex and changing social and cultural milieu – following Frost's (2016) insight, we are biocultural creatures and need to be thought about in this complexity. We are advocating for biosocial education a deep, transdisciplinary encounter – which generates new ways of thinking that traverse social and biological domains and in doing so changes them.

REFERENCES

23andMe. (n/d). *Ancestry Composition*. Retrieved from https://permalinks.23andme.com/pdf/samplereport_ancestrycomp

Adamson, D. (2016). Should you have genetic testing for your embryos? Maybe. *Huffington Post*. Retrieved from Huffpost website www.huffingtonpost.com/dr-david-adamson/should-you-have-genetic-testing-for-your-embryos-maybe_b_8991880.html

Ahmed, S. (2004). *The Cultural Politics of Emotion*. Edinburgh: Edinburgh University Press.

Allan, J. (2008). *Rethinking Inclusion: The Philosophers of Difference in Practice*. Dordrecht: Springer.

Allen, G. (2011). *Early Intervention: The Next Steps*. Retrieved from London www.gov.uk/government/publications/early-intervention-the-next-steps-2

American Psychiatry Association. (2013). *Diagnostic and Statistical Manual of Mental Disorders Fifth Edition*. Retrieved from https://dsm.psychiatryonline.org/doi/book/10.1176/appi.books.9780890425596

Apple, M. (2006). *Educating the 'right' Way: Markets, Standards, God, and Inequality, Second Edition*. London: RoutledgeFalmer.

Armstrong, F. (2003). *Spaced Out: Policy, Difference and the Challenge of Inclusive Education*. London: Kluwer Academic Publishers.

Ashbury, K., & Plomin, R. (2014). *G Is for Genes: The Impact of Genetics on Education and Achievement*. Chichester: Wiley.

Atkinson, E., & DePalma, R. (2009). Un-believing the matrix: Queering consensual heteronormativity. *Gender and Education, 21*(1), 17–29. doi:10.1080/09540250802213149

Atwood, M. (1990). *The Handmaids Tale*. London: Virago.

Baker, B. (2015). From "Somatic Scandals" to "a Constant Potential for Violence"? The culture of dissection, brain-based learning, and the rewriting/rewiring of "the Child". *Journal of Curriculum and Pedagogy, 12*(2), 168–197. doi:10.1080/15505170.2015.1055394

Bakermans-Kranenburg, M. J., & van Ijzendoorn, M. H. (2015). The hidden efficacy of interventions: Gene x environment experiments from a differential susceptibility perspective. *Annual Review of Psychology, 66*, 381–409. doi:10.1146/annurev-psych-010814-015407

Bakhurst, D. (2011). *The Formation of Reason*. Oxford: Wiley-Blackwell.

Bakhurst, D. (2008). Minds, brains and education. *Journal of Philosophy of Education, 42*(3–4), 415–432. doi:10.1111/j.1467-9752.2008.00645.x

Ball, S. J. (2003). The teacher's soul and the terrors of performativity. *Journal of Education Policy*, *18*(2), 215–228.

Ball, S. J. (2013). *Foucault, Power and Education*. London: Routledge.

Barad, K. M. (2007). *Meeting the Universe Halfway*. London: Duke University Press.

Barkley, R. A. (2002, January). International consensus statement on ADHD. *Clinical Child Family Psychology Review*, *5*(2), 89–111.

Barkley, R. A. (2004). Critique or misrepresentation? A reply to Timimi et al. *Clinical Child and Family Psychology Review*, *7*(1), 65–69. doi:10.1023/B:CCFP.0000020193.48817.30

Barton, L. (Ed.). (2001). *Disability, Politics and the Struggle for Change*. London: David Fulton.

Bazan, A., & Detandt, S. (2013). On the physiology of jouissance: Interpreting the mesolimbic dopaminergic reward functions from a psychoanalytic perspective. *Frontiers in Human Neuroscience*, *7*, 709. doi:10.3389/fnhum.2013.00709

Beery, A. K., McEwan, L. M., MacIsaac, J. L., Francis, D. D., & Kobor, M. S. (2016). Natural variation in maternal care and cross-tissue patterns of oxytocin receptor gene methylation in rats. *Hormones and Behaviour*, *77*, 42–52.

Belsky, J., & van Ijzendoorn, M. H. (2015). What works for whom? Genetic moderation of intervention efficacy. *Development and Psychopathology*, *27*(1), 1–6. doi:10.1017/s0954579414001254

Bennett, J. (2010). *Vibrant Matter: A Political Ecology of Things*. London: Duke University Press.

Bergson, H. (1998). *Creative Evolution*. London: Dover.

Bevins, R. A., & Besheer, J. (2006). Object recognition in rats and mice: A one-trial non-matching-to-sample learning task to study 'recognition memory'. *Nature Protocols*, *1*(3), 1306–1311. doi:10.1038/nprot.2006.205_

Bhide, A., Power, A., & Goswami, U. (2013). A rhythmic musical intervention for poor readers: A comparison of efficacy with a letter-based intervention. *Mind, Brain, and Education*, *7*(2), 113–123. doi:10.1111/mbe.12016

Bibby, T. (2009). How do children understand themselves as learners? Towards a learner-centred understanding of pedagogy. *Pedagogy, Culture and Society*, *17*(1), 41–55.

Bibby, T. (2011). *Education – An 'Impossible Profession'? Psychoanalytic Explorations of Learning and Classrooms*. Abingdon: Routledge.

Bibby, T. (2017). *The Creative Self: Psychoanalysis, Teaching and Learning in the Classroom*. London: Routledge.

Bilbo, S. D. (2013a). Frank A. Beach award: Programming of neuroendocrine function by early-life experience: A critical role for the immune system. *Hormones and Behavior*, *63*(5), 684–691. doi:10.1016/j.yhbeh.2013.02.017

Bilbo, S. (2013b). The mysterious relationship between the brain and body. In F. Stasio (Director) and S. Ren (Producer), *The State of Things*. Chapel Hill NC: North Carolina Public Radio – WUNC.

Black, P., Harrison, C., Lee, C., Marshall, B., & Wiliam, D. (2003). *Assessment for Learning: Putting It into Practice*. Maidenhead: Open University Press.

Blane, D. (2016). *How to Combine Sociology with Biology – and Why Do It?* Retrieved from https://blog.esrc.ac.uk/2016/08/12/how-to-combine-sociology-with-biology/

Blane, D., Kelly-Irving, M., Errico, A., Bartley, M., & Montgomery, S. (2013). Social-biological transitions: How does the social become biological? *Longitudinal and Life Course Studies*, *4*(2). doi:10.14301/llcs.v4i2.236

Bock, J., Rether, K., Groeger, N., Xie, L., & Braun, K. (2014). Perinatal programming of emotional brain circuits: An integrative view from systems to molecules. *Frontiers in Neuroscience*, *8*. doi:10.3389/fnins.2014.00011

Boler, M. (1999). *Feeling Power: Emotion and Education*. London: Routledge.

Bomber, L. M., & Hughes, D. A. (2013). *Settling to Learn: Settling Troubled Pupils to Learn – Why Relationships Matter in School*. London: Worth.

Booher-Jennings, J. (2005). Below the bubble: 'Educational Triage' and the texas account-ability system. *American Educational Research Journal, 42*(2), 231–268.

Bou, M., Berge, G. M., Baeverfjord, G., Sigholt, T., Ostbye, T. K., Romarheim, O. H., . . . Ruyter, B. (2.017). Requirements of n-3 very long-chain PUFA in Atlantic salmon (Salmo salar L): Effects of different dietary levels of EPA and DHA on fish perfor-mance and tissue composition and integrity. *British Journal of Nutrition, 117*(1), 30–47. doi:10.1017/S0007114516004396.

Bowman, G. L., Silbert, L. C., Howieson, D., Dodge, H. H., Traber, M. G., Frei, B., . . . Quinn, J. F. (2011). Nutrient biomarker patterns, cognitive function, and MRI measures of brain aging. *Neurology.* doi:10.1212/WNL.0b013e3182436598

Bradbury, A. (2013). *Understanding Early Years Inequality: Policy, Assessment and Young Children's Identity.* Abingdon: Routlede.

Bradbury, A., McGimpsey, I., & Santori, D. (2013). Revising rationality: The use of 'Nudge' approaches in neoliberal education policy. *Journal of Education Policy, 28*(2), 247–267. doi:10.1080/02680939.2012.719638

Braidotti, R. (2013). *Posthuman.* Cambridge: Polity.

Braidotti, R. (Writer) (2016). The posthuman. In J. Gelonesi (Director) and D. Dean (Pro-ducer), *The Philosopher's Zone: ABC Radio National.*

Braidotti, R. (2017, March 1). *Memoirs of a Posthumanist – Tanner Lectures on Human Values.* Retrieved from www.youtube.com/watch?v=OjxelMWLGCo

Britzman, D. (1998). *Lost Subjects, Contested Objects: Towards a Psychoanalytic Inquiry of Learning.* Albany: State University of New York Press.

Butler, J. (1990). *Gender Trouble: Feminism and the Subversion of Identity.* London: Routledge.

Butler, J. (1993). *Bodies That Matter: On the Discursive Limits of 'sex'.* New York: Routledge.

Butler, J. (1997). *Excitable Speech: A Politics of the Performative.* London: Routledge.

Butler, J. (2004). *Precarious Life: The Powers of Mourning and Violence.* London: Verso.

Butler, J. (2005). *Giving an Account of Oneself.* New York: Fordham University Press.

Butler, J., Osbourne, P., & Segal, L. (1994, Summer). Gender as performance: An interview with Judith Butler. *Radical Philosophy, 67*, 32–39.

Byrne, B., Coventry, W. L., Olson, R. K., Samuelsson, S., Corley, R., Willcutt, E. G., . . . DeFries, J. C. (2009). Genetic and environmental influences on aspects of literacy and language in early childhood: Continuity and change from preschool to grade 2. *Journal of Neurolinguistics, 22*(3), 219–236. doi:10.1016/j.jneuroling.2008.09.003

Cacioppo, J. T., Cacioppo, S., & Cole, S. W. (2013). Social neuroscience and social genomics: The emergence of multi-level integrative analyses. *International Journal of Psychological Research, 6*, 1–6.

Calder, P. C. (2014). Very long chain omega-3 (n-3) fatty acids and human health. *European Journal of Lipid Science and Technology, 116*(10), 1280–1300.

Champagne, F. A. (2008). Epigenetic mechanisms and the transgenerational effects of mater-nal care. *Neuroendorinology, 29*(3), 386–397.

Champagne, F. A. (2012). Interplay between social experiences and the genome: Epigenetic consequences for behavior. In M. B. Sokolowski & S. F. Goodwin (Eds.), *Gene-Environ-ment Interplay* (Vol. 77, pp. 33–57). London: Academic Press.

Champagne, F. A. (2013a). Effects of stress across generations: Why sex matters. *Biological Psychiatry, 73*(1), 2–4. doi:10.1016/j.biopsych.2012.10.004

Champagne, F. A. (2013b). Epigenetics and developmental plasticity across species. *Develop-mental Psychobiology, 55*(1), 33–41. doi:10.1002/dev.21036

Chan, T. J. (2004). Towards a global educational justice research paradigm: Cognitive justice, decolonizing methodologies and critical pedagogy. *Globalisation, 2*(2), 191–213.

Chung, E., Cromby, J., Papadopoulos, D., & Tufarelli, C. (2016). Biosocial challenges and opportunities: Epigenetics and neuroscience. *Sociological Review Monographs, 64*(1), 168–185.

Coffield, F., Moseley, D., Hall, E., & Ecclestone, K. (2004). *Should We Be Using Learning Styles? What Research Has to Say to Practice*. London: Learning and Skills Development Agency.

Cohen Kadosh, R., Soskic, S., Iuculano, T., Kanai, R., & Walsh, V. (2010). Modulating neuronal activity produces specific and long-lasting changes in numerical competence. *Current Biology, 20*(22), 2016–2020. doi:https://doi.org/10.1016/j.cub.2010.10.007

Cole, S. W. (2014). Human social genomics. *PLOS Genetics, 10*(8), e1004601. doi:10.1371/journal.pgen.1004601

Cole, S. W., Conti, G., Arevalo, J. M. G., Ruggiero, A. M., Heckman, J. J., & Suomi, S. J. (2012). Transcriptional modulation of the developing immune system by early life social adversity. *Proceedings of the National Academy of Sciences of the United States of America, 109*(50), 20578–20583. doi:10.1073/pnas.1218253109

Coole, D., & Frost, S. (2010). Introducing the new materialisms. In D. Coole & S. Frost (Eds.), *New Materialisms: Ontology, Agency, and Politics* (pp. 1–45). London: Duke University Press.

Cooper, P. (2008). Like Alligators bobbing for poodles? A critical discussion of education, ADHD and the biopsychosocial perspective. *Journal of Philosophy of Education, 42*(3–4), 457–474.

CooperGenomics. (2018, March 1). *Genetic Testing for Every Step in the Family Planning Journey*. Retrieved from www.coopergenomics.com

Cortese, S., Faraone Stephen, V., & Sergeant, J. (2011). Misunderstandings of the genetics and neurobiology of ADHD: Moving beyond anachronisms. *American Journal of Medical Genetics Part B: Neuropsychiatric Genetics, 156*(5), 513–516. doi:10.1002/ajmg.b.31207

Cromby, J. (2015). *Feeling Bodies: Embodying Psychology*. London: Palgrave Macmillan.

Dagkas, S., & Burrows, L. (Eds.). (2016). *Families, Young People, Physical Activity and Health: Critical Perspectives*. London: Routledge.

Davies, B. (2003). *Shards of Glass: Children Reading and Writing beyond Gender Identities*. New York: Hampton.

De Pian, L., Evans, J., & Rich, E. (2014). Mediating biopower: Health education, social class and subjectivity. In K. Fitzpatrick & R. Tinning (Eds.), *Health Education: Critical Perspectives* (pp. 129–141). London: Routledge.

Dean, D. (Producer). (2016, December 4). *The Posthuman*. Retrieved from https://radio.abc.net.au/programitem/perQlbr5qD?play=true

Dedovic, K., Renwick, R., Mahani, N. K., Engert, V., Lupien, S. J., & Pruessner, J. C. (2005). The montreal imaging stress task: Using functional imaging to investigate the effects of perceiving and processing psychosocial stress in the human brain. *Journal of Psychiatry and Neuroscience, 30*(5), 319–325.

DeLanda, M. (2006). *A New Philosophy of Society: Assemblage Theory and Social Complexity*. London: Continuum.

Deleuze, G. (2006). *The Fold*. London: Continuum.

Deleuze, G., & Guattari, F. (1983). Rhizome. In G. Deleuze & F. Guattari (Eds.), *On the Line*. New York: Semiotext(e).

Deleuze, G., & Guattari, F. (2008). *A Thousand Plateaus*. London: Continuum.

Delgardo, R., & Stefancic, J. (2001). *Critical Race Theory: An Introduction*. New York: New York University Press.

Derrida, J. (1978). *On Writing and Difference*. London: Routledge.

Derrida, J. (1988). Signature event context. In J. Derrida (Ed.), *Limited Inc* (pp. 1–23). Elvanston: Northwestern University Press.

Dikker, S., Wan, L., Davidesco, I., Kaggen, L., Oostrik, M., McClintock, J., . . . Poeppel, D. (2017). Brain-to-brain synchrony tracks real-world dynamic group interactions in the classroom. *Current Biology, 27*(9), 1375–1380. doi:10.1016/j.cub.2017.04.002

Dillon, A., & Craven, D. G. (2014). Examining the genetic contribtion to ADHA. *Ethical Human Psychology and Psychiatry, 16*(1), 20–28. doi:http://dx.doi.org/10.1891/1559-4343.16.1.20

Duana, F. (2008). The biologistical construction of race: 'Admixture' technology and the new genetic medicine. *Social Studies of Science, 38*(5), 695–735. doi:10.1177/0306312708090796

Dunbar, R. I. M., Baron, R., Frangou, A., Pearce, E., van Leeuwen, E. J. C., Stow, J., . . . van Vugt, M. (2012). Social laughter is correlated with an elevated pain threshold. *Proceedings of the Royal Society of London B: Biological Sciences, 279*(1731), 1161–1167.

DuPraw, E. J. (1968). *Cell and Molecular Biology.* New York: Academic Press.

Duschinsky, R., Greco, M., & Solomon, J. (2015). The politics of attachment: Lines of flight with Bowlby, Deleuze and Guattari. *Theory, Culture & Society, 32*(7–8), 173–195. doi:10.1177/0263276415605577

Education Endowment Fund. (2016). *Teensleep.* Retrieved from https://educationendowmentfoundation.org.uk/projects-and-evaluation/projects/teensleep/

Edwards, R., Gillies, V., & Horsley, N. (2015). Brain science and early years policy: Hopeful ethos or 'cruel optimism'? *Critical Social Policy, 35*(2), 167–187.

Eicher, J. D., Powers, N. R., Miller, L. L., Mueller, K. L., Mascheretti, S., Marino, C., . . . Gruen, J. R. (2014). Characterization of the DYX2 locus on chromosome 6p22 with reading disability, language impairment, and IQ. *Human Genetics, 133*(7), 869–881. doi:10.1007/s00439-014-1427-3

Engerstrom, Y. (2009). Expansive learning: Towards an activity-theoretical reconceptualization. In K. Illeris (Ed.), *Contemporary Theories of Learning: Learning Theorists in Their Own Words* (pp. 53–73). London: Routledge.

Evans, J. (2014). Ideational border crossings: Rethinking the politics of knowledge within and across disciplines. *Discourse: Studies in the Cultural Politics of Education, 35*(1), 45–60. doi:10.1080/01596306.2012.739466

Evans, J., & Davies, B. (2015). Physical education, privatisation and social justice. *Sport, Education and Society, 20*(1), 1–9.

Evans, J., De Pian, L., Rich, E., & Davies, B. (2011). Health imperatives, policy and the corporeal device: Schools, subjectivity and children's health. *Policy Futures in Education, 9*(3), 328–340.

Exley, S. (2013). Making working class parents think more like middle-class parents: Choice advisers in English schools. *British Journal of Eduational Studies, 61*(3), 345–362.

Fagiolini, M., Jensen, C. L., & Champagne, F. A. (2009). Epigenetic influences on brain development and plasticity. *Current Opinion in Neurobiology, 19*(2), 207–212. doi:10.1016/j.conb.2009.05.009

Faraone, S. V., & Mick, E. (2010). Molecular genetics of attention deficit hyperactivity disorder. *Psychiatric Clinics of North America, 33*(1), 159–180. doi:https://doi.org/10.1016/j.psc.2009.12.004

Feinstein, L. (2003, Summer). Very early: How early can we predict future educational achievement. *Centre Piece,* 24–30.

Feldman, R., Zagoory-Sharon, O., Weisman, O., Schneiderman, I., Gordon, I., Maoz, R., . . . Ebstein, R. P. (2012). Sensitive parenting is associated with plasma oxytocin and polymorphisms in the OXTR and CD38 genes. *Biological Psychiatry, 72*(3), 175–181. doi:10.1016/j.biopsych.2011.12.025

Fielding, M., & Moss, P. (2010). *Radical Education and the Common School.* London: Routledge.

Fine, C. (2011). *Delusions of Sex: The Real Science behind Sex Differences.* London: Icon Books.

Fine, C. (2017). *Testosterone Rex: Uunmaking the Myth of Our Gendered Minds*. London: Icon Books.

Fine, C., & Jordan-Young, R. (2017). We've been labelled 'anti-sex difference' for demanding greater scientific rigour. *The Guardian*. Retrieved from www.theguardian.com/commentisfree/2016/apr/06/anti-sex-difference-scientific-rigour-gender-research-feminism

Fischer Kurt, W., Goswami, U., & Geake, J. (2010). The future of educational neuroscience. *Mind, Brain, and Education*, *4*(2), 68–80. doi:10.1111/j.1751-228X.2010.01086.x

Fisher, P. A., Beauchamp, K. G., Roos, L. E., Noll, L., Flannery, J., & Delker, B. C. (2016). The neurobiology of intervention and prevention in early adversity. *Annual Review of Clinical Psychology*, *12*, 331–357. doi:10.1146/annurev-clinpsy-032814-112855

Fitzgerald, D., Rose, N., & Singh, I. (2016). Living well in the neuropolis. *Sociological Review Monographs*, *64*(1), 221–237.

Foster, R. G., & Kreitzman, L. (2014). The rhythms of life: What your body clock means to you! *Experimental Physiology*, *99*(4). doi:10.1113/expphysiol.2012.071118

Foucault, M. (1990). *The History of Sexuality: An Introduction* (Vol. 1). London: Penguin.

Foucault, M. (1991). *Discipline and Punish: The Birth of the Prison*. London: Penguin.

Foucault, M. (2002). *The Order of Things*. London: Routledge.

Fox Keller, E. (2010). *The Mirage of a Space between Nature and Nurture*. Durham, NC: Duke University Press.

Franke, B., Faraone, S. V., Asherson, P., Buitelaar, J., Bau, C. H. D., Ramos-Quiroga, J. A., . . . Reif, A. (2012). The genetics of attention deficit/hyperactivity disorder in adults, a review. *Molecular Psychiatry*, *17*(10), 960–987. doi:10.1038/mp.2011.138

Franke, B., Neale, B. M., & Faraone, S. V. (2009). Genome-wide association studies in ADHD. *Human Genetics*, *126*(1), 13–50. doi:10.1007/s00439-009-0663-4

Franklin, S. (2007). *Dolly Mixtures: The Remaking of Genealogy*. London: Duke University Press.

Franklin, S. (2013). *Biological Relatives: IVF, Stem Cells, and the Future of Kinship*. London: Duke University Press.

Freire, P. (1970). *Pedagogy of the Oppressed*. New York: Herder & Herder.

Frost, S. (2016). *Biocultural Creatures: Towards a New Theory of the Human*. Durham, NC: Duke University Press.

Fullwiley, D. (2007). The molecularization of race: Institutionalizing human difference in pharmacogenetics practice. *Science as Culture*, *16*(1), 1–30. doi:10.1080/09505430601180847

Fullwiley, D. (2008). The biologistical construction of race: 'Admixture' technology and the new genetic medicine. *Social Studies of Science*, *38*(5), 695–735.

Fullwiley, D. (2015). Race, genes, power. *British Journal of Sociology*, *66*(1), 36–45.

Fuss, D. (1990). *Essentially Speaking: Feminism, Nature and Difference*. London: Routledge.

Gardener, H. (1993). *Multiple Intelligences: The Theory in Practice, a Reader*. New York: Basic Books.

Gardener, H. (2006). *Multiple Intelligences: New Horizons*. New York: Basic Books.

Gartler, S. M. (2006). The chromosome number in humans: A brief history. *Nature Reviews Genetics*, *7*(8), 655–660.

Gevers, D., Knight, R., Petrosino, J. F., Huang, K., McGuire, A. L., Birren, B. W., . . . Huttenhower, C. (2012). The human microbiome project: A community resource for the healthy human microbiome. *PLoS Biology*, *10*(8), e1001377. doi:10.1371/journal.pbio.1001377

Gillborn, D. (2008). *Racism and Education: Coincidence or Conspiracy?* London: Routledge.

Gillborn, D. (2010). The colour of numbers: Surveys, statistics and deficit-thinking about race and class. *Journal of Education Policy*, *25*(2), 253–276.

Gillborn, D. (2016). Softly, Softly: Genetics, intelligence and the hidden racism of the new genism. *Journal of Education Policy*. doi:10.1080/02680939.2016.1139189

Gillborn, D., & Youdell, D. (2000). *Rationing Education: Policy, Practice, Reform and Equity*. Buckingham: Open University Press.

Gillies, V. (2008). Childrearing, class and the new politics of parenting. *Compass*, *2*(3), 1079–1095.

Goldhill, O. (2016). The concept of different 'learning styles' is one of the greatest neuroscience myths. *Quartz*. Retrieved from https://qz.com/585143/the-concept-of-different-learning-styles-is-one-of-the-greatest-neuroscience-myths/

Gore, J., Griffiths, T., & Ladwig, J. (2004). Towards better teaching: Productive pedagogy as a framework for teacher education. *Teaching and Teacher Education*, *20*, 375–387.

Goswami, U. (2006). Neuroscience and education: From research to practice? *National Review of Neuroscience*, *7*(5), 406–411.

Goswami, U. (2014). The neural basis of dyslexia may originate in primary auditory cortex. *Brain*, *137*(12), 3100–3102. doi:10.1093/brain/awu296

Goswami, U. (2015). Sensory theories of developmental dyslexia: Three challenges for research. *National Review of Neuroscience*, *16*(1), 43–54.

Gov, H. (2016). *School Meals Healthy Eating Standards*. Retrieved from www.gov.uk/school-meals-healthy-eating-standards

Graham, L. (2010). Teaching ADHD? In L. Graham (Ed.), *(De)Constructing ADHD* (pp. 1–20). Oxford: Peter Lang.

Grande, S. (2004). *Red Pedagogy: Native American Social and Political Thought*. Maryland: Rowman and Littlefield.

Groeger, A. L., Cipollina, C., Cole, M. P., Woodcock, S. R., Bonacci, G., Rudolph, T. K., . . . Schopfer, F. J. (2010). Cyclooxygenase-2 generates anti-inflamatory mediators from omega-3 fatty acids. *Nature Chemical Biology*, *6*, 433–441.

Groeneveld, M. G., Vermeer, H. J., Linting, M., Noppe, G., van Rossum, E. F. C., & van Ijzendoorn, M. H. (2013). Children's hair cortisol as a biomarker of stress at school entry. *Stress-the International Journal on the Biology of Stress*, *16*(6), 711–715. doi:10.3109/10253890.2013.817553

Grosz, E. (1990). *Jacques Lacan: A feminist introduction*. London: Routledge.

Grosz, E. (1995). *Space, Time, and Perversion*. London: Routledge.

Gruber, R., Laviolette, R., Deluca, P., Monson, E., Cornish, K., & Carrier, J. (2010). Short sleep duration is associated with poor performance on IQ measures in healthy school-age children. *Sleep Medicine*, *11*(3), 289–294. doi:10.1016/j.sleep.2009.09.007

Gudsnuk, K., & Champagne, F. A. (2012). Epigenetic influence of stress and the social environment. *Ilar Journal*, *53*(3–4), 279–288. doi:10.1093/ilar.53.3-4.279

Gudsnuk, K. M. A., & Champagne, F. A. (2011). Epigenetic effects of early developmental experiences. *Clinics in Perinatology*, *38*(4), 703. doi:10.1016/j.clp.2011.08.005

Gulson, K. N., & Webb, P. T. (2016). Emerging biological rationalities for policy: (Molecular) biopolitics and the new authorities in education. In Parker Stephan, Kalervo N. Gulson & Gale Trevor (Eds.), *Policy and Inequality in Education*. Dordrecht: Springer.

Gulson, K. N., & Webb, P. T. (2017). 'Life' and education policy: Intervention, augmentation and computation. *Discourse: Studies in the Cultural Politics of Education*, 1–16. doi:10.1080/01596306.2017.1396729

Hallam, S., Ireson, J., & Davies, J. (2013). *Effective Pupil Grouping in the Primary School*. London: Routledge.

Hamalainen, J. A., Rupp, A., Soltesz, F., Szucs, D., & Goswami, U. (2012). Reduced phase locking to slow amplitude modulation in adults with dyslexia: An MEG study. *NeuroImage*, *1*(59), 2952–2961. doi:10.1016/j.neuroimage.2011.09.075

Haraway, D. (2008). *When Species Meet*. Minniapolis: University of Minnesota Press.

Harding, S. (1986). *The Science Question in Feminism*. Ithaca: Cornell University Press.

Harwood, V., & Allan, J. (2014). *Psychopathology at School: Theorising Mental Disorders in Education*. London: Routledge.

Harwood, V., Hickey-Moody, A., McMahon, S., & O'Shea, S. (2017). *The Politics of Widening Participation: Making Educational Futures*. Oxford: Routledge.

Hattie, J. A. C. (2009). *Visible Learning: A Synthesis of over 800 Meta-Analyses Relating to Learning*. London: Routledge.

Hayashi-Takanaka, Y., Yamagata, K., Wakayama, T., Stasevich, T. J., Kainuma, T., Tsurimoto, T., . . . Kimura, H. (2011). Tracking epigenetic histone modifications in single cells using fab-based live endogenous modification labeling. *Nucleic Acids Research, 39*(15), 6475–6488. doi:10.1093/nar/gkr343

Hayes, D. (2018). New research shows what makes a difference in teaching literacy and why 'evidence-based' is not enough. *EduResearch Matters: A Voice for Australian Educational Researchers*. Retrieved from www.aare.edu.au/blog/?p=2749

Heaney, L. M. (2016). *Exhaled Breath Analysis in Exercise and Health*. (Doctor of Philosophy). Loughborough University, Loughborough.

Heaney, L. M., Ruskiewicz, D. M., Arthur, K. L., Hadjithekli, A., Aldcroft, C. L., Lindley, M. R., . . . Reynolds, J. C. (2016). Real-time monitoring of exhaled volatiles using atmospheric pressure chemical ionization on a compact mass spectrometer. *Bioanalysis, 8*(13), 1325–1336.

Heatherton, T. F. (2011). Neuroscience of self and self-regulation. *Annual Review of Psychology, 62*, 363–390. doi:10.1146/annurev.psych.121208.131616

Henriques, J., Holloway, W., Urwin, C., Venn, C., & Walkerdine, V. (1998). *Changing the Subject: Psychology, Social Regulation and Subjectivity*. London: Routledge.

Herold, B. (2017). The case(s) against personalized learning. *Education Week*. Retrieved from www.edweek.org/ew/articles/2017/11/08/the-cases-against-personalized-learning.html

Hertzman, C. (2013). The significance of early childhood adversity. *Paediatrics & Child Health, 18*(3), 127–128.

Hickey-Moody, A. (2009). *Unimaginable Bodies: Intellectual Disability, Performance and Becomings*. Rotterdam: Sense.

Hickey-Moody, A. (2013). *Youth Arts and Education: Reassembling Subjectivity through Affect*. New York: Routledge.

Hickey-Moody, A. (2014). Affect as method: Feelings, aesthetics, and affective pedagogy. In R. Coleman & J. Ringrose (Eds.), *Deleuze and Research Methodologies* (pp. 79–95). Edinburgh: Edinburgh University Press.

Hickey-Moody, A., & Malins, P. (2007). *Deleuzian Encounters: Studies in Contemporary Social Issues*. Basingstoke: Palgrave Macmillan.

Hill, C. M., Hogan, A. M., & Karmiloff-Smith, A. (2007). To sleep, perchance to enrich learning. *Archives of Disease in Childhood, 92*, 637–643. doi:10.1136/adc.2006.096156

Hodgson, P. (1944). *The Cloud of Unknowing and the Book of Privy Counselling*. Oxford: Oxford University Press.

Hogenboom, M. (2014). Warning over electrical brain stimulation. *BBC News*. Retrieved from www.bbc.co.uk/news/health-27343047

Hoogman, M., Bralten, J., Hibar, D. P., Mennes, M., Zwiers, M. P., Schweren, L. S. J., . . . Franke, B. (2017). Subcortical brain volume differences in participants with attention deficit hyperactivity disorder in children and adults: a cross-sectional mega-analysis. *The Lancet Psychiatry, 4*(4), 310–319. doi:10.1016/S2215-0366(17)30049-4.

Hoogman, M., Bralten, J., Mennes, M., Zwiers, M., Van Hulzen, K., Schweren, L., . . . Franke, B. (2015). P. 1.b.020 subcortical volumes across the life span in ADHD: An ENIGMA collaboration. *European Neuropsychopharmacology, 25*(Supplement 2), S189. doi:https://doi.org/10.1016/S0924-977X(15)30184-X

Howard-Jones, P.A. (2014). Neuroscience and education: Myths and messages. *Nature Reviews Neuroscience, 15*, 817–824. doi:10.1038/nrn3817

Hruby, G., & Goswami, U. (2011). Neuroscience and reading: A review for reading education researchers. *Reading Research Quarterly, 46*(2), 156–172.

Hughes, D. A., & Baylin, J. (2012). *Brain-Based Parenting: The Neuroscience of Caregiving for Healthy Attachment*. London: W.W. Norton & Co.

Hughes, N., & Strong, G. (2016). Implementing the evidence on young adult neuromaturation: the development of a specialist approach in probation services. *Probation Journal, 63*(4), 452–459. doi:10.1177/0264550516648398.

Igarashi, M., Santos, R. A., & Cohen-Cory, S. (2015). Impact of maternal n-3 polyunsaturated fatty acid deficiency on dendritic arbor morphology and connectivity of developing xenopus laevis central neurons in vivo. *The Journal of Neuroscience, 35*(15), 6079–6092. doi:10.1523/JNEUROSCI.4102-14.2015

Illeris, K. (Ed.). (2009). *Contemporary Theories of Learning: Learning Theorists in Their Own Words*. London: Routledge.

International Food Policy Research Institute. (2014). *Global Nutrition Report 2014: Actions and Accountability to Accelerate the World's Progress on Nutrition*. Washington DC: International Food Policy Research Institute.

International Human Genome Sequencing Consortium. (2004). Finishing the euchromatic sequence of the human genome. *Nature, 431*, 931. doi:10.1038/nature03001. www.nature.com/articles/nature03001#supplementary-information

Ivinson, G. (2012). The body and pedagogy: Beyond absent, moving bodies in pedagogic practice. *British Journal of Sociology of Education, 33*(4), 489–506. doi:10.1080/01425692.2012.662822

Jackson, M. C., Morgan, H. M., Shapiro, K. L., Mohr, H., & Lindon, D. E. J. (2011). Strategic resource allocation in the human brain supports cognitive coordination of object and spatial working memory. Human Brain Mapping, 32, 1330–1348.

Jackson, P. A., Deary, M. E., Reay, J. L., Scholey, A. B., & Kennedy, D. O. (2012). No effect of 12 weeks' supplementation with 1 g DHA-rich or EPA-rich fish oil on cognitive function or mood in healthy young adults aged 18–35 years. *The British Journal of Nutrition, 107*(8), 1232. doi:10.1017/S000711451100403X

Jakel, S., & Dimou, L. (2017). Glial cells and their functions in the adult brain: A journey through the history of their ablation. *Frontiers in Cellular Neuroscience, 11*(24). doi:10.3389/fncel.2017.00024

James, M., Black, P., Carmichael, P., Conner, C., Dudley, P., Fox, A., . . . Wiliam, D. (2006). *Learning How to Learn: Tools for Schools*. Abingdon: Routledge.

James, M., & Pollard, A. (Eds.). (2012). *Principles for Effective Pedagogy: InternationalResponses to Evidence from the UK Teaching and Learning Research Programme*. Abingdon: Routledge.

Jerrim, J., Vignoles, A., Lingam, R., & Friend, A. The socio-economic gradient in children's reading skills and the role of genetics. *British Educational Research Journal, 41*(1), 6–29. doi:10.1002/berj.3143

Johnston, S., Linden, D. E. J., & Shapiro, K. L. (2011). Functional imaging reveals working memory and attention interact to produce the attentional blink. *Journal of Cognitive Neuroscience, 24*, 28–38.

Keenan, J. M., Betjemann, R. S., Wadsworth, S. J., DeFries, J. C., & Olson, R. K. (2006). Genetic and environmental influences on reading and listening comprehension. *Journal of Research in Reading, 29*(1), 75–91. doi:10.1111/j.1467-9817.2006.00293.x

Kelley, P., Slockley, S. W., Foster, R. G., & Kelley, J. (2015). Synchronizing educaiton to adolescent biology: 'let teens sleep, start school later'. *Learning, Media and Technology, 40*(2), 210–226. doi:http://dx.doi.org/10.1080/17439884.2014.942666

Kenney, M., & Müller, R. (2016). Of rats and women: Narratives of motherhood in environmental epigenetics. *BioSocieties*, 1–24. doi:10.1057/s41292-016-0002-7

Kenway, J., & Youdell, D. (2011). Emotional geographies of education: Beginning a conversation. *Emotion, Space and Society*, 4, 131–136.

Khalsa, S., Hale, J. R., Goldstone, A., Wilson, R. S., Mayhew, S. D., Bagary, M., & Bagshaw, A. P. (2017). Habitual sleep durations and subjective sleep quality predict white matter differences in the human brain. *Neurobiology Sleep Circadian Rhythms*, 3, 17–25.

Khalsa, S., Mayhew, S. D., Przezdzik, I., Wilson, R. S., Hale, J. R., Goldstone, A., . . . Bagshaw, A. P. (2016). Variability in cumulative habitual sleep duration predicts waking functional connectivity. *Sleep*, 39(1), 97–105.

Kirby, A., Woodward, A., & Jackson, S. (2010a). Benefits of omega-3 supplementation for schoolchildren: Review of the current evidence. *British Educational Research Journal*, 36(5), 699–732. doi:10.1080/01411920903111557

Kirby, A., Woodward, A., Jackson, S., Wang, Y., & Crawford, M. A. (2010b). A double-blind, placebo-controlled study investigating the effects of omega-3 supplementation in children aged 8–10 years from a mainstream school population. *Research in Developmental Disabilities: A Multidisciplinary Journal*, 31(3), 718–730. doi:10.1016/j.ridd.2010.01.014

Kirby, A., Woodward, A., Jackson, S., Wang, Y., & Crawford, M. A. (2010c). Childrens' learning and behaviour and the association with cheek cell polyunsaturated fatty acid levels. *Research in Developmental Disabilities*, 31(3), 731–742. doi:10.1016/j.ridd.2010.01.015

Klein, M., Onnink, M., van Donkelaar, M., Wolfers, T., Harich, B., Shi, Y., . . . Franke, B. (2017). Brain imaging genetics in ADHD and beyond – Mapping pathways from gene to disorder at different levels of complexity. *Neuroscience & Biobehavioral Reviews*, 80(Supplement C), 115–155. doi:https://doi.org/10.1016/j.neubiorev.2017.01.013

Knutson, K. L., Spiegel, K., Penev, P., & Van Cauter, E. (2007). The metabolic consequences of sleep deprivation. *Sleep Medicine Reviews*, 11(3), 163–178. doi:10.1016/j.smrv.2007.01.002

Kok, R., Thijssen, S., Bakernnans-Kranenburg, M. J., Jaddoe, V. W. V., Verhulst, F. C., White, T., . . . Tiemeier, H. (2015). Normal variation in early parental sensitivity predicts child structural brain development. *Journal of the American Academy of Child and Adolescent Psychiatry*, 54(10), 824–831. doi:10.1016/j.jaac.2015.07.009

Kraftl, P. (2013). Beyond 'voice', beyond 'agency', beyond 'politics'? Hybrid childhoods and some critical reflections on children's emottional geographies. *Emotion, Space and Society*, 9, 13–23. doi:http://dx.doi.org/10.1016/j.emospa.2013.01.004

Kraftl, P. (2015). *Geographies of Alternative Education: Diverse Learning Spaces for Children and Young People*. Bristol: Policy Press.

Kringelbach, M. L., & Berridge, K. C. (2010). The neuroscience of happiness and pleasure. *Social Research*, 77(2), 659–678.

Kumar, A., Mastana, S. S., & Lindley, M. R. (2016). N-3 fatty acids and asthma. *Nutrition Research Reviews*, 29(1), 1–16.

Kuppen, S. E. A., & Goswami, U. (2016). Developmental trajectories for children with dyslexia and low IQ poor readers. *Developmental Psychology*, 52(5), 717. doi:10.1037/a0040207

Kuppen, S., Huss, M., & Goswami, U. (2014). A longitudinal study of basic auditory processing and phonological skills in children with low IQ. *Applied Psycholinguistics*, 35(6), 1109–1141. doi:10.1017/S0142716412000719

Kuyken, W., Weare, K., Ukoumunne, O. C., Vicary, R., Motton, N., Burnett, R., . . . Huppert, F. (2013). Effectiveness of the mindfulness in schools programme: Non-randomised controlled feasibility study. *British Journal of Psychiatry*, 203(2), 126–131. doi:10.1192/bjp.bp.113.126649

Kyle, F., Kujala, J. V., Richardson, U., Lyytinen, H., & Goswami, U. (2013). Assessing the effectiveness of two theoretically motivated computer-assisted reading interventions in the United Kingdom: GG Rime and GG Phoneme. *Reading Research Quarterly, 48*(1), 61–76.

Leahy, D. (2009). Disgusting pedagogies. In V. Wright & V. Harwood (Eds.), *Biopolitics and the 'Obesity Epidemic': Governing Bodies* (pp. 172–182). London: Routledge.

LeDoux, J. (2003). *The Synaptic Self: How Our Brains Become Who We Are*. London: Penguin.

Lee, S. S., Chronis-Tuscano, A., Keenan, K., Pelham, W. E., Loney, J., Van Hulle, C. A., . . . Lahey, B. B. (2010). Association of maternal dopamine transporter genotype with negative parenting: Evidence for gene x environment interaction with child disruptive behavior. *Molecular Psychiatry, 15*(5), 548. doi:10.1038/mp.2008.102

Lee, Y-Y., & Hsieh, S. (2014). Classifying different emotional states by means of EEG-based functional connectivity patterns. *PloS one, 9*(4), e95415. doi:10.1371/journal.pone.0095415

Leger, M., Quiedeville, A., Bouet, V., Haelewyn, B., Boulouard, M., Schumann-Bard, P., & Freret, T. (2013). Object recognitionest in mice. *Nature Protocols, 8, 12*, 2531–2537. doi:10.1038/nprot.2013.155

Lenz Taguchi, H., Gerholm, T., Bodén, L., Frankenberg, S., Kjällander, S., Kallionen, P., . . . Tonér, S. (n/d). Challenging the ideas of applying scientific facts and achieving reciprocity in an educational neuroscience RCT study in early childhood education. *Journal of Child Development*, in review.

Lens Taguchi, H. (2018). Retrieved from www.buv.su.se/english/research/research-areas/learning-brain-practice-1.197236, www.buv.su.se/english/research/research-projects/early-childhood-education/enhancing-preschool-children-s-attention-language-and-communication-skills-1.209094

Leonardo, Z. (2005). *Critical Race Pedagogy*. Oxford: Blackwell.

Li, Z., Chang, S. H., Zhang, L. Y., Gao, L., & Wang, J. (2014). Molecular genetic studies of ADHD and its candidate genes: A review. *Psychiatry Research, 219*(1), 10–24. doi:10.1016/j.psychres.2014.05.005

Lindley, M. R., & Youdell, D. (2016). The absent body: Bio-social encounters with the effects of physical activity on the wellbeing of children and young people In S. Dagkas & L. Burrows (Eds.), *Families, Young People, Physical Activity and Health: Critical Perspectives* (pp. 13–28). London: Routledge.

Lingard, B. (2014). *Politics, Policies and Pedagogies in Education: Selected Works of Bob Lingard*. Oxon: Routledge.

Lingard, B., Ladwig, J., Mills, M., Bahr, M., Chant, D., Warry, M., . . . Luke, A. (2001). *The Queensland School Reform Longitudinal Study Vol. 1 and 2*. Retrieved from Brisbane.

Lock, M. (2015). Comprehending the body in the era of the epigenome. *Current Anthropology, 56*(2), 151–177. doi:10.1086/680350

Logan, J., Petrill, S. A., Flax, J., Justice, L. M., Hou, L., Bassett, A. S., . . . Bartlett, C. W. (2011). Genetic covariation underlying reading, language and related measures in a sample selected for specific language impairment. *Behavior Genetics, 41*(5), 651. doi:10.1007/s10519-010-9435-0

Lucassen, N., Kok, R., Bakermans-Kranenburg Marian, J., Van Ijzendoorn Marinus, H., Jaddoe Vincent, W. V., Hofman, A., . . . Tiemeier, H. (2015). Executive functions in early childhood: The role of maternal and paternal parenting practices. *British Journal of Developmental Psychology, 33*(4), 489–505. doi:10.1111/bjdp.12112

Luijk, M. P. C. M., Linting, M., Henrichs, J., Herba, C. M., Verhage, M. L., Schenk, J. J., . . . van Ijzendoorn, M. H. (2015). Hours in non-parental child care are related to language development in a longitudinal cohort study. *Child Care Health and Development, 41*(6), 1188–1198. doi:10.1111/cch.12238

Lyotard, J. (1984). *The Postmodern Condition: A Report in Knowledge*. Minnesota: University of Minnisota Press.

Malabou, C. (2009). *Changing Difference*. Cambridge: Polity.

Mankad, D., Dupuis, A., Smile, S., Roberts, W., Brian, J., Lui, T., . . . Anagnostou, E. (2015). A randomized, placebo controlled trial of omega-3 fatty acids in the treatment of young children with autism. *Molecular Autism, 6*(1), 18.

Margery, K. (1990). *The Book of Margery Kempe*. London: Penguin.

Margulis, L. (1998). *Symbiotic Planet*. New York: Basic Books.

Marmot, M. (2010). *Fair Society, Healthy Lives: The Marmot Review: Strategic Review of Health Inequalities in England Post-2010*. Retrieved from www.parliament.uk/documents/fair-society-healthy-lives-full-report.pdf

May, T. (2016, October 5). Teresa May's keynote speech at Tory conference. *Independent*. Retrieved from www.independent.co.uk/news/uk/politics/theresa-may-speech-tory-conference-2016-in-full-transcript-a7346171.html

Mayes, E. (2013). Negotiating the hidden curriculum: Power and affect in negotiated classrooms. *English in Australia, 48*(3), 62–71.

McGimpsey, I., Bradbury, A., & Santori, D. (2017). Revisions to rationality: The translation of 'new knowledges' into policy under the coalition government. *British Journal of Sociology of Education, 38*(6), 908–925. doi:10.1080/01425692.2016.1202747

Meloni, M. (2014). The social brain meets the reactive genome: Neuroscience, epigenetics and the new social biology. *Fontiers in Human Neuroscience, 8*, 1–12. doi:10.3389/fnhum.2014.00309

Meloni, M. (2015). Epigenetics for the social sciences: Justice, embodiment and inheritance in the postgenomic age. *New Genetics and Society, 34*(2), 125–151. doi:10.1080/1463677 8.2015.1034850

Meloni, M. (2016). *Political Biology: Science and Social Value in Human Heredity from Eugenics to Epigenetics*. Basingstoke: Palgrave Macmillan.

Meloni, M., Williams, S., & Martin, P. (2016). The biosocial: Sociological themes and issues. *The Sociological Review Monographs, 64*(1), 7–25. doi:10.1111/2059-7932.12010

Mendenhall, R., Henderson, L., Scott, B., Butler, L., Turi, K. N., Mallett, L., & Wren, B. (n/d). *Involving Urban Single Low-Income African American Mothers in Genomic Research: Giving Voice to How Place Matters in Health Disparities and Prevention Strategies*. Urbana-Champaign: University of Illinois.

Metzl, J. (2016). By the year 2040, embryo selection could replace sex as the way nost of us make babies. *Quartz*. Retrieved from https://qz.com/677335/by-the-year-2040-embryo-selection-will-replace-sex-as-the-way-most-of-us-make-babies/

Mickleborough, T. D., & Lindley, M. R. (2013). Omega-3 fatty acids: A potential future treatment for asthma? *Expert Review of Respiratory Medicine, 7*(6), 577–780.

Mileva-Seitz, V. R., Bakermans-Kranenburg, M. J., & van Ijzendoorn, M. H. (2016). Genetic mechanisms of parenting. *Hormones and Behavior, 77*, 211–223. doi:10.1016/j.yhbeh.2015.06.003

Miller, G. A., Crocker, L. D., Spielberg, J. M., Infantolino, Z. P., & Heller, W. (2013). Issues in localization of brain function: The case of lateralized frontal cortex in cognition, emotion, and psychopathology. *Frontiers in Integrative Neuroscience, 7*, 2. doi:10.3389/fnint.2013.00002

Mills, M., Goos, M., Keddie, A., Honan, E., Pendergast, D., Gilbert, R., . . . Wright, T. (2009). Productive pedagogies: A redefined methodology for analysing quality teacher practice. *Australian Educational Researcher, 36*(3).

Molfese, D. L. (2011). Advancing neuroscience through epigenetics: Molecular mechanisms of learning and memory. *Developmental Neuropsychology, 36*(7), 810–827. doi:10.1080/87 565641.2011.606395

Moore, A. (2004). *The Good Teacher: Dominant Discourses in Teaching and Teacher Education.* London: Routledge.

Moore, D. S. (2015). *The Developing Genome: An Introduction to Behavioural Epigenetics.* Oxford: Oxford University Press.

Morley, L. (1998). All you need is love: Feminist pedagogy for empowerment and emotional labour in the academy. *International Journal of Inclusive Education, 2*(1), 15–27. doi:10.1080/1360311980020102

Muscatell, K. A., Dedovik, K., Slavich, G. M., Jarcho, M. R., Breen, E. C., & Bower, J. (2016). Neural mechanisms linking social status and inflammatory response. *Social Cognition and Affective Neuroscience, 11*(6), 915–922. doi:10.1093/scan/nsw025

Newton, P. M. (2015). The learning styles myth is thriving in higher education. *Frontiers in Psychology, 6,* 1908.

Ngun, T. C., Ghahramani, N., Sanchez, F. J., Bocknadt, S., & Vilain, E. (2011). The genetics of sex differences in brain and behavior. *Frontiers in Neuroendicrinology, 32*(2), 227–246. doi:10.1016/j.yfrne.2010.10.001

Noble, K. G., Houston, S. M., Brito, N. H., Bartsch, H., Kan, E., Kuperman, J. M., . . . Sowell, E. R. (2015). Family income, parental education and brain structure in children and adolescents. *Nature Neuroscience, 18*(5), 773–778. doi:10.1038/nn.3983. www.nature.com/neuro/journal/v18/n5/abs/nn.3983.html#supplementary-information

Osborne, T., & Jones, P. I. (2017). Biosensing and geography: A mixed methods approach. *Applied Geography, 87,* 160–169. doi:https://doi.org/10.1016/j.apgeog.2017.08.006

Pangelinan, M. M., Zhang, G., VanMeter, J. W., Clark, J. E., Hatfield, B. D., & Haufler, A. J. (2011). Beyond age and gender: Relationships between cortical and subcortical brain volume and cognitive-motor abilities in school-age children. *NeuroImage, 54*(4), 3093–3100. doi:https://doi.org/10.1016/j.neuroimage.2010.11.021

Pappa, I., Mileva-Seitz, V. R., Bakermans-Kranenburg, M. J., Tiemeier, H., & van Ijzendoorn, M. H. (2015). The magnificent seven: A quantitative review of dopamine receptor d4 and its association with child behavior. *Neuroscience and Biobehavioral Reviews, 57,* 175–186. doi:10.1016/j.neubiorev.2015.08.009

Pashler, H., McDaniel, M., Rohrer, D., & Bjork, R. (2008). Learning styles: Concepts and evidence. *Psychological Science in the Public Interest, 9*(3), 103–119.

Pernu, T. K. (2011). Minding matter: How not to argue for the causal efficacy of the mental. *Reviews in Neuroscience, 22*(5), 483–507. doi:10.1515/RNS.2011.043.

Pernu, T. K. (2013). *Interactions and Exclusions: Studies on Causal Explanation in Naturalistic Philosophy of Mind.* (PhD). Helsinki University, Helsinki.

Pflughoeft, K. J., & Versalovic, J. (2012). Human microbiome in health and disease. *Annual Review of Pathology: Mechanisms of Disease, 7*(1), 99–122. doi:10.1146/annurev-pathol-011811-132421

Pickersgill, M. (2016). Epistemic modesty, ostentatiousness and uncertainties of epigenetics: On the knowledge machinary of (social) science. *Sociological Review Monographs, 64*(1), 108–202.

Plak, R. D., Merkelbach, I., Kegel, C. A. T., van Ijzendoorn, M. H., & Bus, A. G. (2016). Brief computer interventions enhance emergent academic skills in susceptible children: A gene-by-environment experiment. *Learning and Instruction, 45,* 1–8. doi:https://doi.org/10.1016/j.learninstruc.2016.06.002

Plomin, R., & Deary, I. J. (2015). Genetics and intelligence differences: Five special findings. *Molecular Psychiatry, 20*(1), 98–107. doi:10.1038/mp.2014.105

Pollard, A., Collins, C., Maddock, M., Simco, N., Swaffield, S., Warin, J., & Warwick, P. (2005). *Reflective Teaching 2nd Edition.* London: Continnum.

Prain, V., Cox, P., Deed, C., Dorman, J., Edwards, D., Farrelly, C., . . . Yager, Z. (2013). Personalised learning: Lessons to be learnt. *British Educational Research Journal, 39*(4), 654–676. doi:10.1080/01411926.2012.669747

Rasmussen, M. L. (2009). Beyond gender identity. *Gender and Education, 21*(4), 431–477.

Reynolds, J. C., Turner, M. A., Carr, P., Lindley, M. R., & Creaser, C. (forthcoming). Direct analysis of volotile organic compounds in foods using compact mass spectrometry. *Rapid Communications in Mass Spectrometry*.

Rich, E., Evans, J., & De Pian, L. (2011). Chidren's bodies, surveillance and the obesity crisis. In E. Rich, L. F. Monaghan, & L. Aphramore (Eds.), *Debating Obesity: Critical Perspectives* (pp. 139–163). Basingstoke: Palgrace Macmillan.

Roberts, C. (2013). Evolutionary psychology, feminism and early sexual development. *Feminist Theory, 14*(3), 295–304.

Roberts, C. (2015). *Puberty in Crisis: The Sociology of Early Sexual Development*. Cambridge: Cambridge University Press.

Romens, S. E., McDonald, J. S., & Pollak, S. D. (2015). Associations between early life stress and gene methylation in children. *Child Development, 86*(1), 303–309. doi:10.1111/cdev.122270

Rose, N. (2000). Government and control. *British Journal of Criminology, 40*, 321–339.

Rose, N. (2013). The human sciences in a biological age. *Theory, Culture and Society, 30*(3), 3–34.

Rose, N., & Abi-Rached, J. M. (2013). *Neuro: The New Brain Sciences and the Managment of the Mind*. Oxford: Princeton University Press.

Rose, S., & Rose, H. (2013). *Genes, Cells and Brains: The Promethean Promise of the New Biology*. London: Verso.

Rosen, M. (2017). Our children's education has been wrecked by Sats. Time to say no more. *The Guardian*. Retrieved from www.theguardian.com/education/2017/jul/13/our-childrens-education-has-been-wrecked-by-sats-time-to-say-no-more

Rotimi, C. N. (2004). Are medical and nonmedical uses of large-scale genomic markers conflating genetics and 'race'? *Nature Genetics Supplement, 36*(11), 37–43. doi:10.1038/ng1439

Said, E. (1997). *Covering Islam: How the Media and the Experts Determine How We See the Rest of the World*. New York: Vintage.

Said, E. (2003). *Orientalism*. London: Penguin.

Save the Children. (2016). *Lighting Up Young Brains: How Parents Carers and Nurseries Support Brain Development in the First Five Years*. Retrieved from London.

Schneider, G. W., & Winslow, R. (2014). Parts and wholes: The human microbiome, ecological ontology, and the challenges of community. *Perspectives in Biology and Medicine, 57*(2), 208–223. doi:https://doi.org/10.1353/pbm.2014.0016

Schuch, V., Utsumi, D. A., Costa, T. V. M. M., Kulikowski, L. D., & Muszkat, M. (2015). Attention deficit hyperactivity disorder in the light of the epigenetic paradigm. *Frontiers in Psychiatry, 6*, 126. doi:10.3389/fpsyt.2015.00126

Scott, B. H., Semple, M. N., & Malone, B. J. (2010). Temporal codes for amplitude contrast in auditory cortex. *Neuroscience, 30*(2), 767–784. doi:10.1523/JNEUROSCI.4170-09.2010

Sellar, S., & Lingard, B. (2014). The OECD and the expansion of PISA: New global modes of governance in education. *British Educational Research Journal, 40*(6), 917–936. doi:10.1002/berj.3120

Selzam, S., Krapohl, E., von Stumm, S., O'Reilly, P. F., Rimfeld, K., Kovas, Y., . . . Plomin, R. (2016). Predicting educational achievement from DNA. *Mol Psychiatry*. doi:10.1038/mp.2016.107

Sheed, F. J. (1978). *The Confessions of Saint Augustine*. London: Sheed and Ward.

Shei, R. J., Lindley, M. R., & Mickelborough, T. (2014). Omega-3 polyunsaturated fatty acids in the optimization of physical performance. *MIlitary Medicine, 179*(11), 144–156.

Shipman, P. (2002). *The Evolution of Racism: Human Differences and the Use and Abuse of Science*. Cambridge, MA: Harvard University Press.

Slee, R. (2011). *The Regular School*. London: Routledge.

Sparkes, A. C. (2013). Qualitative research in sport, exercise and health in the era of neoliberalism, audit and new public management: Understanding the conditions for the (im)possibilities of a new paradigm dialogue. *Qualitative Research in Sport, Exercise and Health, 5*(3), 440–459. doi:10.1080/2159676X.2013.796493

Spinoza, B. (1996). *Ethics*. London: Penguin.

Stolz, S. A. (2015). Embodied learning. *Educational Philosophy and Theory, 47*(5), 474–487. doi:10.1080/00131857.2013.879694

Swaffield, S. (Ed.). (2008). *Unlocking Assessment: Understanding for Reflection and Application*. Abbingdon: Routledge.

Tammam, J., Steinsaltz, D., Bester, D. W., Semb-Andenaes, T., & Stein, J. F. (2015). A randomised double-blind placebo-controlled trial investigating the behavioural effects of vitamin, mineral and n-3 fatty acid supplementation in typically developing adolescent schoolchildren. *British Journal of Nutrition, 115*, 361–373.

Tanaka, K., Farooqui, A. A., Siddiqi, N. J., Alhomida, A. S., & Ong, W-Y. (2012). Effects of docosahexaenoic acid on neurotransmission. *Biomolecules & Therapeutics, 20*(2), 152–157. doi:10.4062/biomolther.2012.20.2.152

Teague, L. (2015). *Pegagogy, Subjectivity and Counter Politics in the Primary School: An Ethnography of a Teacher's Practices*. (Doctor of Philosophy). UCL Instittute of Education, London.

Teague, L. (2017). The curriculum as a site of counter politics: Theorising the 'domain of the sayable'. *British Journal of Sociology of Education*, 1–15. doi:10.1080/01425692.2017.1304814

Thapar, A., Cooper, M., Eyre, O., & Langley, K. (2013). Practitioner Review: What have we learnt about the causes of ADHD? Journal of child psychology and psychiatry, and allied disciplines, 54(1), 3-16. doi:10.1111/j.1469-7610.2012.02611.x

Thomas, G. (2016). After the gold rush: Questioning the 'Gold Standard' and reappraising the status of experiment and randomized controlled trials in education. *Harvard Educational Review, 86*(3), 390–411. doi:10.17763/1943-5045-86.3.390

Thompson, G. (2016). Computer adaptive testing, big data, algorithmic approaches to education. *British Journal of Sociology of Education, 36*(3), 398–408. doi:10.1080/01425692.2016.1158640

Time4Learning. (n/d). *Teaching to Kids' Learning Styles*. Retrieved from www.time4learning.com/learning-styles.shtml

Timimi, S. (2004). A critique of the international consensus statement on ADHD. *Clinical Child and Family Psychology Review, 7*(1), 59–63. doi:10.1023/B:CCFP.0000020192.49298.7a

Tjio Joe, H. I. N., & Levan, A. (1958/2010). The chromosome number of man. *Hereditas, 42*(1–2), 1–6. doi:10.1111/j.1601-5223.1956.tb03010.x

Tognini, P., Napoli, D., & Pizzorusso, T. (2015). Dynamic DNA methylation in the brain: A new epigenetic mark for experience-dependent plasticity. *Frontiers in Cellular Neuroscience, 9*. doi:10.3389/fncel.2015.00331

Trabzuni, D., Ramasamy, A., Imran, S., Walker, R., Smith, C., Weale, M. E., . . . North American Brain Expression Consortium. (2013). Widespread sex differences in gene expression and splicing in the adult human brain. *Nature Communications, 4*, 2771. doi:10.1038/ncomms3771, www.nature.com/articles/ncomms3771#supplementary-information

Turner, M. A., Bandelow, S., Edwards, L., Patel, P., Martin, H. J., Wilson, I. D., & Thomas, C. L. (2013). The effect of a paced auditory serial addition test (PASAT) intervention on the profile of volatile organic compounds in human breath: A pilot study. *Journal of Breath Research, 7*, 017102.

van Ijzendoorn, M. H., Bakermans-Kranenburg, M. J., & Ebstein, R. P. (2011). Methylation matters in child development: Toward developmental behavioral epigenetics. *Child Development Perspectives, 5*(4), 305–310. doi:10.1111/j.1750-8606.2011.00202.x

Vasich, T. (2015). Brain development suffers from lack of fish oil fatty acids, UCI study finds. *UCI News*. Retrieved from https://news.uci.edu/2015/04/15/brain-development-suffers-from-lack-of-fish-oil-fatty-acids-uci-study-finds/

Walker, S. C., & McGlone, F. P. (2013). The social brain: Neurobiological basis of affiliative behaviours and psychological well-being. *Neuropeptides, 47*(6), 379–393. doi:10.1016/j.npep.2013.10.008

Wastell, D., & White, S. (2012). Blinded by neuroscience: Social policy, the family and the infant brain. *Families, Relationships and Societies, 1*(3), 397–414.

Weale, S. (2017). More primary school children suffering stress from Sats, survey finds. *The Guardian*. Retrieved from www.theguardian.com/education/2017/may/01/sats-primary-school-children-suffering-stress-exam-time

Webb, T. (2013). Policy problematization. *International Journal of Qualitative Studies in Education*. doi:10.1080/09518398.2012.762480

Wenger, E. (2009). A social theory of learning. In K. Illeris (Ed.), *Contemporary Theories of Learning: Learning Theorists in Their Own Words* (pp. 209–218). London: Routledge.

Wiliam, D. (2011). *Embedded Formative Assessment*. Bloomington, ID: Solution Tree Press.

Williams, J., Stonner, C., Wicker, J., Krauter, N., Derstroff, B., Bourtsoukidis, E., . . . Kramer, S. (2016). Cinema audiences reproducibly vary the chemical composition of air during films, by broadcasting scene specific emissions on breath. *Scientific Reports, 6*, Article number: 25464. doi:10.1038/srep25464

Williamson, B., & Payton, S. (2009). *Curriculum and Teaching Innovation: Transforming Classroom Practice and Personalisation*. Retrieved from www.nfer.ac.uk/publications/FUTL03/FUTL03.pdf

Williamson, B., Pykett, J., & Nemorin, S. (2017). Biosocial spaces and neurocomputational governance: Brain-based and brain-targeted technologies in education. *Discourse: Studies in the Cultural Politics of Education*, 1–18. doi:10.1080/01596306.2018.1394421

Wilson, E. (2015). *Gut Feminism*. New York: Duke University Press.

Winnicott, D. W. (1960). The theory of the parent-infant relationship. *The International Journal of Psychoanalysis, 41*, 585–595.

Winnicott, D. W. (2017). *The Collected Works of D. W. Winnicott*. Oxford: Oxford University Press.

Wong, M. M., Browwe, K. J., Fitzgerald, H. E., & Zucker, R. A. (2004). Sleep problems in early childhood and early onset of alcohol and other drug use in adolescence. *Alcoholism: Clinical and Experimental Research, 28*(4), 578–587.

Wong, C. C. Y., Caspi, A., Williams, B., Craig, I. W., Houts, R., Ambler, A., . . . Mill, J. (2010). A longitudinal study of epigenetic variation in twins. *Epigenetics, 5*(6), 516–526. doi:10.4161/epi.5.6.12226

Woods, J. (2014). Why does the government want to teach mindfulness in schools? *Telegraph*. Retrieved from www.telegraph.co.uk/lifestyle/wellbeing/10694775/Why-does-the-Government-want-to-teach-mindfulness-in-schools.html

World Health Organisation. (2013). *Health 2020: A European Policy Framework and Strategy for the 21st Century*. Retrieved from Copenhagen www.euro.who.int/__data/assets/pdf_file/0011/199532/Health2020-Long.pdf?ua=1

Wright, J., & Halse, C. (2014). The healthy child citizen: Biopedagogies and web-based health promotion. *British Journal of Sociology of Education, 35*(6), 837–855.

Wright, J., & Harwood, V. (Eds.). (2009). *Biopolitics and the 'Obesity Epidemic': Governing Bodies*. London: Routledge.

Youdell, D. (2004). Engineering school markets, constituting schools and subjectivating students: the bureaucratic, institutional and classroom dimensions of educational triage. *Journal of Education Policy*, *19*(4), 407–431. doi:10.1080/0268093042000227474

Youdell, D. (2005). Sex-gender-sexuality: How sex, gender and sexuality constellations are constituted in secondary schools. *Gender and Education*, *17*(3), 149–170.

Youdell, D. (2006a). *Impossible Bodies, Impossible Selves: Exclusions and Student Subjectivities*. Dordrecht: Springer.

Youdell, D. (2006b). Subjectivation and performative politics – Butler thinking Althusser and Foucault: Intelligibility, agency and the raced-nationed-religioned subjects of education. *British Journal of Sociology of Education*, *27*(4), 511–528.

Youdell, D. (2010). Pedagogies of becoming in an end-of-the-line 'special' school. *Critical Studies in Education*, *51*(3), 313–324.

Youdell, D. (2011). *School Trouble: Identity, Power and Politics in Education*. London: Routledge.

Youdell, D. (2015). Assemblage theory and education policy sociology. In K. Gulson, A. Metcalfe, & M. Clarke (Eds.), *Education Policy and Contemporary Theory* (pp. 111–121). London: Routledge.

Youdell, D. (2017a). Bioscience and the sociology of education: The case for biosocial education. *British Journal of Sociology of Education*, 1–14. doi:10.1080/01425692.2016.1272406

Youdell, D. (2017b). Genetics, epigenetics and social justice in education: Learning as a complex biosocial phenomenon. In M. Meloni, J. Cromby, D. Fitzgerald, & S. Lloyd (Eds.), *The Palgrave Handbook of Biology and Society* (pp. 295–316). London: Palgrave Macmillan.

Youdell, D., & Armstrong, F. (2011). A politics beyond subjects: The affective choreographies and smooth spaces of schooling. *Emotion, Space, Society*, *4*(1), 144–150.

Youdell, D., Harwood, V., & Lindley, M. R. (2017). Biological sciences, social sciences and the languages of stress. *Discourse: Studies in the Cultural Politics of Education*, 1–23. doi:10.1080/01596306.2018.1394420

Youdell, D., & McGimpsey, I. (2015). Assembling, disassembling and reassembling 'youth services' in austerity Britain. *Critical Studies in Education*, *56*(1), 116–130.

Zembylas, M. (2007). *Five Pedagogies, a Thousand Possibilities: Struggles for Hope and Transformation in Education*. Rotterdam: Sense.

Zembylas, M. (2013). Critical pedagogy and emotion: Working through 'troubled knowledge' in posttraumatic contexts. *Critical Studies in Education*, *54*(2), 176–189. doi:10.1080/17508487.2012.743468

INDEX

Page numbers in *italics* indicate figures; page numbers in **bold** indicate tables.

ability and learning 143–145, 149
acetylation 22, 24
ADHD *see* attention deficit/hyperactivity disorder (ADHD)
affect 79–80; *see also* feeling
Allan, Julie 100–101
alleles 19
anabolism 25
ancestry industry 12
'anxiety' and high-stakes testing 2–4
assemblages 32
assessment for learning 128
associations in ADHD 102–103, 117
atoms 25
attention deficit/hyperactivity disorder (ADHD): bioscience of 101–105, 110–112; biosocial approaches to 120–123; brain and **113**; as case study 9; complexity of 116–118, *119*, 120; diagnostic criteria for 97–99; interaction of genes and environment in 113–114; Omega-3 deficiency and 45, 47; pharmaceuticals for 115; research on 94; sociology of 99–101; stigma of 115–116
auditory processing and dyslexia 137–141, *139*

Bakhurst, David 68
being human 56–58; *see also* person
Bilbo, Staci 70–71

biology: body as focus of 6; of feeling 82–84, *83*, *85*, 86, *87*; love affair with 4–5; naturalizing and fixing effects of 1–2
bio-psycho-socio-cultural human 73–75
bioscience orientations to 'optimizing humans' 38–40
biosciences: ADHD and 101–105, 110–112; critique of 4–5, 35; influence of environment and 15–16; interaction between biological, social or environmental and 6–7; learning and 132; *see also* epigenetics; nutrition
biosocial approach: to ADHD 120–123; to feeling, in classroom 91–93; to learning 147–149, *148*; multifactorial complex causality and 12–13; overview 14–15, 32–34
biosocial assemblages: overview 9; special education needs as 96–97, 122
biosocial plasticity model 15, 37, 44
body: biology of 62–70; brain as 63–64; as focus of biology 6; food practices of schools and 44–45, 47; impairment/disability distinction and 95; interactions with brain 70–72
body-brain-environment-person 75–76
body-brain-person 70–72
Braidotti, Rosie 60, 61

brain: activation, networks and connectivity of 27; biology of 62–70; as body 63–64; chemistry of 28; interactions with body 70–72; neuroscience of 64–67; overview 26; plasticity of 7, 49–50, 146; regions and functions of 27, 64–67, *66*, 111–112, **113**
'brain-based' education 134
brain imaging and ADHD 110–112
brainism 68
brain-mind-person 67
brain volume 26, 110–111
Butler, Judith 36, 60, 61

candidate genes 105
catabolism 25
cell membranes 24
cells: defined 24; glial 26; pluripotent 20
chromatin 22
chromosomes 17, *18*
classrooms: biosocial understanding of feeling in 91–93; relationships in 50
communities of practice 129, *130*
consumer choice in education 78
critical approaches to learning 128–132
critical/political pedagogy 29–30
Critical Race Theory 150
critical social science scholarship and biosciences 4–5
curriculum and learning 128

DAT gene 111, 117
decentering of subject 59–60
deficit emotional self-regulation 112
deletions 20
deoxyribonucleic acid (DNA) 17
depression, role of gut in 70
destressing schools 149
DHA (docosahexaenoic acid) 44–45, 141
Diagnostic and Statistical Manual (DSM 5) 97, 98–99, 100
difference: gender differences 10–11; problem of 9–10; racial differences 11–12
disability 95
Disability Studies 51–52
discourses 29
DNA (deoxyribonucleic acid) 17
docosahexaenoic acid (DHA) 44–45, 141
dopamine 28
DSM 5 (Diagnostic and Statistical Manual) 97, 98–99, 100
duplications 20
dyslexia and auditory processing 137–141, *139*

early intervention policy 101, 146
early sexual development 37–38, 73–74
economic and social structures, economy and institutions 28–29
education: biosocial, difficulties, dangers and 149–151; destressing 149; feeling and 77–79, 91–93; 'neuro-myths' in 134; as optimization 41–42
Education Endowment Fund 39
eicosapentaenoic acid (EPA) 44–45
electroencephalography (EEG) 27
embodiment 6, 31, 60–62
emotional self-regulation 78, 112; *see also* feeling
emotional signaling molecules 84, 92
endocrine system 28
endophenotype 104
ENIGMA working group 110, 111
entanglements 56–57
environment 6–7, 15–16, 57–58, 75–76, 113–114
EPA (eicosapentaenoic acid) 44–45
epigenetics: accounts of epigenetic effects 21–22; ADHD and 113–114; brain and 66; developmental 82; environment in 57; learning and 132, *133*, 134; mechanisms of gene regulation *21*; overview 7, 12
ethics and optimization of humans 40–41
eugenics 1, 40
event related potential 27

Fair Society, Healthy Lives 142
feeling: affectivity and 31; biology of 82–84, *83, 85,* 86, *87*; education and 77–79, 91–93; encountering affect 79–80; happiness 89–91; learning and VOCs 87–89, *88*; sociological research on 80–82; *see also* 'stress'
fMRI (functional Magnetic Resonance Imaging) 5, 27
'folded reading of science' 73
Fox Keller, Evelyn 38, 41
frameshift mutations 20
Freire, Paolo 128–129
Frost, Samantha 6, 9; *Biocultural Creatures* 74–75
functional Magnetic Resonance Imaging (fMRI) 5, 27

'g' (generalized genetic intelligence) 5, 43, 44
gamma-aminobutyric acid (GABA) 28
gender differences 10–11

gene and environment interaction (G x E) 113–114
gene locus 17, 19
gene regulation and expression 24
genes: candidate 105; DAT 111, 117; defined 16; 'hot genes' 104–105, **106–109**; interaction with environment 113–114
genetics: of ADHD 105, 110; of racial difference 11–12; turn to 1–2
gene variants *19*, 19–20
genome 16
genome wide association studies 21, 43
genotype 16, 103–104
germ lines 21
Gillborn, David 42, 44, 144–145
glial cells 26
glutamate 28
gonadotropin-releasing hormone (GnRH) analogues 38, 74
Goswami, Usha 50, 134, 136, 137–138, 140
Graham, Linda 99–100
Graphogame 54, 149
grey matter of brain 26

happiness: neuroscience of 89–91; promoting 149
Harwood, Valerie 100–101
Health 2020 (WHO) 142
health and learning 142–143
hearing and reading 137–141, *139*
heritability of ADHD 103
high-stakes testing 2–4, 125
histones 22
holobiont 71–72
'hot genes' 104–105, **106–109**
Howard-Jones, Paul 126
HPA axis 47–50
human genome project 43, 102
Human Microbiome Project 71–72
humans, bio-psycho-socio-cultural 73–75; *see also* 'optimizing humans'; person; posthuman

identity 30
Ilyenkov, Evald 68
impairment 95
inclusive education and disability studies 95–96, 120
indole 89
inequality of educational experience 8–9
inflammatory immune response 71
insertions 20
intelligence 42–44, 143
intermediate phenotype 104

jouissance 89–91

Kenway, Jane 81
Kraftl, Peter 79

learning: biosocial approach to 147–149, *148*; capacities for 145–147; critical approaches to 128–132; curriculum, pedagogy and assessment in 128; dynamic and situated nature of 131–132; epigenetics and 132, *133*, 134; health and 142–143; impeding 143–145; neuroscience of 134–136, *135*; nutrition and 141–142; as phenomena 124–125; to read 136–141, *139*; sleep and 142; as testing 125; volatile organic compounds and 87–89, *88*
learning styles 125–126, *127*, 128

magnetoencephelography 27
Magnocellular theory 137
Malabou, Catherine 6
mass spectrometry and feeling 84, *85*, 87–89, *88*
materiality 60–62
Meloni, Maurizio, *Political Biology* 37
'mental disorders' 100–101
meritocratic principle 42
metabolism 25
methylation 22, *23*
methylphenidate (Ritalin) 115
Metzl, Jamie 39
microbiome 71–72
microglia 71
mindfulness in education 78, 91–92
missense mutations 20
molecules 24–25
Montreal Imaging Stress Task 86, *87*
mutations 19–20

neurons 26
neuroscience: of brain 64–67; of happiness 89–91; of learning 134–136, *135*; overview 7, 25–26; of reading 52–53; turn to 1–2; using 149
neurotransmitters 28
'new biological age' 4
new materialism 32
nonsense mutations 20
nucleotides 17
nutrition: defined 25; fish oil supplementation 148; learning and 141–142; optimizing humans and 44–45, 47

Omega-3 44–45, *46*, 141–142
Omega-3 fish oil 44, 45, 47, 148
'optimizing humans': bioscience
    orientations to 38–40; education as
    41–42; ethics and 40–41; hopes and
    fears of 35–36; intelligence and 42–44;
    nutrition and 44–45, 47; overview 55;
    relationships and 47–50, *48*; remediation
    of reading dysfunction and 50–55; social
    science orientations to 37–38

parenting: ADHD and 115–116; biosciences
    and 4–5; learning and 146
pedagogy: critical/political 29–30; learning
    and 128; 'neuro-sensitive' 147; productive
    129
performativity 30–31
Pernu, Pierre 69–70
person: being human 56–57, 58; biologies
    of brain and body 62–70; bio-psycho-
    social-cultural human 73–75; body-
    brain-environment-person 75–76; body-
    brain-person 70–72; environment and
    57–58; as focus of sociology 6; as social
    subject 59–62
personalism 68–69
personalization of learning 144
pharmaceuticals for ADHD 115
phenomena, learning as 124–125
phenotype 16, 99, 103–104
philosophy of mind 68–70
phrenology 64, *65*
pluripotent cells 20
pluripotent genes 20
policy: ability and 143–144; biosciences
    and 4–5; difficulties and dangers of using
    science in 149–150; early intervention
    101, 146; trans-national education and
    early years 35–36
polygeneticity 21, 118
posthuman 32, 60
power 29
prenatal testing 39
productive pedagogy 129
proteins 19
psychoanalysis 31

racial differences 11–12
Rasmussen, Mary Lou 61
reading: dysfunction and 51–52;
    interventions for 53–55; learning to read
    136–141, *139*; neuroscience of 52–53;
    research on 50–51

receptors 28
reflective approaches to pedagogy
    128
relationality 129, *130*
relationships: classroom 50; importance of
    47–50, *48*; learning and 148–149
repeat expansions 20
resources, allocation of 149
Ritalin (methylphenidate) 115
RNA (ribonucleic acid) 17
Roberts, Celia 6, 9, 73–74; *Puberty in Crisis*
    37–38
Rose, Nikolas 4
'running the line' ethnographic data 80–82,
    93

SATs (Standardized Assessment Tests)
    2–4
scales of granularity *33*
'self' and neuroscience 67
serotonin 28
sex differences 10–11
single nucleotide polymorphisms 19
sleep and learning 142
social science orientations to 'optimizing
    humans' 37–38
social sciences: affective turn in 78; focus of
    28–32
sociology: of ADHD 99–101; people as
    focus of 6
sociology of education: critique of
    biosciences by 4–5, 35; inequality
    of educational experience and 8–9;
    overview 28; research in 79
special education needs (SEN): as biosocial
    assemblage 96–97; reading and 51–52;
    sociology of 95–96
Standardized Assessment Tests (SATs)
    2–4
standardized tests and learning 125
stigma of ADHD 115–116
'stress': biology of school feelings and 84,
    86, *87*; high-stakes testing and 2–4;
    'trauma' and 82; VOCs and 87–89,
    88
stress (HPA) axis 47–50
subject, person as 59–62
subjectivation 30, 58
synaptic pruning 71

testing, learning as 125
time4learning website 126, 128
transcription 19

transdisciplinarity 14–15, 32–34, 76
transgender young people 38, 74
trans-national education and early years
    policy context 35–36
Turner, Matthew 87–89

van Ijzendoorn, Marnius 49
Visual Word Form Area 53,
    136–137

volatile organic compounds (VOCs) 24, 84,
    85, 87–89, *88*
white matter of brain 26, 111
Wilson, Elizabeth 6, 9, 14–15, 122; *Gut
    Feminism* 70, 73
working memory 134, *135*

Youdell, Deborah 42, 44, 61, 80–81, 96,
    131, 144–145